SECOND EDITION

REBUILDING

WHEN YOUR RELATIONSHIP ENDS

DR. BRUCE FISHER

FOREWORD BY VIRGINIA M. SATIR

Impact Publishers®
SAN LUIS OBISPO, CALIFORNIA 93406

First Edition, 1981
Second Edition, October, 1992
Copyright © 1981, 1992
by Bruce Fisher
Eighth Printing, October, 1997

Library of Congress Cataloging-in-Publication Data

Fisher, Bruce, 1931-
  Rebuilding: when your relationship ends / Bruce Fisher. 2nd ed.
      p. cm.
  Includes bibliographical references and index.
  ISBN 0-915166-95-X
  1. Divorce—Psychological aspects. 2. Man-woman relationships.
  I. Title.
HQ814.F53 1992
306.89 — dc20   92-17193
                                                 CIP

Author photo back cover by Susan Scherer, Columbus, Ohio
Cover design by Sharon Schnare, San Luis Obispo, California
Illustrations by Sharon Schnare and Emilie Kong, North Hollywood,
    California. Page 295 illustration by Anne Bain, Boulder, Colorado
Printed in the United States of America

Published by **Impact** 〰 **Publishers**®
POST OFFICE BOX 1094
SAN LUIS OBISPO, CALIFORNIA 93406

This book is dedicated to...

...the thousands of people that, while I was attempting to teach them in the Rebuilding Classes, taught me much of what is written in this book.

...my children, Todd, Sheila, and Bobby who have often through their love given me more reality, feedback, and truth than I have been ready to hear.

...my parents, Bill and Vera, because the more I understand life, families, and myself, the more I appreciate the gifts of life and love they gave me.

...Nina, who, with her love, often gives me what I need instead of what I want.

AND A WORD OF THANKS

to my editor and publisher, Bob Alberti, who helped it turn out the way I wanted it to.

Contents

FOREWORD

Virginia M. Satir, M.S.W.

Divorce is a metaphorical surgery which affects all areas of life of the individual. I have often said that the roots of divorce are in the circumstances and hopes at the time of marriage. Many, many, many people marry with the idea that life is going to be better. Perhaps only a fool would enter into marriage thinking that would not be the case. The depth of disappointment at the time of divorce will depend upon how much more one wants to get out of life or how much more one feels it necessary to add someone to one's life to make life worthwhile.

For many people, divorce is a broken experience, and before they can go on with their lives, they need to be able to pick up the pieces. This period often includes deep emotional feelings of despair, disappointment, revenge, retaliation, hopelessness and helplessness. They need to develop a whole new orientation to the life that will come. And they need time to mourn what was hoped and to realize that the hope will not manifest itself.

Many books on divorce talk only about the problems. Of course, there are the injury to the ego, diminished feeling of self-worth, constant nagging questions about what went wrong, and many fears about the future. Dr. Fisher has given a very practical and useful framework within which to examine the brief period, to take a look at where one is, and to point directions for the future. He offers step-by-step guides to getting oneself in a position to enjoy the life that comes after the divorce. He presents it as a period in which one can learn from the past, get to know oneself better, and also to help to develop new parts of the self that were previously unknown. An apt analogy would be that of a convalescence which occurs after any kind of surgery.

The emotional levels one needs to work through during and following divorce are very much parallel to the stages one goes through at the time of death. At first, there is a denial of the events that have taken place and a consequent feeling of wanting to isolate oneself from the whole situation. Then anger, wherein one blames someone else for one's predicament. The third level is bargaining; a kind of situation in which one wants to look at the ledger to see that things are equal. This is often manifest over the custody of children and property settlements at the time of divorce. Then comes a period of depression, which is where much self-hatred, self-blame and feelings of failure are present. Finally, after all of this, one comes to the acceptance of the situation and an acceptance of the self. Out of this comes hope for what can happen.

I believe Bruce Fisher's book makes it possible for people to work through these various levels, stage-by-stage. It is important to give this "rebuilding" period the time it needs, to awaken parts of the self that have been paralyzed, repressed, or unknown. Let each self — in this case the divorced person — come into the next part of life with hope rather than failure !

Menlo Park, California
September 1980

Editor's Note: Virginia Satir (1916-1988) was one of the most well-loved and highly respected contributors to the field of marriage and family therapy. She was recognized as a founder of family systems theory. Her many books, including her best-seller PEOPLEMAKING, were influential in establishing the framework for family therapy, and comprise a major component of the foundation of the profession as it is currently practiced . Ms. Satir wrote this foreword for the first edition of REBUILDING.

FROM STUMBLING BLOCKS
TO REBUILDING BLOCKS

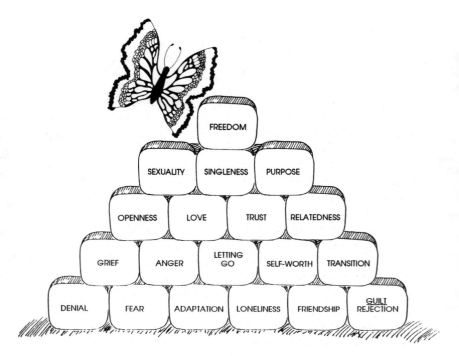

You are probably experiencing the painful feelings that come when a love relationship ends. There is a proven 19-step process of adjustment to the loss of a love. This chapter provides an overview and introduction to the Rebuilding Blocks which form that process.

Chapter 1

Are you hurting? If you have recently ended a love relationship, you are. Those who appear not to hurt when their love relationships end have either already worked through a lot of hurt, or have yet to feel the pain.

So go ahead, acknowledge that you're hurt. It's natural, expected, healthy, even *okay* to hurt. Pain is nature's way of telling us that something in us needs to be healed, so let's get on with the healing.

Can I help? Well, I can share with you some of the learning that takes place in the divorce process seminars I've been conducting for the last two decades. The growth that takes place in people during a ten-week seminar is remarkable. Maybe by sharing with you some of these ideas and some of the feedback I've had from the hundreds of thousands of readers of the first edition of this book, I can help you learn how to get through the hurt also.

There is an adjustment process — with a beginning, an end, and specific steps of learning along the way. While you are feeling some of the pain, you're more anxious to learn how to be healed. If you are like most of us, you probably have had some destructive patterns of behavior for years — maybe since your childhood. While you were in a love relationship, it was difficult to change, and you might have been comfortable enough that you felt no need to change. But now there is that pain. What do you do? Well, you can use the pain as motivation to learn and to grow. It's not easy. It takes a lot of hard work. But you can.

I have arranged the steps of the adjustment process into a pyramid of "Rebuilding Blocks" to symbolize a mountain. Re-building means climbing that mountain, for most of us a difficult journey. Some people don't have the strength and stamina to make this difficult journey; they stop off somewhere on the trail. Some of us become seduced into another important love relationship before learning all that we can from the pain. They too drop out before reaching the top, and they miss the magnificent view of life that comes from climbing the mountain. (You may have guessed by now that I live in Colorado near the mountains!) Some of us withdraw into the shelter of a cave in our own little world and watch the procession go by — another group which never reaches the top. And, sadly, there are a few who choose self-destruction, jumping off the first cliff that looms along the trail.

Let me assure you that the climb is worth it! The rewards at the top make the tough climb worthwhile.

How long will it take to climb the mountain? My studies with the *Fisher Divorce Adjustment Scale* indicate that on the average it takes about a year to get up above the tree line (past the really painful, negative stages of the climb), longer to reach the top. Some will make it in less time, others in more. Some research suggests that a few in our climbing party will need as long as three to five years. Don't let that discourage you. Finishing the climb is what counts, not how long it takes. Just remember that you climb at your own rate, and don't get rattled if some pass you along the way. Like life itself, the process of climbing and growing is the source of your greatest benefits!

I've learned a great deal about what you're going through by listening to the people in my seminars, and by reading hundreds of letters from readers. People sometimes interrupt one of my talks and ask, "Were you eavesdropping when my ex and I were talking last week? How did you know what he (she) was saying?" Well, although each of us is an individual, with unique experiences, there are similar patterns that all of us go through while ending a love relationship. When I talk about patterns, you will likely find it will be more or less the pattern you're experiencing.

These patterns are similar not only for the ending of a love relationship, but for any ending crisis that comes along in your life. Frank, a participant in one of my seminars, reports that he followed the same patterns when he left the priesthood of the Catholic Church. Nancy found the same patterns when she was fired from her job, Betty when she was widowed. Maybe one of the most important personal skills we can develop is how to adjust to a crisis. Probably there will be more crises in our lives, and learning to shorten the pain time will be a highly valuable learning experience.

In this chapter I will briefly describe the trail that we will be taking up the mountain. In the following chapters we will get on with the emotional learning of actually "climbing" the mountain. I suggest that you start keeping a journal right now to make the climb more meaningful. After the journey is over, you can re-read your journal to gain a better perspective on your changes and growth during the climb. More about journals at the end of this chapter.

The rebuilding blocks model graphically shows 19 specific feelings and attitudes, arranged in the form of a pyramid to symbolize the mountain that must be climbed. The adjustment process can be as difficult a journey as climbing a mountain. At first the task is overwhelming. Where to start? How do I climb? How about a guide and a map to help us climb this difficult mountain? That is what the rebuilding blocks are — a guide and a map prepared by others who have already traveled the trail. As you climb, you'll discover that tremendous personal growth is possible, despite the emotional trauma you've experienced from the ending of your love relationship.

In the first edition of this book, published in 1981, I described just 15 rebuilding blocks. My work since then, with thousands of people who've gone through the divorce process, has led to the addition of four new blocks, and some changes in the original 15. I'm grateful to those whose lives have touched mine, through this book and through the classes. I've learned much from them, and I'll be sharing their experiences with you in these pages.

Throughout the book you will find specific ways of dealing with each rebuilding block to prevent it from becoming a stumbling block. (You have probably already stumbled enough!) People often report that they can immediately identify their blocks which need work. Others are unable to identify a problem block because they have effectively buried their feelings and attitudes about it. As a result, at some higher point on the climb, they may discover and explore the rebuilding blocks they overlooked at first. Cathy, a volunteer helper in one of my seminars, suddenly recognized one during an evening class: "I've been stuck on the Rejection and Guilt rebuilding block all along without realizing it!" The following week she reported considerable progress, thanks to identifying the problem.

On the following pages is a pre-journey briefing on the climb, presenting the blocks as they come on the trail up the mountain. Beginning at the bottom, we find *denial* and *fear*, two painful stumbling blocks which come early in the process of adjustment. They can be overwhelming feelings, and may make you reluctant to begin the climb.

DENIAL: "I Can't Believe This Is Happening to Me"

The good news is we humans have a wonderful mechanism that allows us to only feel as much pain as we can handle without becoming overwhelmed. Pain that is too great is put into our "denial bag" and held until we are strong enough to experience and learn from it.

The bad news is some of us experience so much denial that we are reluctant to attempt recovery — to climb the mountain. There are many reasons for this. Some are unable to access and identify what they are feeling and will have difficulty adjusting to change of any sort. They must learn that "what we can feel, we can heal." Others have such a low self-concept, that they don't believe they are capable of climbing the mountain. And some feel so much fear that they are afraid to climb the mountain.

How about you? What feelings are underneath your denial? Nona talked hesitantly about taking the ten-week seminar, and finally was able to describe her hesitation. "If I took the divorce seminar, it would mean that my marriage is over, and I don't want to accept that yet."

FEAR: "I Have Lots of It!"

Have you ever been in a winter blizzard? The wind is blowing so hard that it howls. The snow is so thick you can see only a few feet ahead of you. Unless you have shelter, it feels — and it can be — life threatening. It's a very fearful experience.

The fears you feel when you first separate are like being in a blizzard. Where do you hide? How do you find your way? You choose not to climb this mountain because even here at the bottom you feel overwhelmed. How can you find your way up when you believe the trail will become more blinding, threatening, fearful? You want to hide, find a lap to curl up in, and get away from the fearful storm.

Mary called several times to sign up for the seminar but each opening night came and went without her. I finally discovered she had been hiding in her empty apartment, venturing out only for an occasional trip to the grocery store when she ran out of food. She wanted to hide from the storm, from her fears. She was overwhelmed with fear; coming to opening night of the divorce class was way too scary for her.

How do you handle your fears? What do you do when you discover your fears have paralyzed you? Can you get the courage to face them so you can get ready to climb the mountain? Each fear you overcome gives you strength and courage to continue your journey through life.

ADAPTATION: "But It Always Worked When I Was a Kid!"

I have many healthy parts. I can be inquisitive, creative, nurturing of myself, have good feelings of self-worth, and be appropriately angry. As I was growing up, my healthy parts were not always encouraged by my family, my school, my church, or other influences in my life, such as movies, books, and magazines. Sometimes I suffered stress, trauma, lack of love, and other hindrances to health from my family of origin and from society.

When I was not able to meet my emotional and psychological needs for nurturing, attention, and love, I developed adaptive behaviors to help me to meet my needs. An adaptive behavior might take the form of being over-responsible for others, becoming a perfectionist, trying to always be a people-pleaser, or developing my "urge-to-help" part. Adaptive behaviors which are too well developed leave me out of balance. I try to restore my balance through a relationship with another person.

For example if I am over-responsible, I look for an under-responsible person. If the person I find is not under-responsible enough, I will *train* him or her to be under-responsible! This leads me to "polarize" responsibility: I become more and more over-responsible, the other person becomes more and more under-responsible. This polarization is often fatal to the success of a love relationship and is a special kind of co-dependency.

Jill stated it clearly: "I have four children — I'm married to the oldest one." She resents having all of the responsibility, such as keeping track of the checkbook and writing all of the checks. Instead of blaming Jack for not being able to balance the checkbook, she needs to understand that the relationship is a system, and as long as she is over-responsible, chances are Jack will be under-responsible.

Adaptive behaviors you learned as a child will not always lead to healthy adult relationships. Does that help you understand why you need to climb this mountain?

The next few blocks represent the "divorce pits" — *loneliness,* loss of *friendships, guilt & rejection, grief, anger, letting go.* These blocks represent difficult feelings, and pretty tough times. It will take a while to work through them before you'll start feeling good again.

LONELINESS: "I've Never Felt So Alone"

When a love relationship ends, the feeling is probably the greatest loneliness you have ever known. Many daily living habits must be altered now that your partner is gone. As a couple, you may have spent time apart before, but your partner was still in the relationship, even when not physically present. When the relationship is ending, your partner is not there at all. Suddenly you are totally alone.

The thought, "I'm going to be lonely like this forever," is overwhelming. It seems you're never going to know the companionship of a love relationship again. You may have children living with you and friends and relatives close by, but the loneliness is somehow greater than all of the warm feelings from your loved ones. Will this empty feeling ever go away? Can you ever feel okay about being alone?

John had been doing the bar scene pretty often. He took a look at it and decided that, "I've been running from and trying to drown my lonely feelings. I think I'll try sitting home by myself, writing in my journal to see what I can learn about myself." He was beginning to change feeling lonely into enjoying aloneness.

DENIAL | FEAR | ADAPTATION | LONELINESS | FRIENDSHIP

FRIENDSHIP: "Where Has Everybody Gone?"

As you've discovered, the rebuilding blocks that occur early in the process tend to be quite painful. Because they are so painful, there is a great need for friends to help one face and overcome the emotional pain. Unfortunately, many friends are usually lost as one goes through the divorce process, a problem that is especially evident for those who have already physically separated from a love partner. The problem is made worse by withdrawal from social contacts because of emotional pain and fear of rejection. Divorce is threatening to friends, causing them to feel uncomfortable around the dividing partners.

Betty says that the old gang of couples had a party this weekend, but she and her ex were not invited. "I was so hurt and angry. What did they think — that I was going to seduce one of the husbands or something?" Social relationships may need to be rebuilt around friends who will understand our emotional pain without rejecting us. It is worthwhile to work at retaining some old friends, and finding new friends to support and listen.

GUILT/REJECTION: Dumpers 1, Dumpees 0

Have you heard the terms *dumper* and *dumpee* before? No one who has experienced the ending of a love relationship needs definitions for these words. Usually there is one person who is more responsible for deciding to end the love relationship; that person becomes the dumper. The more reluctant partner is the dumpee. Most dumpers feel guilty for hurting the former loved one. Dumpees find it tough to acknowledge being rejected.

The adjustment process is different for the dumper and the dumpee, since the dumper's behavior is largely governed by feelings of guilt, and the dumpee's by rejection. Until our seminar discussion of this topic, Dick had maintained that his relationship ended mutually. He went home thinking about it, and finally admitted to himself that he was a dumpee. At first, he became really angry! Then he began to acknowledge his feelings of rejection, and recognized that he must deal with them before he could continue the climb.

GRIEF: "There's This Terrible Feeling of Loss"

Grieving is an important part of the recovery process. Whenever we suffer the loss of love, the death of a relationship, the death of a loved one, or the loss of a home, we must grieve that loss. Indeed, the divorce process has been described by some as largely a grief process. Grief combines overwhelming sadness with a feeling of despair. It drains us of energy by leading us to believe we are helpless, powerless to change our lives. Grief is a crucial rebuilding block.

One of the symptoms of grief is a loss of body weight, although a few people do gain during periods of grief. I was not surprised when I overheard Glenda telling Harriet, "I need to lose weight — guess I'll end another love relationship!"

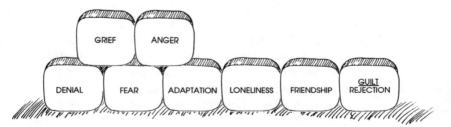

ANGER: "Damn the S.O.B.!"

It is difficult to understand the intensity of the anger felt at this time unless one has been through divorce. When I lecture, I frequently tell a true story that appeared in the Des Moines *Register* a few years ago. It helps me to find out if the audience is primarily composed of divorced or married people: While driving by the park, a female dumpee saw her male dumper lying on a blanket with a new girl friend. She drove into the park and ran over the former spouse and his girl friend with her car! Divorced people respond by exclaiming, "Right on! Did she back over them again?" Married people, not understanding the divorce anger, will gasp, "Ugh! How terrible!"

Most divorced people were not aware that they would be capable of such rage because they had never been this angry before. This special kind of rage is specifically aimed towards the ex-love partner and it can be really helpful to your recovery, since it helps you gain some needed emotional distance from your ex.

LETTING GO: "Disentangling Is Hard To Do"

It's tough to let go of the strong emotional ties which remain from the dissolved love union. Nevertheless, it is important to stop investing emotionally in the dead relationship.

Stella, whom you'll meet again in chapter nine, came to take the seminar about four years after her separation and divorce. She was still wearing her wedding ring! To invest in a dead relationship, an emotional corpse, is to make an investment with no chance of return. The need instead is to begin investing in productive personal growth, which will help in working your way through the divorce process.

SELF-WORTH: "I'm Not Really So Bad After All!"

Feelings of self-worth and self-esteem greatly influence behavior. Low self-esteem and a search for stronger identity are major causes of divorce. Divorce, in turn, causes lowered self-esteem and loss of identity. For many people, self-concept is lowest when they end the love relationship. They have invested so much of themselves in the love relationship that when it ends, their feelings of self-worth and self-esteem are devastated.

"I feel so worthless that I can't even get out of bed this morning," reports Jane. "I know of no reason for doing anything today. I just want to be little and stay in bed until I can find a reason why I should get up. No one will even miss me so what's the use of getting up?"

As you improve your feelings of self-worth, you're able to step out of the divorce pits and start feeling better about yourself. With improved self-worth also comes the courage you'll need to face the journey into yourself which is coming up.

TRANSITION: "I'm Waking Up and Taking Out the Trash"

I want to understand why my relationship ended. I need to perform an autopsy upon my past dead relationship. If I can figure out why it ended, I can work on changes that will allow me to create and build different relationships in the future.

Transition is beginning to realize the influences from your family of origin, and to realize you married someone very much like the parent you've not made peace with. Waking-up is when you realize that whatever growing-up tasks you didn't finish in childhood, you're trying to work out in your adult relationships. This process of waking-up happens when you're tired of doing the "shoulds" that you've always done, and instead want to make choices about how you will live your life. Any one of these stumbling blocks that is not resolved can result in the ending of your primary love relationship. John began waking up when he stated, "I married my mother and she married her father, and together we lived out their lives."

Some folks seem to have a need to bring home "stray cats" to nurture back to good health; they often end up marrying one of those cats. They continue to bring home stray cats until they make some basic personality changes. I asked one woman how she would feel if she discovered she had taken home another stray cat the next time she got married. The big male policeman in the class interrupted to ask, "How do you think it feels to *be* a stray cat?"

It's time to take out your trash, to dump the leftovers which remain from your past and your previous love relationship and your earlier years. You thought you had left these behind; but when you begin another relationship, you find they're still there. As Ken said to me, "Those damn neuroses follow me everywhere!"

Transition represents a period of transformation, as you learn new ways of relating to others. It is the beginning of becoming free to be *yourself*.

The next four blocks are hard work, but highly satisfying, as you face yourself, learn about who you really are, and rebuild your foudation for healthy relationships. *Openness, love,* and *trust,* will take you on a journey into yourself. *Relatedness* will ease you back into intimate contact with others.

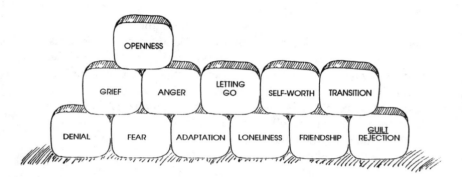

OPENNESS: *"I've Been Hiding Behind a Mask"*

A mask is a feeling or image that you project, trying to make others believe that is who you are. But it keeps people from knowing who you really are, and sometimes even keeps you from knowing yourself. I remember when I was a child the neighbor who always had a smiling face. When I became older, I discovered the smiling face covered up a mountain of angry feelings inside the person.

Many of us are afraid to take off our masks because we believe that others won't like the real person underneath the mask. But when we do take off the mask, we often experience more closeness and intimacy with friends and loved ones than we believed was possible.

Jane confided to the class that she was tired of always wearing the Barbie-doll™ happy face. "I would just like to let people know what I am really feeling instead of always having to appear to be happy and joyful." Her mask was becoming heavy, which indicates she might be ready to take it off.

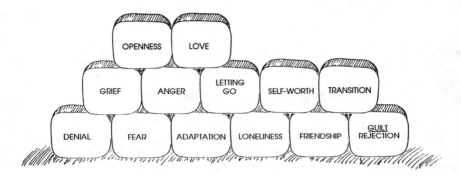

LOVE: "Could Somebody Really Care for Me?"

The typical divorced person says, "I thought I knew what love was, but I guess I was wrong." Ending a love relationship should encourage one to re-examine what love is. A feeling of *unloveableness* may be present at this stage. Here's how Leonard put it: "Not only do I feel unlovable now, but I'm afraid I never *will* be lovable!" This fear can be overwhelming.

Long ago I heard a sermon titled, "Love Thy Neighbor as Thyself," which asked, "What happens if you don't love yourself?" Many of us place the center of our love in another person rather than in ourselves. When divorce comes, the center of our love is removed, adding to the trauma of loss. An important element in the rebuilding process is to learn to love yourself. If you don't love yourself, how can you expect anybody else to love you?

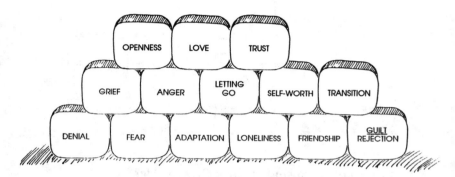

TRUST: "My Love Wound Is Beginning To Heal"

Located in the center of the pyramid, the Trust rebuilding block symbolizes the fact that the basic level of trust, within myself, is the center of the whole adjustment process. Divorced people frequently point their fingers and say they cannot trust anyone of the opposite sex. There is an old cliché which fits here: when you point a finger at something, there are three fingers pointing back to you. When divorced people say they don't trust the opposite sex, they are saying more about themselves than about the opposite sex.

The typical divorced person has a painful love wound resulting from the ending of the love relationship, a love wound which prevents him/her from loving another. It takes a good deal of time to be able to risk being hurt and to become emotionally close again. Incidentally, keeping that distance can be hazardous, too! Lois says that when she returned home from her first date, there was a mark on the side of her body caused by the door handle on the car — she was attempting to get as far away from him as possible!

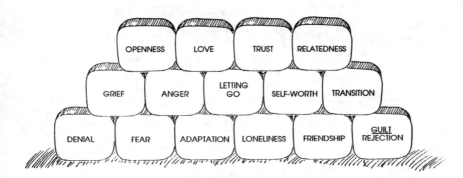

RELATEDNESS: "Healthy Relationships Help Me Rebuild"

Often after a love relationship has ended, one finds another relationship — one which appears to have everything the previous union lacked. I believe I have found the one and only with whom I will live forever. Because this new relationship appears to solve all of my problems, I hold onto it very tightly. And I believe the new partner is the one who is making me happy.

I need to realize that what feels so good is that I am becoming who I would like to be. I need to take back my power and take responsibility for the good things I am feeling.

The new relationship after a breakup is often called a "rebound" relationship, a label which is partly true. When this relationship ends, it is often more painful than when the primary love relationship ended. One symptom of that pain: about twenty percent of the people who have signed up for the divorce class didn't enroll after their marriages ended; they enrolled after their rebound relationships ended.

You may not be quite ready to think about the next block just yet. But it's time.

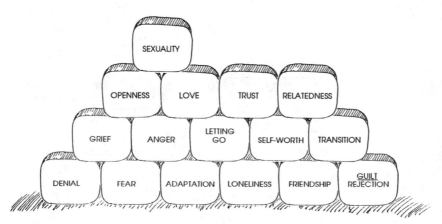

SEXUALITY: *"I'm Interested, but I'm Scared"*

What do you think of when the word sex is mentioned? Most of us tend to react emotionally and irrationally. Our society over-emphasizes and glamorizes sex. Married couples often imagine divorced people as oversexed and free to "romp and play in the meadows of sexuality" the whole night long. In reality, single people often find the hassles of sexuality among the most trying in the divorce process.

A sexual partner was available in the love relationship. Even though the partner is gone, sexual needs go on. In fact, at some points in the divorce process, the drive is greater than before.

Most people are more or less terrified by the thought of dating — feeling like teenagers again — especially when they sense that somebody has changed the rules since they dated earlier. They feel old, unattractive, unsure of themselves, and fearful of awkwardness. And to top it off, they have the "parent morality" that tells them to be "good little boys ands girls." Not only are their parents telling them what they should do, their own teenagers may delight in parenting them! ("Be sure to get home early, Mom.") Thus, for many, dating is confusing and uncertain. No wonder sexual hang-ups are so common!

As we near the top of our climb, the remaining blocks offer comfort, and a feeling of accomplishment for the work you've done to get this far: *singleness, purpose,* and *freedom.* Here at last is a chance to sit down and enjoy the view from the mountain top!

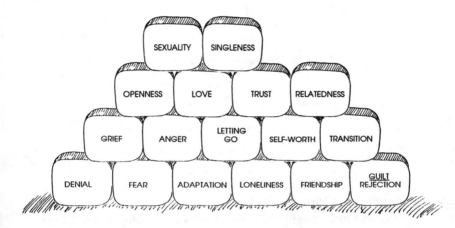

SINGLENESS: "You Mean It's Okay?"

People who went directly from their parental homes into "marriage homes," without having a period of singleness, often missed this important growth period entirely. Even college may have been supervised by "parental" figures and rules.

Regardless of your previous experience, however, a period of singleness — growth as an independent person — will be valuable now. Such an adjustment to the ending of a love relationship will allow you to really let go of the past, to learn to be whole and complete within yourself, and to invest in yourself. Singleness is not only *okay,* it is necessary!

Joan came up to me in a seminar after I had discussed singleness. She was elated and said, "I'm enjoying being single so much that I felt I must be abnormal. You make me feel normal being happy as a single person. Thanks."

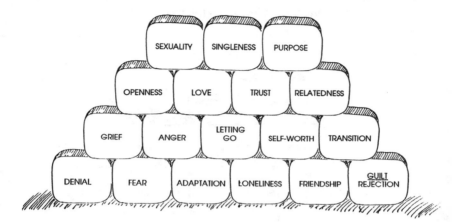

PURPOSE: "I Have Goals for the Future"

Do you have a sense of how long you are going to live? I was very surprised during my divorce when it occurred to me that at age forty I might be only half-way through my life. If you have many years yet to live, what are your goals? What do you plan to do with yourself after you have adjusted to the ending of your love relationship?

I think it is helpful to make a lifeline and take a look at the patterns in your life, and at the potential things you might accomplish for the rest of your time. Planning helps bring the future into the present.

FREEDOM: From Chrysalis to Butterfly

At last, the top of the mountain!

The final stage has two dimensions. The first is freedom of *choice*. When you have worked through all of the rebuilding blocks that have been stumbling blocks in the past, you're free to enter into another relationship. You can make it more productive and meaningful than your past love relationships. You are free to choose happiness as a single person or in another love relationship

There is another dimension of freedom: the freedom to *be yourself*. Many of us carry around a burden of unmet needs, needs which may control us and not allow us freedom to be the persons that we want to be. As we unload this burden and learn to meet needs that were formerly not met, we become free to be ourselves. This may be the most important freedom.

Looking Backward

We have now looked at the process of adjustment as it relates to ending a love relationship. While climbing the mountain, one occasionally slips back to a rebuilding block which may have been dealt with before. I listed the blocks from one to nineteen, but they are not necessarily dealt with in that order. In fact, one is more or less working on all of them together. And a big setback, such as court litigation or the ending of another love relationship, may result in a backward slide some distance down the mountain.

Rebuilding Your Faith

Some people ask how religion relates to the rebuilding blocks. Many people working through divorce find it difficult to continue their affiliation with the church they attended while married for several reasons. Some churches still look upon divorce as a sin. Many people continue to feel guilty within themselves whether the church condemns them or not. Churches frequently are very family oriented. Single parents and children of divorced people may be made to feel different, to not belong in church. Many people become distant from the church since they are unable to find comfort and understanding as they are going through the divorce process. This distance leaves them with more loneliness and rejection.

Happily, many churches do express concern for the needs of people in the divorce process. I encourage you to inform the church of your needs by developing a singles group, talking to an adult class, sharing with the minister feelings of rejection and loneliness which may be fostered by church members.

Ask your church to inform others of the needs of people who are ending their love relationships.

My personal belief is that the rebuilding block concept is what religion is all about. I believe the way we live reflects our faith, and God wants us to develop and grow to our fullest potential. Learning to adjust to a crisis is a spiritual process as well. The quality of our relationships with the people around us, and the amount of love, concern, and caring we're able to show others are good indications of our relationship with God.

Children Must Rebuild Too

"What about the children?" Many people ask about kids and how the rebuilding blocks relate to them. The process of adjustment for kids is very similar to that for adults. The rebuilding blocks apply to the children (as they may to other relatives such as grandparents, aunt, uncles and close friends). Many parents get so involved in trying to help their kids work through the adjustment process that the parents neglect to meet their own needs.

If you're a parent who is embarking on the Rebuilding journey, my suggestion is that you learn to take care of yourself and work through the adjustment process. You will find that your children will tend to adjust more easily as a result. The nicest thing you can do for your kids is to get your own act together. Kids tend to get hung up in the same rebuilding blocks as their parents, so by making progress for yourself, you will be helping your children too.

In our discussion of each rebuilding block in the chapters to come, we will take up the implications of that stage for the kids. Appendix A may become the basis for you to set up and implement a "Children of Divorce" workshop in order to help your children do a better job of adjusting to the divorce.

Homework: Learning by Doing

Many people are reading self-help books these days, learning the vocabulary and gaining awareness, yet not really learning emotionally from the experience. Emotional learning includes those experiences which register in your feelings, such as: mothers are usually comforting; certain kinds of behavior will bring punishment; ending a love relationship is painful. What we learn emotionally affects our behavior a great deal, and much of the learning we have to do to adjust to a crisis is emotional relearning. The things we believed all of our lives may not be true and we have to relearn. In these matters, intellectual learning is of little value until we learn emotionally.

Because emotional learning is so important, I have included in this book exercises to help you relearn emotionally. Most chapters have some specific exercises for you to do before reading the next chapter in the book.

Here are your first homework exercises:

1. *Keep a journal or a diary in which you write down your feelings.* You might do it daily, weekly, or whenever it fits your schedule. Start a lot of the sentences in the journal with "I feel," because that should help you write more feelings. Writing a journal will not only be an emotional learning experience that will enhance your personal growth, but it will also provide a yardstick to measure your personal growth. People often come back months later to read what they wrote and are amazed at the changes they have been able to accomplish. I cannot remember anyone who has written a journal who has not found it to be a worthwhile experience. I suggest you start writing the journal as soon as you finish reading this chapter. You may want to write in your journal after reading each chapter.

2. *Build a support group for yourself.* Because a support system is so important, this is a key part of your first homework assignment. I suggest you find one or more friends, preferably of both sexes, and discuss the rebuilding blocks with which you're having difficulty. This sharing may be easier for you with a person who has gone or is going through the divorce process himself/herself, because many married people may have difficulty relating to your present feelings and attitudes. Most important , however, is your trust in that person.

If you choose to form a discussion group of supportive friends, you may find this book a helpful guide.

3. *Learn to ask another person for help.* Call someone whom you feel you would like to get to know better and start building a friendship. Use any reason you need to get started. Tell the person about this homework assignment if you like. You're learning to build a support system of friends. Make that connection when you're still feeling somewhat secure, so that when you are down in the pits (it's tough to reach out when you're down there!), you will know you have at least one friend who can throw you an emotional life-line.

4. *Answer the checklist questions.* At the end of each chapter you will find a series of statements, most of them adapted from my *Fisher Divorce Adjustment Scale*, which I have included as checklists for you.

Take the time to answer them, and let your responses help you decide how ready you are to proceed to the next rebuilding block.

(If you would like to take the complete *Fisher Divorce Adjustment Scale*, contact a professional counselor or psychologist, who can administer, score, and interpret the *Scale* for you. For more information about the *FDAS*, see page 314.)

5. (Optional) You may find it helpful to *listen to my audio cassette, Rebuilding* (see page 326), as you make your way up the mountain. I also have a 60-minute video cassette (see page 314), which will give you another perspective on how to climb the mountain. These tapes summarize the ideas in the book, and may help you focus your attention on the material in the chapters.

How Are You Doing?

Here is the first set of checklist statements for you to respond to before you start reading the next chapter. Assess your response to each question as *satisfactory, I need to improve,* or *unsatisfactory.*

1. *I have identified the rebuilding blocks that I need to work on.*
2. *I understand the adjustment process.*
3. *I want to begin working through the adjustment process.*
4. *I want to use the pain of this crisis to learn about myself.*
5. *I want to use the pain of this crisis as motivation to experience personal growth.*
6. *If I am reluctant to grow, I will try to understand what feelings are keeping me from growing.*
7. *I will keep my thoughts and feelings open to discover any rebuilding blocks that I may be stuck in at the present time.*
8. *I have hope and faith that I can rebuild from this crisis and make it into a creative learning experience.*
9. *I have discussed the rebuilding blocks model of adjustment with friends in order to better understand where I am in the process.*
10. *I am committed to understanding some of the reasons why my relationship ended.*
11. *If I have children of any age, I will attempt to help them work through their adjustment process.*

How to Use this Book

On Your Own. Most readers of *Rebuilding* are recently-divorced individuals who are reading this book on their own. If that description fits you, I suggest you start at the beginning and take it one chapter at a time. Do each chapter's homework before going on to the next chapter. The chapters are arranged in the approximate order you will experience them.

On the other hand, I have found many readers want to devour the whole book first, then go back and work their way through it and do all of the homework. Whichever approach you choose, I suggest you use a highlighter as you read the book in order to better understand the information. Some readers have found it helpful to use a different colored highlighter each time they read the book. Each time you read it, you will find new and different concepts that you missed before. You hear only what you are ready to hear — depending upon where you are in your personal growth process.

There are many different reactions from individuals who read this book. Some of you will be overwhelmed with some of the information. Some of you will realize you left your relationship too soon and need to go back and work on some of the unfinished business with your love partner. George (a member of my divorce class a few years ago) told me that after he had read the first chapter, he experienced a great deal of anger and threw the book against the wall just as hard as he could!

In a Group. Even better than reading the book on your own is to form a small group to discuss a chapter per week together. It takes a minimum of leadership to do this and you will be pleased to discover how much support you get, and how much more you learn from the book by discussing it with others. Many churches have implemented such a discussion group as part of their singles ministry.

Experience has shown that the most personal growth and transformation comes in a group which follows my *Teacher's Guide* that explains how to implement the "Fisher Rebuilding Ten-Week Class." The ten-week program uses this book as a textbook for the class. The *Teacher's Guide* has lesson plans for each of the ten sessions, explains how to use the *Fisher Divorce Adjustment Scale* as a test to give you feedback about your adjustment, and describes the use of "Volunteer Helpers" who are graduates of the class selected and asked to come back to support the present class participants. The *Teacher's Guide* has information designed to answer any question you might have in implementing the ten-week seminar.

Most people are amazed at the transformation that takes place in the participants in the ten-week class. It might be called a "Divorce Recovery Program," but it's really about helping people take control of their lives and learn to make "loving choices" in the way they live. My research suggests that this is the most helpful form of treatment you can experience when you're putting your life back together after the ending of a love relationship — even more helpful than individual therapy.

Caution. I need to warn you about an ineffective way of using this book which I've observed occasionally in my visits to communities around the U.S. and in other countries. Many churches and other groups have implemented their own programs, in which they use the book along with an "expert" lecture each week on a related topic. With this method, you not only must adjust to your crisis, but also to a new viewpoint each week. It's like spoon feeding you. Instead of giving you an opportunity for active discussion and learning from your peers — a "laboratory" in how to take control of your life — the lecture approach keeps you listening passively to someone else's ideas. It keeps your group from bonding and connecting with each other the way you do in the Fisher Rebuilding Class. It puts band-aids on your pain but doesn't allow you to really heal and transform your life.

If you are a part of such a group, I urge you to take control of your life and assertively ask the group leaders to investigate the Fisher Rebuilding Class. Thousands have found it a powerful and helpful way to make this crisis into a creative experience.

I hope this book helps you adjust to your crisis and take control of your life. I acknowledge and affirm your desire to learn, to grow, to heal, to become more nearly the person you would like to be. Good luck in climbing the mountain!

DENIAL
"I Can't Believe This Is Happening to Me!"

Ending a love relationship may be the greatest emotional pain you will ever experience. The pain is so great, in fact, you may react with denial or disbelief. This only prevents you from facing the important question, "Why did my love relationship have to end?" There are rarely simple answers, so it will take some time and effort. Until you can accept the ending, you will have difficulty adjusting and rebuilding.

Chapter 2

Owl is crying forlornly in the dark,
I heard him calling to his mate last night.
I waited with him to hear the familiar answering cry,
And my heart fell with his
as the silence fell, louder than a cry.
He is still calling tonight,
Only to be answered by longer silences.
*   I have never seen the owl.*
*   I have only heard him calling*
*   And waiting...*

                                    — Nancy

Look at the big crowd gathered at the trailhead waiting to climb the mountain! There are so many kinds of people waiting — all sizes and colors, all ages, both men and women, some wealthy, some poor. Some people think that only losers get divorced, but many of these look like winners. Some are eager to start the climb and are doing calisthenics. Some look in shock — as though they have just witnessed a death. There are some who look up the mountain and act overwhelmed, as though they never expect to be able to climb to the top. Many are waiting around, expecting their former love partners to pick them up so they won't have to make the climb.

Many act confused and disoriented. John is shaking his head and mumbling, "I thought we had a good marriage. I had been the captain of the football team in high school, she was a cheerleader. Everyone predicted we would be perfect together. Then last week she dropped the bombshell on me. She said she was unhappy, that she didn't love me, and she wanted a divorce. She left with our two children to stay with her parents. I was dumbfounded. I thought it would never happen to me."

Mary is impatient to start the climb. She is telling a passerby, "I was so unhappy in our marriage. I wanted a divorce but was afraid to initiate any actions. Then he was killed in a train wreck, and everyone thought I was weird because I felt so little grief. But his death left me free to climb this mountain — when do we start?"

We hear Rita saying, "He has left me and is living with another woman, but I know in my heart that he will always be my husband. God made this marriage and God will have to end it. I refuse to climb this mountain and will stay married until I die. Maybe when we get to Heaven we will be together again."

David is warming his feet by stomping on the ground and appears to be cold and in shock. "I had a good marriage. We never fought. But last night she told me she had fallen in love with my best friend and she was packing her bags to leave. I went in the bathroom and was sick. This morning I called my lawyer and asked him to start divorce proceedings."

Maria is a grey-haired grandmother. "I lived with him and gave him my whole life. I planned to share the harvest of our years in old age with him. But he left without giving any reasons. My harvest is destroyed and I am too old to plant another crop."

I could fill this whole book with stories similar to these. Similar, yet unique stories of people who are reacting in many different ways to the ending of their love relationship.

It is hard for me or anyone to be comforting when you are hurting so much. The most help I can offer at this point is to listen to your reality of the crisis. You feel as though you have failed, as though you have been hit in the stomach and had your emotional wind knocked out, as though you had just experienced death even though you are still living. The initial shock is easier for those of you who made the decision to leave and who were more prepared for this crisis, but the ending is still painful no matter what the circumstances.

Why Did It Have To End?

The big question most of you are asking is "Why?" You need to understand what went wrong, to perform an autopsy upon the dead relationship. You want to know why, yet denying the pain often prevents you from accepting the results of this emotional autopsy. To understand why helps to overcome the denial, so in this chapter and the next we'll discuss some of the reasons love relationships die.

I like to start my talks to teenagers by asking them, "How many of you plan to get married?" Usually about half of them raise their hands. Then I ask, "How many of you plan to get divorced?" I never see any raised hands after this question.

No one plans to get a divorce. And most of us deny it at first if it does happen. We want to bury our heads in the sand like ostriches to avoid the storm. But, like the ostrich, we have problems in our love relationships which are more obvious to others than they are to us.

There are three entities in a love relationship — two people and the relationship between them. It is analogous to a bridge: the two people are the foundations at each end of the bridge; the relationship is the span which connects these two foundations. When change occurs in one or both of the foundations at the end of the bridge, it strains the bridge itself. Some changes are too great for the bridge to handle, and it falls into the river. In people, such changes may result from personal growth, education, religious experiences, attitude change, anxiety, anger, relocation, or maybe a reaction to stress or trauma.

(One way to prevent such stress upon the relationship is to never grow or change — not a very healthy way, is it?)

You may recognize that you or your love partner recently went through a period of change and personal growth, and that this upset the system of interaction in your love relationship — tumbling your bridge into the river.

If you need to doubt and question yourself and your abilities, you may feel that you *should* have been able to adjust to this stress resulting from change. My answer is this: Two of the most important abilities we need to learn in our lives are how to build and maintain this bridge between two people in a love relationship, and how to parent our children. And where do we receive education and training for these two important roles? Mostly in our families — certainly not in school.

I was talking to a group of about 100 women recently, and asked them how many would like to have a marriage like that of their parents. There was only one who raised her hand! Did the rest receive good training from their families on how to have a happy love relationship? Did you receive good training and education on how to adjust to a strain in your love relationship?

Perhaps relationship counseling would have helped you to adjust? Perhaps. I state proudly that I am a terrific marriage counselor when both parties want to work on the relationship! But I am a lousy marriage counselor when only one wants to work.

What was the reality in your love relationship? Were both you and your partner wanting to work and improve the system, or did only one of you want to work on the relationship? If only one is willing, then it is not very likely that the relationship will improve. A team of horses will not pull a very big load when one of the horses is lying down.

You may be punishing yourself with feelings of failure in your love relationship by playing the *if only* game: "If only I had listened more; if only I hadn't become so angry; if only I had made love to her every time she wanted to; if only I hadn't been such a bitch."

I hope by now you have satisfied your need to punish yourself. I suggest you let it go. Your hindsight is much better now. You have learned a great deal about life and about yourself since the troubles began in your love relationship. Your awareness and your insights are much improved. How about using the new awareness and insight as a basis for further *growth,* rather than self-punishment? Do something for the rest of your life, not the past. Try saying, "I did the best I could with what I knew and what I had to work with," and leave it at that. Now, you're going to work on today, and tomorrow, and the next day, and the next....

Maybe your relationship failed because there was a third party involved. It is easier to be angry at that third party than it is to be angry at your former love partner or yourself. There is a "Catch-22" in being angry at your former love partner — you are damned if you do, and damned if you don't. How can you be angry at the person you loved? It is easier to be angry at the person who came in and "took your spouse away from you."

There are many reasons why one partner leaves a relationship to become involved with another. You may feel that the other person had something to offer that you didn't have. That may be true in some cases. But every love relationship has some cracks in its foundation, and in many cases — for many reasons — these cracks may result in a breakup. Patterns of development and interaction start long before love relationships end. If there were such serious cracks in your relationship, it may be difficult for you to see and understand them at this time.

Let me give you an example. Many people have not freed themselves from their parents' influence when they marry. They don't have identities of their own, separate from being children of their parents. Such a person may later decide to dump a love partner. But when you examine what is really going on, you see that he or she is actually dumping the parents' control and influence. To rebel against the spouse may be, in reality, to rebel against the parents.

So the crack in your relationship may have begun even *before* you married. And if there was a crack in your relationship, it is easy for a third party to become involved by filling that crack. It often is easier — or seems easier — for a person outside of the relationship to fill the deficiency than it is for a person who is part of the relationship. A good marriage counselor may be able to help you to explore and understand some of the cracks and deficiencies in your past love relationship.

There is another important phenomenon that frequently contributes to the demise of a marriage. Many couples make the mistake of investing all of their time and energy into a project external to the love relationship. Examples might be building a new house or business, or going to school. This external project may keep the couple so occupied they have little energy or time to invest in their love relationship. In fact, the project may become a method of avoiding each other. When the house is finished, the couple finds they have nothing in common anymore, and the new house becomes a monument to their divorce.

Why Did It Begin In the First Place?

Many people ask, "Why did so-and-so get a divorce?" Sometimes a more relevant question is, "Why did that couple marry?" Many people marry for the wrong reasons, such as 1) to overcome loneliness, 2) to escape an unhappy parental home, 3) because they think that everybody is expected to marry, only "losers" who can't find someone to marry stay single, 4) out of a need to parent, or be parented by, another person, and, 5) because "we fell in love."

I will talk more about love in another chapter, but let it suffice for now that there are many levels of love and not all are mature enough to provide a sound basis for getting married. Quite frequently we have an idealized image of that other person. We fell in love with that *image* rather than the person. When the honeymoon is over (a long time passes before reality hits), we are disillusioned because that person is not living up to the image we have idealized. Perhaps "falling in love" is an attempt to fill some of our emptiness, rather than a sound basis on which to build a marriage.

Those who get married for these wrong reasons (including "falling in love") might be described as half-people who are trying to become whole, and to find happiness by getting married. Even the usual wedding vows talk about "two people becoming one." During a talk with a group of ministers, one asked if I thought the marriage vows were contributing to divorce. I replied, "Yes." The discussion was lively, and I believe a few of the ministers began to consider changing the vows in the marriage ceremony.

When you are ready to face life alone and have found happiness as a single person, then you are ready to face life together with another person. Two whole people who have climbed the mountain of personal growth and self-awareness will tend to have a much more dynamic relationship than two half-people joining together in an attempt to become whole.

Most of the wrong reasons may be summarized by stating that the unhappy person expects that getting married will bring happiness. Do you remember the movies we saw about marriage in the *old days* — the '30s, '40s and '50s? (Television has seen to it that no one is too young to remember them!) The movie was all about the *courtship* of the couple. When they married, the movie ended. The subtle message was that you became married and — with no effort— lived happily ever after. Such a fairy tale!

My son Todd writes his ideas and thoughts on paper and often they are profound. He described a good reason for getting married:

"At some time in the future during my growth toward becoming a full person, there will come a day when my cup runneth over so profusely that the need will arise for another person to soak up the excess."

When It's Over... It's Over

Recognizing the ending of an unhappy and unproductive relationship may help you look at your divorce as a decision reflecting good mental health. Take a look at your former relationship, your former partner, and yourself. Set aside for a moment all of society's reasons why you were "meant for each other." This is the time for painful honesty. Ask yourself:

Were you and your partner friends?

Did you confide in one another?

What interests did you share? Hobbies? Attitudes toward life? Politics? Religion? Children?

Were your goals — for yourself, each other, the relationship — similar/compatible?

Did you agree on methods for solving problems between you (not necessarily the solutions, the methods)?

When you got angry with each other, did you deal with it directly, or hide it, or try to hurt each other?

Did you share friendships?

Did you go out together socially?

Did you share responsibilities for earning money and household chores in a mutually-agreed-upon way?
Did you make at least major decisions jointly?
Did you allow each other time alone?
Did you trust each other?
Was the relationship important enough for each of you to make some personal sacrifices for it when necessary?

I hope these questions were not too painful for you. Your honest answers will probably help you recognize that your relationship really was — in most cases — at an end, even before the formal separation/divorce. It is tough to acknowledge some of those shortcomings. It is even tougher to accept that I was part of the problem (easy enough to blame my partner, or society, or...). Acceptance, however, is the all important positive side to this first rebuilding block called Denial.

Take some time with this. And remember: You do not have to take on a load of guilt in order to accept that your relationship is over! Stay out of the "if only" game. The reasons, the contributing factors are as complex as those structures which support a bridge. It takes a great deal of analysis of *known* forces and stresses and loads and strength of materials to build a successful bridge. How infinitely more complex is a successful love relationship! And how little most of us really *know* about the interpersonal forces and stresses and loads and strength of our own materials!

You'll learn much more as the journey up our mountain continues. For now, take a deep breath and say it — "My love relationship has ended."

Now let yourself cry for a while.

From Denial to Acceptance

Now that you are up to your tears in the reasons why relationships end, and you have taken a hard look at the cracks in your own former love relationship, you may be feeling "sadder but wiser." And maybe a bit down on yourself. You are not alone at this point either.

A computer taught me a key aspect of learning to accept a love relationship is ending. On my *Fisher Divorce Adjustment Scale* was a subtest designed to measure how well you had accepted the ending of your love relationship. When the statistics had been analyzed by the computer, the items of the self-acceptance subtest had disappeared! I checked to find where they had gone, and discovered that many were related to feelings of self-worth. The data are clear, and confirmed by others: the better your feelings of self-worth, the easier it is for you to accept the ending of your love relationship.

If you have difficulty starting the journey up this mountain because you refuse to accept the ending of your love relationship, you may need to work on improving your self-concept. I know that when you are in the shock of a recent ending, telling you to improve your self-concept is like blowing in the wind — it does not change much. Still, you will find it true. Especially after we deal with self-concept more in chapter eleven, you will experience the difference for yourself as you discover more of your own value.

As you come closer to standing alone, to accepting that your relationship has really ended, the emotional pain will get pretty intense. And the pain you are feeling is real. Divorce and death of a spouse are probably the two most painful experiences you will feel in your life. Millions of other people have felt the same things you are feeling as your relationship ends. It hurts. And even knowing you're not alone helps only a little. But we need to use our pain to learn. To flow with the pain rather than denying it. To use it as motivation to grow and make the crisis into an opportunity, rather than an experience that leaves us with wounds that never heal. We can use the pain as an excuse to remain bitter, angry, unhappy; or we can use the pain to grow. Which do you choose to do?

Those of you who believe that you will be getting back together with your former love partner probably feel there is no reason to climb this mountain of adjustment. In Colorado about 20 to 30 percent of the people who file for divorce do not obtain a final decree (the percentage varies from year to year). We do not know what happens to these couples, but it can be assumed that many resurrect their love relationships, and get back together again.

What's the best plan of action for those of you who want to get back together? Do you have to climb this mountain of adjustment? If your relationship has become fractured to the point of physical separation and you are talking about divorce, you may need time apart to change the old patterns of interaction. You may need to close off the bridge to traffic while you shore up the foundations. Experience individual personal growth before you start working on the bridge. It's pretty easy just to move in together again, but it's difficult to make the old *relationship* more meaningful and productive unless the *people* go through changes. You may need to climb the mountain before you go back to your former love partner!

About Friends and Lovers

I want to become somewhat parental and talk to you about how vulnerable you are to becoming involved in another love relationship as a way of making your pain go away. My belief is that you need *friends* rather than *lovers* right now.

Have you read Homer's Odyssey? The Greek myth tells of sailors on a journey filled with various obstacles. One of these obstacles is an island where beautiful female sirens attempt to seduce the sailors into stopping. (The sailors have been forewarned that stopping will lead to their destruction). They prevent the sirens from tempting them by tying themselves to the mast and blindfolding themselves.

Like Homer's sailors, you will need to tie yourself to the mast of self-discipline and avoid becoming too deeply involved in another love relationship until you have healed some of the emotional pain. Almost always a relationship which is started when you are in deep pain will add to your misery in the long run. But friendships are helpful; and if you can build friendships rather than love relationships, it will be more productive, for the present.

Imagine a circus tightrope act. The platform at one end represents the security you had in the love relationship. The platform at the other end represents the security you need to find within yourself. You need to walk across the tightrope in your adjustment process to find that inner security. You can fall off one side by withdrawing into your apartment or home and not making any friends.

You can fall off the other side by becoming deeply involved in another long-term, committed love relationship — if you're investing more in the relationship than you are in your own personal growth. You wake up one morning and discover you're trying to please the other person and trying to make the relationship work, but you're not trying to become the person you wish to be.

The balance pole is having friends that help you keep your balance as you walk across the tightrope. They give you honest feedback that is not biased by a need to have your love. Friends are more objective than lovers, and you need objectivity at this point in your life. Set yourself a goal: learn to be happy as a single person before you become coupled again!

Suffer the Children

There are three areas relating to denial that cause problems for kids. First is that children of divorce will continue to maintain some sort of a fantasy image of their parents getting back together again, with much emotional investment in that dream. They have difficulty accepting the reality that their parents' relationship is over. It may be a surprise to learn how strong this fantasy is in your children. You continually need to present them with the reality that the relationship is over, so they don't continue to invest in this fantasy. Kids may use all kinds of manipulative behavior trying to get the two of you back together again, trying to have you spend time together, or trying to get you talking to each other. Your kids have a large emotional investment in not accepting the ending of their parents' relationship, and in hoping that their parents will get back together again. Respond gently but firmly and persistently with your own decision — that the marriage is over.

An important second aspect with kids and the denial/acceptance block is their belief that they did something to cause their parents' breakup. The last time that they disobeyed — when they did not go to bed or clean up their food at mealtime or do their household chores — they think this led to their parents' fight and then to their divorce. Try hard to help your kids see that it's not their fault and that divorce is a grown-up problem.

A third aspect has to do with the children's fear that now they have "lost" one parent, will they lose the other parent? They tend to be very clinging and dependent upon the parents, and they need a lot of reassurance that the parents will not leave. Parents do divorce each other, but they do not divorce their children. You need to reassure your children that even though Mom and Dad are divorced from each other, they will never divorce the children.

How Are You Doing?

You may be making this journey even though you don't want to, even though you are still married in your heart. The emotional pain is so great that you know you have to climb. It will benefit you to learn as much from this journey as possible, so decide to make it a positive experience, rather than a begrudging one.

In the next chapter, we'll continue our exploration of why love relationships end. Before you go on, however, take time to complete this chapter's checklist, to help you decide if you are ready to move on to the next portion of the trail. Use it to check out your progress. No one is grading you, so be very honest with yourself.

1. *I am able to accept that my love relationship is ending.*
2. *I am comfortable telling my friends and relatives that my love relationship is ending.*
3. *I have begun to understand some of the reasons why my love relationship did not work out, and this has helped me overcome the feelings of denial.*
4. *I believe that even though divorce is painful, it can be a positive and creative experience.*
5. *I am ready to invest emotionally in my own personal growth in order to become the person I would like to be.*
6. *I want to learn to become happy as a single person before committing myself to another love relationship.*
7. *I will continue to invest in my own personal growth even if my former love partner and I plan to get back together.*

FEAR
"I Have Lots of It!"

Fear can be paralyzing until we're able to recognize it as a part of us that is our friend. Fear then becomes a motivator and a way to learn more about ourselves. Fears are a major part of the feelings we experience when we are in the pits of divorce.

Chapter 3

Fear was my biggest obstacle. I was afraid of all the changes I had no control over, and at the same time, I was afraid nothing would ever change. My whole life was being influenced by my fears! I was afraid of being alone, and at the same time isolating myself, afraid of never really being loved again and yet pushing love away when it got too close... I was completely stuck, paralyzed by my own fear... It wasn't until I admitted my fears, listed them and talked about them openly, that they lost their power over me.

—Jere

I spent thirty-three years as a homemaker, raising a large family. I had the security and comfort of upper-middle-class living. When I became a single parent, with responsibility for our youngest child and faced with the task of becoming self-supporting (with few if any marketable skills), I was literally paralized with fear.

—Joanne

Look at the large crowd looking up at the trail. They are making comments such as: "Don't take that trail; you'll fall off the side of the mountain." "The trail is too steep. I'm afraid I can't climb it." "I don't know what kind of wild animals will jump out at me while I'm climbing." "I don't think I want to do this." "I'm afraid of what I'll learn about myself if I make this climb."

Ending a love relationship results in fears of all kinds. Some fears you didn't know you would ever feel. Some are old fears you've had most of your life but had been successfully denying.

It's easy to allow fears to immobilize you. You feel too afraid to climb the mountain, and become almost paralyzed by your fears. A little fear can be motivating. But too many fears makes it difficult to function and to get on with your life.

There are a couple of key things I've learned about fears which can be helpful in learning to deal with them. The first is that fears not yet identified are the most powerful. When you identify them, take a look at them, and face them, you'll find they aren't as scary and powerful as you thought. One simple thing you can do which really helps is to make a list of your fears. Identify the things you're afraid of, so you can get in touch with just what you're feeling.

Another useful insight about fears is that *feared situations which you don't face are the very ones that are likely occur.* If I'm afraid of being rejected, I find many ways of avoiding rejection. I may become a people pleaser, or develop an over-responsible part, or avoid expressing anger. While these behaviors might appear to insulate me from rejection, they actually can increase my chances of being rejected. People sense I am not being real, honest, authentic, and may reject me for that. Until we face our fears, what we are afraid of will most likely happen to us. So, as you become aware of your fears, it's best not to deny them, but to face them openly. That alone may be enough to chase some of them away!

What Are YOU Afraid Of?

Let's take a look at some of the common fears I have heard people experience in the past. I think this list of fears which come up often in the divorce process will help you access and identify your own fears. How many of these fears are you experiencing?

One of the greatest fears is fear of *the unknown future.* I don't know what the trail up this mountain is like. I don't know what I'll learn about myself or about others. I can't visualize how I'll be able to make it as a single person.

These fears about the unknown are based in our formative years. Like the ghosts you thought you saw when you woke up in the middle of the night, the fear is real, but the objects aren't really there; they're figments of your imagination. You need to learn that you can face the ghosts of the unknown future, and live one day at a time. You can learn to trust the process and know that you'll be able to face eventually every new experience that occurs as you experience the ending of a love relationship.

There is a common fear of *becoming a divorced person*. What will people think? They will discover what a failure I am. If I can't work out the problems in my love relationship, what is there left for me? It's as if I spilled food on my clothes while eating and now everyone is shouting, "Look at that person who is so stupid and foolish that she spilled food all over herself." I feel embarrassed, awkward, found out, ashamed, and afraid people won't like me anymore.

It is fearful *to have everyone discover our family secrets*. Often we haven't thought about it but many of our family secrets are not secret anymore. When we were together, I could have a fight with my love partner but no one knew about it. We felt ashamed of having problems in our marriage, but at least the whole world didn't know about it then. When you separate, it's hard to keep the kids' teachers from knowing. Friends soon discover there is another phone number to reach my ex. The post office found out right away that her mail was to be forwarded to another address. The utility company had to be notified that the bill wouldn't be paid until some of the financial decisions had been made. It seems everyone in the whole world knows about the dirty linen that only the two of us knew about before.

I feel fearful because I don't know *how to make the decisions I have to make*. What lawyer do I contact? What therapist will I go see? How do I decide which bills to pay when I won't have enough money to pay them all? My spouse handled the check book. Now how do I learn to manage the checking account? I don't have any idea of how to have my car serviced. I'm sure the men at the repair shop will take advantage of me because I never had to take the car in before. Just learning all I need to know so I can make good decisions is a full-time job. I'm too overwhelmed emotionally to care much about my car.

I am fearful about *money*. How can I make it financially when there are now two houses to maintain? I'm afraid I'll be fired because all I do is cry at work. I can't concentrate and do an adequate job. Why would anyone want to have me work for them when I'm so inefficient? I don't know where I'll find enough money to pay the bills and feed my children.

And speaking of children, I'm afraid of *being a single parent*. I'm barely functioning on my own and I just don't have the patience, courage, and strength to meet the needs of my kids by myself. I no longer have a partner to take over when I'm overwhelmed. I have to be there for my kids 24 hours a day, seven days a week. I want to crawl into bed and hide my head under the covers. I wish there were someone whose lap I could crawl up in, someone who would hold me, instead of me having to pretend I'm strong enough to hold my kids on my own lap.

I'm afraid of *losing my kids*. My ex-partner is talking about going for custody. I've always been the significant parent for my kids and they say they want to be with me. But my ex has more money and is able to buy the things the kids want. I'm sure my kids will be swayed by the promise of so many material things that I can't provide; surely they'll want to live with him. If we have a custody hearing, what will my kids say? Will they talk about how distraught mom is and that she's too busy and upset to spend any time with them?

I'm afraid about *whom to talk to*. I need someone to listen to me but will anyone understand? Most of my friends are married and have not been through a divorce. Will they gossip about what I share with them? Will they still be my friends now that I'm divorced? I must be the only person in the whole world feeling these feelings. No one else can possibly understand me when I can't even understand myself.

I'm afraid of *going to court*. I've never been in court before. I thought only criminals or those who have broken the law go to court. I have heard the "war stories" of what's happened to others in court when they were going through a divorce, and I'm afraid some of the same things will happen to me. I know my ex-partner will find the best barracuda attorney around, and I'll lose everything. I don't want to be mean and nasty but I am afraid I'll have to be in order to protect myself. Why does the court have so much power over what happens to me, my family, my children? What have I done to deserve this kind of treatment?

I'm afraid of *anger*. I'm afraid of my own anger and of my partner becoming angry. As a child I used to feel terror when my parents were angry and fighting. I learned to avoid being around anger. My partner and I never fought or showed anger in any way. I find myself feeling angry sometimes and it really frightens me. What if I became angry? It would take away any chance of getting back together again. I feel angry a lot of the time but it's not safe or right for me to get angry. I do feel depressed and I wonder if there is a connection between my anger and feeling depressed.

I'm afraid of *being out of control*. The anger feelings are so great inside of me. What if I were like my parents when they got angry and lost control? I hear stories of people doing violent actions when they are divorcing. Might I do something violent if I get out of control?

I'm afraid of *being alone and living alone*. If I'm alone now, who will take care of me when I am old? I have seen couples take care of each other and avoid going to a nursing home or retirement center. But with no one to take care of me, I'll spend my old age alone. And what if I get ill? I might just die in my empty apartment and no one will know. There's no one to take care of me when I'm ill, and no one to find me if I become so sick I can't function or call for help.

I also fear *discovering I am unlovable*. If my ex-partner, who knows me better than anyone, doesn't want to live with me, I must be unlovable. How can I live the rest of my life alone and feeling unlovable? I was always afraid of being abandoned and now I feel I have been abandoned. I've been discarded like a toy that isn't wanted anymore.

I feel afraid I am *becoming mentally ill*. I feel crazy enough to be admitted to a mental hospital. I feel crazy enough that the idea of being taken care of completely in a psych ward, with even my meals provided, is almost appealing. Never before in my life could I imagine being crazy enough to think a psych ward would sound desirable. But it does in a way. I want to be little and have someone take care of me, even if I have to go to a psych ward to have it happen.

I'm afraid of *being hurt even more than I have been hurt*. I never knew I could hurt so much. The person I loved — and I thought loved me — has hurt me more than anyone else has ever hurt me in my life. I want to hide so I won't be hurt anymore. I hurt so much I found myself feeling numb, as though I had callouses on my feelings. I'm afraid I will crack and not be able to survive being hurt again.

I am afraid of *change*. What changes are going to happen to me? Will I have to move from my home? Will I have to find a new job? Will I have to make new friends? Will I have to make changes in myself and my personality in order to survive? These unknowns are pretty frightening; I don't know what changes I will have to make as a result of this crisis.

The thought of *dating and being with another person* is so fearful that I don't allow myself to even think about it.

Allowing Fear To Become a Friend.

A few people deal with their fears by doing risky and dangerous things. They want to face their fears and find that taking risks allows them to feel their fears. As part of the divorce process, they will climb cliffs, drive their cars dangerously, or put themselves in other dangerous situations which cause them to feel fearful. Rarely are such extreme behaviors productive. Instead of trying to push the limits of fear, it's more valuable to let fear become a friend.

Therapists often ask those who are feeling a great deal of fear to think of the worst thing that could happen. Are you going to die from this crisis? Are you going to become ill? Are you going to be sent off to prison? Usually the worst thing is that you're going to live with a lot of hurt for a while. The most likely outcome is that the crisis will lead to being transformed, and experiencing life in a deeper more profound way.

Fear is a normal part of each of us, and we can make it a friend. It keeps us from taking unnecessary risks, putting ourselves in situations that are dangerous to us, exposing ourselves and becoming vulnerable. Without fear, we might not live very long, because we would expose ourselves to situations which are life-threatening. We need fear to help protect us. You suffer a physical burn from a fire and learn to respect and fear the fire; you know it can hurt you. The same thing is true with an emotional burn. When you're hurt, you learn to protect yourself from becoming too intimate until you have healed the emotional burn.

Fear also can be a motivator. It can motivate us to develop coping skills in order to survive. It can motivate us to develop better defenses. It can motivate us to become stronger emotionally and physically. We can use fear as a motivator to work through the adjustment process. For example, I may say to myself, "I don't want to be in this much pain. I want to work through the process and overcome my fears."

The best way to overcome fears is to allow yourself to feel them. "The only way out is through." You need to discover your fears, to be committed to overcome them, and to use them as an avenue into understanding yourself better. The things you're afraid of lead you to knowing yourself better.

You may, for example have fears about parenting and dealing with your children. Working through this crisis can result in your being a far better parent than you were before the crisis. Facing and dealing with your fears allows you to have more time and energy to devote to personal growth, career development, developing better relationship skills, becoming a better parent.

Dealing with Fear

When you are feeling fear, go into your body and determine where you are experiencing the fear. It usually is in your solar plexis, that area just above your belly button. But you can feel it in various places in your body, such as down the backs of your legs. Identifying where you are experiencing fear helps you to accept and start to deal with the fearful feelings.

Normally when you are feeling fear, your body will send oxygen and adrenaline to the big muscles in your body in the primitive way your body prepares to fight or defend yourself against the danger you are perceiving. Most of you do not have large muscles in your brain so the result might be that you are not thinking well when you are feeling fear.

I suggest you find a comfortable place to sit or lie down and do some deep breathing exercises. Breathe in as much air as you can.

Fill your lower lungs with air by doing belly breaths. Get the oxygen flowing in your blood, especially to your head.

Now relax. Allow all the muscles in your body, from your toes to your forehead, to release tension and become deeply relaxed. Keep breathing deeply as you relax more and more fully. Close your eyes for a few minutes and imagine yourself in a very calm relaxing scene (on the beach, in a mountain meadow, ...).

Then think: Is this fear life threatening? Where did I learn this fear? Is it a present concern or a remnant from my past? For example, when my partner in exile is expressing anger toward me, does it remind me of how fearful I felt when my father became angry when I was a child? Does my fear remind me of a time when I was emotionally or physically hurt in the past? What would be appropriate action for me to do when I am feeling this fear? Is the fear I am feeling going to overwhelm me or can I use it as a method of better understanding myself? Processing my fear will help me to allow fear to be my friend and help me to take more control of my life. The more choices I can make, the less fear will control me.

You can experience a great deal of personal growth and transformation because of the crisis of ending your love relationship. Facing and overcoming your fears can help you make the crisis into a creative experience.

Children Are Even More Scared Than You

After I told my eight-year-old daughter I was leaving, I went in to pack my clothes. When I came back to kiss her good-bye, she was hiding under the bed. She was so scared she doesn't remember this and denies to this day that she was hiding.

Imagine the fears children feel when their parents divorce! Their whole world is threatened: Do my parents still love me? Where will I live? Will I go with mommy, or with daddy? What will my friends think? Will I even *have* any friends? What's going to happen to me?

Children often fear that they'll be left alone: "Mommy is leaving me; will Daddy leave too?" "I didn't have anything to say about my daddy moving out. I wonder when my mommy will move out and leave me all alone."

The message we need to give our children is that *parents may divorce each other, but they will never divorce their children.* The marriage may end, but parenting is forever. Ressurance on this point, *in words and actions,* is extremely important at this time.

Fears are extremely powerful. Children, like adults, can learn to identify their fears, talk about them, and handle them more comfortably. All of us need to recognize that it's okay to be afraid; everybody is sometimes.

Incidentally, the relaxation and deep breathing methods described in this chapter are very valuable for kids, too. If they learn them early, they can apply them in all kinds of life situations which bring up anxiety and fear (e.g., exams, public speaking).

How Are You Doing?

Here is a check list to help you determine if you have completed this part of the journey. It will be hard to really climb the mountain of adjustment until you have become courageous enough to deal with your fears.

1. *I have identified and made a list of my fears.*
2. *I have found a friend or a helping person with whom I can share my list of fears.*
3. *I am learning that fear can be one of my friends.*
4. *I am changing fear from a paralyzing into a motivating feeling.*
5. *I am learning more about myself by facing my fears directly.*

ADAPTATION
"But It Worked When I Was a Kid!"

Growing up, we all learned a variety of ways to adapt when our needs for love and attention were unfulfilled. Some of those strategies may have helped us get by as children, but they are excess baggage for grown-ups. An over- or under-responsible style for example, is not effective in adult relationships. The process of rebuilding offers many opportunities to change your unhealthy parts into authentic, relationship-enhancing behaviors.

Chapter 4

In my first marriage I was the parent taking care of him. In my next love relationship I would like to have a parent to take care of me and nurture the little girl inside of me. And then in my third love relationship maybe I can become balanced and have a healthy relationship.
— Janice

You're still trying to figure out why your love relationship ended, aren't you?

Before we continue our climb up the mountain of rebuilding blocks, let's take some time to explore that question. Almost everyone going through the divorce process wants to find out more about why their love relationships ended; this chapter will help you answer that question.

Nothing is 100% when you are ending a love relationship. When you were considering divorce, your feelings were probably about 80% favorable to the divorce and 20% against it. When you are in crisis, it is confusing — but quite normal — to hear these competing voices inside of you.

Each of us has many sub-personalities or parts. When you drive by the ice-cream store, one voice says, "Let's stop and get an ice cream cone." Another voice says somewhat critically, "Do you remember your New Year's Resolution to lose twenty pounds? You won't do it by eating ice cream all the time!" Best of all is a mediating voice that says, "It's okay to have a small ice cream cone once a week as a reward for being such a good person."

Listen to your self-talk and you will better understand your different sub-personalities. As you listen to the different voices inside yourself, try to identify the parts that are represented. If you're like most people going through a divorce, there may have been an "internal war" among the parts that eventually became an "external war" with your love partner and resulted in the ending of the relationship.

Getting in touch with the diverse parts of yourself can be of great benefit to your healing process, and will also improve the self-understanding you'll need for building more solid relationships in the future.

Healthy Relationships

Why do so many people, when they have a choice between a healthy relationship and an unhealthy one, often choose the unhealthy one? What does health look like, anyway? How does it feel? How can we create healthy relationships with ourselves and with others?

Let's begin to deal with those questions by looking first at what might be called healthy personality parts.

Each of us has a *feeling part*, which some refer to as the "inner child." It's important to be able to access and identify feelings. There is evidence of a correlation between how much one can *feel* and now much one can *heal*. The person who isn't able to access and talk about feelings will take much longer adjusting to a crisis.

We also have a *creative part* that thinks of new ways of doing things or thinking about things. The creative part is a wonderful gift that allows us not only to be artistic, but original, unique, individual, and self-actualized. Being creative feels good and leads us to be more human and less robot-like.

The *magical part* reads garden seed catalogues and believes that the seeds we plant will produce flowers and plants that look like the catalogue pictures. This part enjoys going to see *Mary Poppins* movies and believes we too could fly with an umbrella. The magical part allows us to balance out our serious and rational sides so we can have fun and not always have to be eating bran, broccoli, and other things that are good for us.

We have a *nurturing part*, but often we become unbalanced with our nurturing. We nurture others quite easily but neglect to nurture ourselves. We bought the idea that it is better to give than to receive, and then often pay the price of giving ourselves away. The healthy part is to give both to others and to ourselves.

We have a *spiritual part* that allows us to connect through faith to whatever our supreme being looks like. This is often more of a childlike part because faith may not be rational, intellectual, and adult. The spiritual child part allows us to surrender to a power greater than we, but at the same time to use our free will to make loving choices in our lives.

Can you name other parts of you that are healthy parts? Take some time and think about it. Write down a list of other healthy parts.

Did You Grow Up Healthy?

I have some important questions for you to think about. How much did your family, your childhood home, encourage your healthy parts? Were you, particularly if you are a male, encouraged to cry? If you're female, were you encouraged to be appropriately angry — and to show it? Were you encouraged to be inquisitive and creative? Were you encouraged to be independent and think for yourself or were you told to "do as I say because I am your parent"?

How about other influences in your childhood, such as school? Were you encouraged to be creative or did being different cause you problems? Were you encouraged to be angry? To cry? To talk about feelings? What grades did you receive for being nurturing, spiritual, believing in magical fairy tales?

What about your religious training? Did your church encourage creative doubts in your beliefs? Did you find encouragement to be angry or was anger looked at as sinful and not religious? Was nurturing of yourself encouraged? Or were you taught it is better to give (and give, and give) than to receive?

Feedback from my seminar participants indicates that some of us received more encouragement to acknowledge our healthy parts than others. Some of us grew up in families that allowed us to be creative, to believe in magic, to give and receive nurturing. Others had schools which, along with teaching the three R's, still allowed us to be individual and unique. Some families and schools and churches taught us how to be more loving, but too many emphasized fear and control to make us behave as we were "supposed to."

For a variety of reasons, many of us failed to learn how to acknowledge and encourage our healthy parts. As adults, we forget to feel, to be creative, to take time for ourselves, to invest in our spiritual well-being. We internalized the rejection of these healthy parts in order to get along, to belong, to get grades, to make money, to be what others want us to be. Now, we feel more or less unloved, not nurtured, not okay. We may have low self-esteem, and look for ways of feeling better from our relationships instead of looking inside ourselves. No wonder we're uncomfortable when we find healthy relationships with others. We're uncomfortable with any healthy parts we may have *within* us.

Developing Adaptation Strategies

Those of us whose emotional and psychological needs were slighted in our formative years found it necessary to discover ways to adapt to our non-nourishing situations. We developed alternative "adaptive behavior" parts that allowed us to better meet our needs. The more stressful and traumatic a childhood was, the greater the need for such adaptive behavior parts. Let's take a look at what some of these adaptation strategies look like.

Caren developed an *"urge-to-help"* part. If others in the family were unhappy, quarreling, angry, using drugs to excess, she felt better when she "helped" them. Her pain and discomfort was less when she focused on their pain and discomfort. Now in her adult relationships, whenever she sees someone needing help, she wants to pitch in: picking up hitch-hikers along the road; talking to anyone in the grocery store who appears to be feeling sad or irritable; finding stray cats and bringing them home. She may choose to marry someone in need, because she's looking for someone who needs help to balance out her "urge-to-help" part.

Gerald learned an adaptive *over-responsible* behavior. An oldest child, he changed his siblings' diapers, baby-sat the younger ones, helped with preparing meals. These activities gained him recognition, attention, and love. He grew up continuing to take care of the rest of the family — just what he had resented doing as a child. And he found someone to marry who is under-responsible (and when she wasn't under-responsible enough, he "trained" her to be more under-responsible!)

Lots of us grew up with adults who were very critical. Joe was given the job of taking care of the yard at an early age. He learned that if he mowed every blade of grass off evenly with no long stems sticking up, if he trimmed around each tree and along the sidewalk, mowed the grass diagonally so it looked like a major league baseball diamond, he might receive less criticism. He gave up early on looking for any "atta-boys," praise, or encouragement. He found the only way he could receive compliments was to go to the neighbors: his father often bragged about his son to others, but never praised him directly.

When Joe grew up, it was very difficult to go shopping with him because he had a great deal of difficulty making up his mind what to buy. He was afraid of making the wrong decision because he had internalized a part of his father which might be called an *inner critic* part. Many of us have a big adaptive "inner critic" part which keeps reminding us that we should strive to be perfect and we are definitely not behaving as perfectly as we "should." All decisions, even what to buy when we go shopping, should be the best decision possible. Like Joe, we strive to be perfect so the inner critic will not shout so loudly inside.

What does this adaptive behavior perfectionist look for in a partner? Maybe a people-pleaser who will continually please the inner critic, which easily becomes an "outer-critic" in our adult relationships. The only thing more difficult than living with another person who is a perfectionist is living with one's own internal perfectionist part. Some perfectionists marry an opposite — like the

"Pig-Pen" comic strip character — so the perfectionist can continually find something to criticize in the other person's messy behavior.

Bob grew up with a lot of chaos in his childhood home: family members always coming home drunk, being off-the-wall emotionally, behaving irrationally, or just angry and emotional all of the time. Bob made a choice to always be rational, logical, sensible, intellectual, and to avoid feelings of any kind. He learned to adapt to the chaos by being completely *intellectual and unfeeling,* because when he got into feelings, he was hurt, criticized, and felt not-okay. He learned to stuff feelings of any kind, particularly any angry feelings he might have. Becoming angry was okay for the "big people" but not for him.

What kind of person would a buried-feelings person like Bob look for in a relationship? He had become unbalanced by being all intellect and with no feelings so he needed a partner who would balance him out — a person who was very emotional and expressive of her feelings! (It seems to be easier for males to become non-feeling people but it can be either sex. Often the female is the more feeling person because growing up female in our society usually means learning to be aware of and to trust feelings.)

When emotional individuals marry their non-feeling opposites like Bob, the emotional partners keep trying to draw feelings of any kind out of their reluctant mates. And the harder they try, the more intellectual the other person becomes ("intellectual" here refers to a focus on thinking rather than feeling; it doesn't necessarily mean the person is interested in intellectual pursuits). And the more intellectual one is, the more emotional the other becomes. Such relationships may become polarized, with one person carrying virtually all of the intellectual parts, and the other carrying all of the feelings for the relationship.

Most folks think they married because they "fell in love." I've decided that falling in love is an unstable condition — maybe even an emotional illness! Oftentimes it has to do with *the way the partners are unbalanced,* rather than having anything to do with love. Some of us marry our disowned or disused personality parts and call it "falling in love."

Why Relationships End

What do our adaptation strategies have to do with the ending of relationships?

Think about personality as a car with one of the adaptive behavior parts in the driver's seat. Other people in the person's life are going to have to put up with the way that part is driving, particularly if the "driver" is a rigid, adaptive behavior. And the more unmet needs there are which led to the adaptive behavior style, the more rigid and controlling the adaptive behavior is likely to be. If the driver is over-responsible, for example, everyone will have to deal with a lot of controlling behavior, and will learn to be under-responsible (if they elect to stay in the relationship). If the personality in the driver's seat is a people-pleaser, everyone will have to tell the driver how and where to drive — people-pleasers don't like to make any decisions on their own.

Everything can work okay for a while with an adaptive personality part in control. Sooner or later, however, one partner is likely to grow tired of the imbalance.

Nancy was an over-responsible person (O-R) who tired of always being in control. She developed a lot of resentment at Jack, her partner, because he was a walking example of that part of her which she didn't want to own or admit. Nancy saw Jack having more fun, being less responsible, and not carrying his share of the load. She became angry and resentful because Jack couldn't even handle the checkbook; checks were bouncing all over town because of insufficient funds. Sometimes Jack never got the checks written or the bills paid until the phone calls started coming. Nancy decided to end the relationship.

Like Nancy, over-responsible partners quite frequently become tired of the role and leave the marriage. As for Jack and other under-responsible people (U-R), the crisis can be an opportunity to wake-up and become more responsible. If not, they will look for another mommy or daddy to marry so they can carry on the same pattern in the next relationship.

Had Jack decided to take more responsibility, he might have resented Nancy for not "allowing" him to grow up; *he* may have decided to end the relationship. U-R's often become rebellious, frustrated, irritable and angry, and want to get away from the O-R's smothering behavior.

If Nancy doesn't take the opportunity to look at herself and her adaptation strategy, she will probably seek out and find another stray cat to take care of so her O-R part can keep driving the personality car.

I have asked many people to identify when they first noticed an event that upset the system in their love relationship. They usually mention things like a baby being born, the wife starting to work outside of the home, the husband being transferred to a new job, a grandparent becoming ill or dying, being in and barely surviving a major flood. If I ask them how they were able to adjust to this change in the relationship, they usually say the relationship was too rigid to adjust. The change was the beginning of the end of their relationship.

Did you have an event that upset your system which resulted eventually in your relationship ending?

The Bridge Across Responsibility

Here is a metaphor to help you think about this over/under-responsible relationship. Imagine the love partners (Jack and Nancy; you and your partner) as the ends of a bridge. The two of them are supporting the relationship bridge: it is the connection between them. The over-responsible person (Nancy) is the bridge sweeper who keeps the whole bridge clean — all the way across to Jack's end of the bridge. The under-responsible person (Jack) is sitting on his end of the bridge with a fishing pole. Nancy resents Jack fishing all of the time instead of keeping his end of the bridge swept. Fisherman Jack resents Nancy never taking time to enjoy fishing herself, not to mention her scaring away the fish with her persistent sweeping.

I'm talking about this particular over/under responsible adaptive behavior more than some of the others because it was the most common adptation strategy with the 2,000 people I've taught personally in the divorce class. The over/under responsible pattern seems to be a major cause of divorce. It might be called a parent-child relationship, caretaker/taker relationship, or an alcoholic/enabler relationship. It is a specific form of co-dependency, in which each person is dependent upon the other to keep the system in balance. (Or rather, *imbalance*.) What kinds of adaptive behaviors have you developed? Are they driving your personality car? Would you like to be better able to choose which of your parts you want to be driving? How will you go about changing and taking charge of your life?

Feelings Underneath Adaptive Behavior

I've found that over-responsible people are usually giving to others what they would like to have someone give to them. They have unmet needs — usually from an unsatisfying childhood — which lead them to develop adaptive behavior so they'll feel better and more comfortable. The same is true of the other adaptation strategies. The way to take charge of your life is to learn how to meet the needs which were not met in your formative years. This starts with understanding some of the feelings underneath adaptive behavior.

Julie developed an adaptive behavior pattern because, "I don't want to feel *rejected* and *abandoned*. If I take care of him, he won't dare leave me. He'll feel obligated to not reject me." She takes care of others so she will feel less rejected.

Wayne takes care of Susan because, he told the class, "I would feel *guilty* if I didn't. If I do things for myself, my inner critic starts telling me how selfish I am. How I never do enough for others. How I need to be more loving. By giving to Susan, I feel less guilt."

Fear of criticism is one of the most common feelings behind adaptation strategies. Bill tells it this way: "I learned to feel somewhat anxious inside because of the large amount of criticism I heard from one or more of the significant adults in my childhood. I need to make my world as perfect as possible because I feel *fearful* when my external world is not perfect. I've developed my adaptive behavior so I will feel less fear."

Here is Edward's story: "The only time I feel worthwhile is when I am doing something for others. I don't have much *self-esteem*, but I feel better when I am doing my adaptive behavior. I didn't feel loved

loved as a child and I learned to be seen and not heard. So I am a people-pleaser because I feel worthless if I am not pleasing you."

"I feel *angry*," Alec admitted, "and I don't know how to express it or even allow myself to feel it. So I become very critical of you as a way of adapting. I saw my father as being angry but never showing it openly. But he was very critical of others. I become critical and controlling as a way of disguising my dis-owned anger."

Jennifer grew up with an all-too-common experience: "As a female I saw my mother being the caretaker of the family so my adaptive behavior was learned from her *modeling* — take care of others."

Michael also learned from parental *modeling*: "As a male I saw my father being the breadwinner of the family so the adaptation strategy I learned is to make enough money to be as good a bread-winner as my father was. It is more important to me to work long hours than it is to spend time with my family."

Making Peace with My Inner Critic

Most of us have a well-nourished and thriving "inner critic" part, which often has been the part driving our personality car. The inner critic is good at finding ways of controlling us, just as critical people in childhood found ways of controlling us.

I asked the members of one class to think of a name for their inner critics, and most gave them the same name as one of their parents. Most of us developed our inner critics from the criticism we heard from one or both of our parents.

"I've often thought of the inner critic as me, or as *who I am*," Beverly told me. I pointed out to her that it is important to identify it as just one of the many parts of her personality, and to put up some internal boundaries between the essence of who she is and the part of her that is critical. When we understand that the inner critic is just one of many parts, we have begun to diminish the power it has over us. *My inner critic is smaller than I, and I can be bigger than it is.*

Many of us tend to respond to our inner critics in much the same way we did to our parents. If we believed our parents' criticism, which often resulted in lower feelings of self-esteem, we similarly believe our inner critics and allow the criticism to continually lower our esteem. Those of us who rebelled against our parents may well rebel against our inner critics.

We must remember that we are controlled if we always *obey* one of our parts. But we are also controlled if we are forced to always *rebel against* one of our parts. If we tuned out our parents and didn't listen, we probably will tune out the inner critic voice as well.

How do you react to the voice of your inner critic? Do you react the same way as you did to your parents? Do you want to react differently? How will you do that?

Instead of trying to dis-own or dis-use your inner critic by not listening to it or by ignoring it or by believing it, start listening to what it is saying. Think of it this way: a person sitting next to you whom you keep ignoring will probably try harder and harder to get your attention. He or she might even start shouting at you, or inflict some physical pain or discomfort.

The inner critic is even more powerful than that frustrated person at your elbow, and it's harder to keep ignoring it when it lives inside your head! Consciously make a decision to start listening to that part. You might even write down what you hear it saying. It probably has been talking with "you" messages: "You are really dumb." "Can't you ever do it right?" Acknowledge it, and eventually it will start softening the words it uses. When it is feeling heard, feeling important, and feeling understood, it will start changing from "you" messages to "I" messages: "I didn't like the way I handled that situation." Notice how much more constructive that statement is, and how much more valuable to you when you accept it as your own.

When your critic is finished each time, respond with the familiar cliche', "Thank you for sharing."

What is really happening is that you are making peace with your "inner-parent." The inner critic is usually very much like the admonitions of your parent(s) when you were a child. As you listen to and begin to own your inner critic, it becomes a new and healthy "good-parent."

Homework To Help You Take Charge of Your Life.
One of the major goals of this *Rebuilding* book and the 10-week class is to help you understand what went wrong with your past relationship by learning how your adaptive behavior keeps you unbalanced. Here's a homework assignment designed to help you start becoming more balanced.

(If you want to try to change your relationships either with your past love-partner or with a new partner, I suggest you read my follow-up book and take the ten-week class titled, "Rebuilding Relationships." The follow-up book and class emphasize the next stages of relationship, and teach key communication skills. You'll find more information in the back of this book.)

If your adaptive behavior in the past relationship was *over-responsible*, you were probably a good giver and a poor taker. You were responsible for others, but were not responsible for yourself. You need to become balanced in your giving and receiving so you can do each one equally well.

Your homework is to ask someone to do something for you. (I can just hear some of you saying, "I can't do that." Not ready to let go of your adaptive behavior, huh?) There is another part of the homework. Say no when someone asks you to do something for them. Do you understand how this homework helps you specifically to balance out your giving and receiving? The important thing for you be aware of when you do this homework is which one of the six feelings you experience when you do the homework: rejected, guilty, fearful, angry, low self-worth, or unable to stop doing the modeled behavior?

If your adaptive behavior in your past relationship was *under-responsible*, you will need to put your money where your mouth is and carry out specific changes in responsible behavior.

Dave shared an example of his homework. In the past his former wife was over-responsible. After they were divorced, he would ask her what their teen-age daughters would like for their birthdays. She, of course, was over-responsibile and able to state exactly what they would like. He continued his under-responsible behavior by purchasing for the girls exactly what his ex-wife recommended. She was happy to continue her over-responsible behavior. His daughters were happy to get what they wanted for their birthdays. And Dave was still in his under-responsible behavior. He shared his homework with the class: "I decided on my own what my daughters would like for birthday presents, and I got it for them without asking anyone what I should buy. It wasn't anything they'd asked for, but they seemed thrilled anyway!"

If your adaptive behavior in your past relationship was being a *perfectionist*, your homework is to not make your bed when you get up this week. ("Oh, I can't do that. I will be thinking about the messy bed all day and not get anything done at work. The room looks really messy when the bed isn't made. What if the plumbing should break down and someone would come and see the messy bedroom?" You're not ready to change, huh?)

Remember to ask yourself what are you feeling when you do the homework so you can become aware of the feelings underneath your adaptive behavior.

If your adaptive behavior in your past relationship was being a *people-pleaser*, your homework is to do something that displeases someone. It might be saying no to a request for a favor, or not doing something that you have been resenting doing but were afraid if you didn't, they would be displeased. The problem here is that, if I suggest homework, you might do it to please me. So it may be valuable for you to create your own homework instead. Be aware of the feelings underneath as you do the homework.

If your adaptive behavior in your past relationship was being the *intellectual, non-feeling person*, your homework is to write ten "I-feel messages" each day for the next week. (An "I-feel message" is simply a statement of your *feelings* — not what you *think*, what you *feel* — at any moment. "I feel angry." "I feel confused." NOT "I feel that you're being unfair." That's an opinion, a thought.) And be aware of how it feels to talk about your feelings!

If your adaptive behavior in your past relationship was being *unorganized* as a way of hiding under the mess, then your homework is to start a "to be done today" list. Be aware of feelings underneath.

If your adaptive behavior in your past relationship was being *rebellious,* your homework is to make a list of ten "I-am statements." ("I-am" statements are self-descriptions without the usual social roles: "I am a person who hates rules" is okay; "I am a resident of Ohio" is not.) This is designed to help you gain an individual identity of your own instead of allowing someone else to be in charge of your life — which is what happens when you feel you *must* rebel.

If your adaptive behavior in your past relationship was *whatever you decided,* then you will have to decide what your homework will be also!

Learning To Nurture Yourself

This is homework for everyone — even if you haven't determined if you have any adaptive behavior: Do something nice for yourself, something that will make you feel good. Stop and get an ice cream cone and eat it all up before you pick up the kids. Take a long bubble-bath. Read a book that you have been wanting to read for a long time. Develop a new hobby. Have a full body massage. Have someone take care of and nurture you for a whole evening. Write twenty things you like about yourself on recipe cards and post them where you can read them until you believe them.

Children and Adaptation

This part of the trail is especially important for children. As we have seen in this chapter, it is the formative years — and usually in response to parents — when adaptive behaviors develop: when we're not getting our needs met; when we feel frightened; when we need more attention and love

Not surprisingly, the need to develop adaptive behavior is even greater when our parents are separating and divorcing. Ever notice how the oldest daughter becomes a pseudo-mom when she is with dad? Or how the boy becomes the "man of the house" when he is with mom? How often I have seen children become over-responsible when the parents are in the divorce pits and are behaving under-responsibly!

We adults often encourage our children to develop adaptive behaviors by our own need to be little. We have difficulty working through our own process, and want somebody "big" around because we don't feel we can do it ourselves. It's understandable, but not a good idea. We need to be careful not to use our children to meet our own needs.

Let's encourage our children to become independent as they grow and develop — to be themselves instead of being caretakers for their parents. Let's help them build their creative and inquisitive parts. Let's help them make peace with their inner critic, and learn how to use it as a friendly guide to a responsible and independent life.

How Are You Doing?

The crowd on the trail is growing restless. Most want to get on with the journey. Before you go, check out the following questions to see if you're ready to move ahead.

1. *I have become aware of my adaptive behavior part(s).*
2. *I am committed to becoming more flexible and balanced by doing self-nurturing.*
3. *I have identified and completed the homework designed to help me take charge of my adaptive behavior.*
4. *I am aware of the feeling or feelings underneath my adaptive behavior.*
5. *I have made a list of healthy parts that I would like to encourage within myself.*
6. *I have a better understanding of why my love relationship ended.*

LONELINESS
"I've Never Felt So Alone"

It is natural to feel extreme loneliness when your love relationship ends. But healing can come from the pain, if you listen to it. You can learn how to grow through loneliness to the stage of aloneness — where you are comfortable being by yourself.

Chapter 5

Loneliness is a disease
That grows slowly and
Undetected. Its symptoms
Are terrifying.
Loneliness is a dark,
Unseeing veil that covers
You with sadness, and a
Desperate race to conquer the
Complete spiritual and
Emotional emptiness. . .

I am experiencing this
Disease, and wish I could
Find a cure —
But even a ray of sunlight
Is a blessed thing.
For loneliness demands; it takes
Everything from you and
In return gives you nothing
But solitude; as if you
Were the only person
In an unmerciful world.

— Elaine

As we look around and watch people climbing this mountain of rebuilding blocks, we see various kinds of loneliness. There are the people who have withdrawn into their cave and just peer out sullenly, looking very sad and dejected. And there are the lonely people who insist on being with somebody else, so they always are holding hands or following somebody around. And then there are the busy people — always busy doing this and that so they never have to face their loneliness.

Loneliness is pain. But it is a pain which tells us we have something important to learn.

Loneliness can be a vacuum or an iceberg. Lonely people need to deal with the vacuum inside by sucking up everyone around in order to fill their void. Or they need to deal with the iceberg inside by trying to gain warmth from everyone around.

The formerly married do not have a corner on the loneliness market. Untold numbers suffer from the affliction. For many, it began in childhood and persisted through the marriage and into divorce. (Another cause of divorce, for those of you who are keeping a list.) This may be a crucial part of the climb for you if loneliness has been a stumbling block for years.

The loneliness that comes when that special person is gone is often more intense than any you have ever felt. You have no one with whom to share meals, bed, or the special comments and behavior of your children. Used to having the sounds, smells, and touch of that other person in the home, you now know nothing but silence. There is a strange emptiness in the house, as though a gong was struck and produced no sound. You can find no one in the whole world to see, hear, or feel as you do. Friends who do try to reach out seem distant, even as you most need them to be close and real.

Voices within scream, "Withdraw, withdraw, and you won't be hurt again!" You want seclusion, but at the same time crave emotional warmth, like the wounded dog who retires to parts unknown until its wound is healed. You want to regress to childhood, to have a mommy care for you.

Some who are lonely in marriage, suddenly are relieved to end the relationship that encouraged loneliness. Never emotionally close to the loved one, life with that person was painful. Whatever kept you from closeness was hard to understand and harder to change. The negative feelings of pain, anger, and frustration toward that person may have led to keeping distance between you. Ending the relationship gained distance while avoiding the painful expression of those negative feelings. (Another cause of divorce — are you keeping track?)

Many of the rebuilding blocks have a three-stage pattern. For *loneliness*, the first stage is withdrawal; one may withdraw or fantasize about it. Some hide in empty apartments and brood, so that others will not suspect their fear. Another approach is to play the "poor-little-me" game, hoping that someone will come along and feel sorry. The goal is to keep others from seeing how much one hurts, while at the same time letting the former partner know.

Quiet is a constant reminder during this stage that the other person is gone — really gone. The silence can be crushing. Inability to concentrate makes reading impossible. TV is boring. Nothing is exciting! There is a nagging, restless desire to do something — but what?

Withdrawal may be appropriate for some during this period because — let's face it — the lonely are not very good company. The need for emotional warmth is insatiable. The need often stifles friends, engulfs them, and denies them space to be themselves, to be friends. I am reminded of a nursery story about millions and billions and trillions of cats who began to eat each other up until there were no cats left. Close friends in this stage can "eat each other up" until there is nothing left of either!

Life may be like a pendulum, swinging from one extreme to the other. Seeking ways to escape this loneliness, many of us enter a second stage, becoming "busyholics," with an activity for each night of the week and two on Saturdays and Sundays. We work long hours at our jobs and find all kinds of excuses to keep working rather than coming home to emptiness. (We also may have been workaholics while married — perhaps to keep from coming home to a lonely marriage.) We go out with people whom we really do not enjoy just to avoid being alone. A party for singles may last all night — no one wants to go home!

We are running from ourselves — as though a frightening ghost lurked inside, a ghost of loneliness. For those who have really been lonely, the ghost may have begun to seem real! We never take time to stop and look at what we are doing or where we are going because we are so busy running. Instead of climbing up the mountain, we are running around it in circles!

This busy-loneliness varies in length and intensity from person to person. Some may only feel that they want to be busy; others may become so busy that they have to walk on tiptoes to keep their posteriors from dragging. Eventually all get tired and begin to realize that there must be more to life than running from the ghost of loneliness. Then they begin to slow down into the aloneness stage.

And Then You're Alone

Aloneness — what one friend called the "all-oneness" stage — is finally achieved at the point of being *comfortable* by yourself. You may *choose* to be at home alone by the fire with a book, rather than going out to be with people you really do not like. Development of inner resources and personality leads to interests, activities, thoughts, and attitudes that make it comfortable to be alone with oneself.

"How do I get there from here?" Start by facing the ghost of loneliness and realizing that it is a ghost! You have run from it, feared it, avoided it. But when you turn to that ghost of loneliness and say "Boo!" often the ghost loses its power and control. You have accepted loneliness as part of being human, and thereby become more comfortable being alone.

Accept also that loneliness has healing qualities. A period of time alone with oneself allows introspection, reflection, growth and development of the inner self. Hollowness and emptiness are replaced by inner fullness and strength. You have made a giant step toward independence when you are comfortable by yourself, no longer dependent on the company of others.

Choosing to be with another person to escape loneliness is a very unhealthy reason to begin another love relationship. There is tremendous therapeutic value in being by yourself, even lonely for a time, before you start another love relationship. Time really is the best healer. A period of loneliness is part of the remedy you need so that you can choose to enter into the next relationship rather than needing the next relationship to overcome loneliness. The mentally healthy person maintains a balance between being with others and being alone. You need to find what the proper balance is for you.

All the Lonely Children

Children suffer loneliness too after their parents are divorced. They have the same kind of empty feelings inside them that the parents have. They have the same need to be with others to fill up that loneliness, but they also fear being close to others.

Kids may feel they are the only divorced kid in school. In one community, divorce was so prevalent that when one youngster told school friends that his parents were getting a divorce, the other kids said, "Your parents are finally getting with it, aren't they?" In another community, divorce can still be so "wrong," so unusual, that the child might be the only divorced kid in the grade.

Daily living habits are altered just as are those of the parents. Instead of coming home and having two parents to spend time with them, play with them, put them to bed, there is only one parent. And the kids feel the loneliness of the new house when one or both parents move. At the home of the noncustodial parent, there may not be familiar toys or books to play with. Often the other parent's home is not set up for children, and may be located in a new neighborhood, away from friends.

The kids need to work through this loneliness — just as the parents do — in order to develop their own healthy feelings of aloneness. Kids need to learn that they have the resources within themselves to spend time alone without having to have another person around.

Many kids may have been lonely before the divorce because the interaction within the family did not help them to feel that they belonged. Divorce tends to increase this feeling of not belonging or not being okay. However, perhaps the crisis itself can be used to help deal directly with the problem. It is a special time for parents to help the children feel that they belong, that they are loved, and that they are an important part of this new family — whether it be a single-parent family or a two-parent family with the parents living apart.

Nevertheless, as with all of the rebuilding blocks, when the parents are dealing with their own loneliness, it is very difficult for them to have enough emotional time and energy left to devote to the kids' needs. It may be necessary, as I mentioned before, for parents to work through their own rebuilding blocks first; then they will be better able to help their children.

How Are You Doing?

Do some work *now* on your own capacity for being alone. If you can honestly answer "yes" to most of the items listed below, you have developed a healthy *aloneness*, and you are ready to move on up the mountain. If more than three or four of these areas need work, spend some time going over this chapter, so you can become more comfortable being by yourself.

1. *I am taking time for myself rather than keeping too busy.*
2. *I am not working such long hours that I have no time for myself.*
3. *I am not hiding from loneliness by being with people I don't enjoy being with.*
4. *I have begun to fill up my time with activities important to me.*
5. *I have stopped hiding and withdrawing into my home or apartment.*
6. *I have stopped trying to find another love relationship just to avoid being lonely.*
7. *I am content doing activities by myself.*
8. *I have stopped running from loneliness.*
9. *I am not letting the feelings of loneliness control my behavior.*
10. *I am comfortable being alone and having aloneness time.*

FRIENDSHIP
"Where Has Everybody Gone?"

The support you receive from life-line friends is very important and can shorten the time it takes you to adjust to the crisis. Friends are more valuable to you than lovers right now. You can develop friends of both sexes without becoming romantically and sexually involved. Divorce is threatening to many married people, so your married friends may slip away from you.

Chapter 6

Maria and I had lots of friends and family around all the time. Most weekends we'd have a bar-b-que or go over to her sister's place or take a picnic with two or three other couples. Since we split up none of those people ever call me or drop by. How come married people don't seem to want us around when we're single?   —Jose

As we climb the mountain, notice the different ways people handle the problems of friendship. While going through the pain of separation, some people insist on walking alone. They tend to withdraw, and they feel uncomfortable being with anybody else. You will notice others who are continually clinging to each other, as though they cannot be alone for a single minute. Always walking arm in arm, they even plan ahead so that they have no part of the journey to walk by themselves. Note also how few people continue to have any communication with friends from the days of their love relationship.

It appears that we have to find new friends as we journey up the path. On this stage of our climb, finding friends seems to be a very difficult problem.

"Ain't It Great To Be Single?"

Did you ever, when you were married, look at your divorced friends with envy and wish you could be part of all of those interesting activities they were into? That you could go to the exciting events that your spouse was reluctant to go to? Well, now you are free! What do you think about the "glamorous" single life now? For most of us, especially when we first separate, the single life is not glamorous — in fact it is downright lonely and scary.

It is lonely, in part, because we tend to lose the friends we had when we were married. There are four main reasons:

• When you are ending a love relationship, you suddenly become an eligible love partner and a possible partner for one of the people in a marriage. Thus, whereas you were formerly invited to all the parties as a couple because you were safe, now you are a single person and a threat. Suddenly people are looking at you as eligible, and invitations to married friends' parties diminish accordingly. When I became divorced, I was working in a situation in which I had considerable contact with a married woman. Three months after my separation, I walked by her desk and she said, "You're sure a lot more sexy now that you are separated and getting a divorce!" I told her, "I don't really believe I've changed very much, but I feel you are looking at me differently now. It makes me feel like an object rather than a person." Though flattered by her interest, I was uncomfortable as a potential threat to her marriage.

• The second reason we tend to lose friends is that a divorce is very polarizing. Friends tend to support either the ex-husband or the ex-wife, rarely both. Thus, we tend to lose the friends who have sided with our former spouse.

• I think the third reason is probably the most important: the fear that "If it can happen to you, it can happen to me." Your divorce is very threatening to many marriages around you, so married "friends" slip away. Although you may feel rejected, actually it is their problem, and a reflection on them rather than on you. It is likely true that the shakier your friends' marriage, the quicker they will leave you. So, instead of feeling rejected, understand that the divorce has caused them to feel very insecure about their marriage. They withdraw from the friendship because they fear divorce may be a contagious disease!

• There is a fourth aspect of friendship which is important to understand while you are going through divorce. Married people are considered to be part of the mainstream, accepted, couple-oriented society that is the cornerstone of our way of life. Divorced people, however, become part of the singles subculture — a part of our society that is less acceptable to many. This singles subculture may be somewhat hidden and difficult to find, especially until you become a single person. To be pushed out of the acceptable mainstream culture into the "questionable" singles subculture is a difficult adjustment.

There is a different standard of mores and values in the singles subculture. People live a little bit looser; they tend to be a little bit freer, sort of a large fraternity or sorority. At a singles gathering, "I'm divorced" becomes a valuable conversation opener, rather than a turn-off. If, as is often the case, the other person is also divorced, suddenly you have something in common and you can start talking to each other. Because the standards and mores are different, formerly-coupled people are not quite sure how to behave in the singles subculture and their first reaction can be somewhat of an emotional shock. You think, "Somebody's changed the rules, and I don't know what the new rules are!"

Building Friendships

As you begin to work at rebuilding your friendships, you will find a three-stage process. In the first stage, you are so hurt, lonely, and depressed that you avoid friends unless it is very safe to be with them. The second stage begins when you can at last take the risk of reaching out to people, even when the fear of rejection looms large. The third stage is becoming comfortable with people, finding out that you are okay, and beginning to enjoy people without fear of being rejected.

Recently divorced persons frequently ask: "How do I make friends after a divorce? Where can I find someone to date?" The problem is that many formerly married people are out looking desperately for another love relationship, instead of enjoying the people around them. The goal should be to get to know people, and some of these new acquaintances may become special friends or even lovers.

Start by expanding your "pool" of acquaintances. You can meet new people wherever you go — the grocery stores; classes in tennis, ceramics, cooking, language, personal growth; community groups; volunteer service organizations; the library; work; or just out walking the dog. If you are genuinely interested in the people with whom you come in contact, you are sending out vibrations that make people want to respond. But if you are coming across as lonely, desperate, and needy, people will not want to be around you.

The vibrations I am talking about include your body movements, the way you walk, the tone of your voice, your eye contact, your style of dress, and all the subtle ways you show how you are feeling. Experienced people in the singles subculture can often tell if you are single by your vibrations. Note that even if you do not intend to do so, you are sending out some sort of signals. Are you inviting others to get to know you?

When you are ready to make friends and feel comfortable doing so, there are some specific steps you might want to take. The people who enroll in classes or groups such as my divorce and personal growth seminar have found one way to handle the rebuilding block of friendships. Participating in such a seminar may help you find deep and meaningful friendships you never thought possible. Check with local churches, colleges, Y's, mental health centers, marriage counselors, and psychologists.

If you don't find such a seminar, you may want to start a group of your own with five to ten people of both sexes who are interested in reading this book and discussing the ideas. Meet in each others' homes. Have a time for work and a time for play; spend some time in group discussion and some time just socializing with each other. Share your common concerns and feelings. It may be advantageous to have people who do not know each other, so you will not get into old patterns of gossip. I found this kind of discussion group provided me with some of my most memorable and enjoyable evenings in my own divorce process. There are literally hundreds of divorce process groups around the country (and in other countries as well) which meet weekly and use this book as a discussion guide.

It's Not Time for Romance Yet!

There is one concept I feel so strongly about that I want to write it in capital letters: I SUGGEST YOU NOT GET INVOLVED IN ANOTHER LONG-TERM, COMMITTED LOVE RELATIONSHIP UNTIL YOU HAVE EMOTIONALLY WORKED THROUGH THE ENDING OF THE PAST LOVE RELATIONSHIP! Getting involved too soon results in carrying emotional garbage from the past relationship into the next one. You would likely marry someone just like the one you left, or someone just the opposite. Either way, the chances of the same problems occurring in the next relationship are great.

A healthy process of divorce might be described as "learning to be a single person." Many people never learned to be independent individuals before they were married. They went directly from their parental home to the marriage home. If you have not learned to be a single person, it is easy for you to *hide* in another relationship. Because your emotional needs are great when you are ending the love relationship, the comfort of another love relationship is appealing. Nevertheless, there is truth in the paradox that when you are ready to face life alone, then you are ready for marriage.

But you do need friends, and relationships with potential love partners based upon friendship. If you can build open, trusting, honest relationships with good communication and opportunities for both persons to experience personal growth, then you will probably work through the divorce process more rapidly.

Sometimes it is hard to tell whether a current relationship is limiting personal growth. The best criterion might be to ask, "Am I learning to be a single person?" If you feel you are losing your identity because of your love relationship, then you probably need to back off from it. (This is easier said than done in many instances! But I stress again how important it is to GET YOURSELF TOGETHER first !)

I'll have more to say about growing relationships in Chapter 16.

Can't We Just Be Friends?

Here is an exciting concept that you may learn for the first time: It is possible to develop a close, nonsexual, nonromantic friendship *with a member of the opposite sex!* This may be the way it happens for you: you tentatively make friends, but you are very cautious because of your fears of closeness and intimacy. The friendship becomes important, and you suddenly realize that you want very badly to maintain this friendship because it feels so good. You have a feeling down inside somewhere that if the quality of the friendship changes to a romantic, sexual one, it will be less meaningful, and it will become not so special anymore. Then you realize that you want to keep this friendship very much, and will go to great lengths to invest emotionally so that it will continue to grow. Such a friendship brings a free and exhilarating feeling. It also destroys the myth about never becoming a friend with a member of the opposite sex.

There was an old wives' tale about this kind of friendship destroying marriages, which you will now recognize as pretty phony logic. There are just as many kinds of friends as there are vegetables; and trying to make a tomato into a zucchini is difficult, if not impossible! You have learned something that will enrich your next marriage if you so choose. To have friends of both sexes is one indication of a healthy relationship.

While you are working to develop new friendships, you may also be hearing a barrage of negative comments about marriage in the singles subculture. There are people who rant and rave and shout from the hilltops that they will never get married again. They compile long lists of all the painful and negative aspects of marriage. And if there is someone who decides to remarry, they even send cards of *sympathy* to the couple! You need to realize that these people are as threatened by marriage as some people are threatened by divorce. Perhaps a bad marriage led to feelings that they could never have a happy marriage, so they project their unhappy biases about marriage onto others.

I admit that there *are* a lot of unhappy married people. But I think that is due to individual personalities. Some folks would be unhappy wherever they are; the marital situation may have little to do with it.

A marriage, after all, can be no happier than the two individuals in it.

Building a support system of life-line friends will shorten the time it takes you to adjust to a crisis. We all need friends who can throw us a life-line when we feel we are "drowning." A friend whom we can talk with is a *real* "life-saver" during a crisis. If you have not developed such a support system, then you need to start doing so — it may save your life.

Children Need Friends Too

Children have a problem with friendships also, often feeling isolated and "different" — as if they are the only children of divorce in the whole school. They may not know anybody else whose parents are divorced, partly because children do not often *talk* about their parents getting divorced — it is still a stigma in many communities.

(On the other hand, there are communities where the kid goes to school and says, "Guess what? My parents are getting divorced! " And the other kids say, "Welcome to the club! ")

Just as their parents tend to become friends with only formerly married and single people, children may begin to seek out friendships from families with single parents. And again, children may withdraw, just as parents withdraw, and shut out all friendships whatsoever. Children who are going through the pain of their parents' divorce really need friends to talk to, but they find it difficult to seek them out or to discuss personal concerns. Schools are concerned about this, and many are providing some sort of service to help kids who shut themselves off because of their parents' divorce. It is a valuable service.

Parents can help their children find somebody to talk to. Maybe it is the time for relatives to get involved (however, relatives who are highly emotional and who may have unresolved concerns themselves are *not* good people for the children to talk to). Also, while it is often helpful for children to talk to adults, this is the time that they need to talk to other children of divorce if possible.

We need to be aware and supportive of the needs of our kids as they are going through this process. We can encourage them to become involved with others through after-school activities and community programs. Having friends to talk with will shorten children's adjustment time, just as it does for the adults involved.

How Are You Doing?

Now might be a good time to sit down off the trail, rest for a moment, and take a look at the people around you. How long has it been since you have taken time to act interested in them, to see them as people rather than as married, potential lovers, or someone to be afraid of? Do any look interesting enough to have as a friend? I am sure you will find it easier to make the rest of the climb up this mountain if you have a friend to hold your hand, to give you a hug, and to catch you when you slip. Why not take time right now to invest emotionally in some friendships? If you worry about rejection, remember that that person may want a friend just as much as you do!

Use the check list below to assess your progress with friendships, before you go on to the next chapter. Remember too, that friendship does not just *happen* — like anything worthwhile, it takes continuous effort !

1. *I am relating with friends in many new ways since my crisis.*
2. *I have at least one life-line friend of the same sex.*
3. *I have at least one life-line friend of the opposite sex.*
4. *I am satisfied with my present social relationships.*
5. *I have close friends who know and understand me.*
6. *People seem to enjoy being with me.*
7. *I have both single and married friends.*
8. *I have discussed ideas from this book with an important friend.*
9. *I communicate frequently about important concerns with a close friend.*

GUILT /REJECTION:
Dumpers 1, Dumpees 0

Dumpers end the love relationship, while dumpees have it ended for them. The adjustment process differs since dumpers feel more guilt and dumpees feel more rejection. Dumpers start their adjustment while still in the love relationship, but dumpees start adjusting later. For the mutuals, people who jointly decide to end the relationship, the adjustment process is somewhat easier.

Chapter 7

I laughed so hard.. .
It was the funniest joke I ever heard;
"He doesn't love you."
And it was even funnier
When you told it yourself;
"I don't love you. "
And I laughed so hard
That the whole house shook,
And came crashing down upon me.

— Nancy

As we begin this segment of our climb through the rebuilding blocks, let me explain where we are headed in the pages ahead. The four key concepts of this chapter are so closely intertwined that it may get confusing at times. We will be viewing the two main characters in the divorce drama as *dumper* and *dumpee*. And we will take a look at two of the very strong feelings which accompany the trauma of divorce — *guilt* and *rejection*.

We notice different groups of people on this portion of the trail. There are those who are in shock, lying on the ground trying to get their emotional wind back. Some are walking around looking guilty and trying not to look at those on the ground. Then there are others who are walking around holding hands with their former lovers! (What are they doing here, anyway?) Everyone looks sad.

On the ground are the *dumpees,* who were walking the pathway of life and enjoying their love relationships when their partners announced they were leaving. Sometimes the dumpees had some warning; sometimes they had none. They have a great deal of difficulty accepting the ending of their relationships.

Those looking guilty are the *dumpers.* They had been thinking about leaving the relationship for some time, maybe a year or two, trying to get their courage up because they knew it would hurt the dumpee a great deal. They avoid looking at the dumpees because that makes them feel more guilty. They are usually better climbers because they had been thinking about the climb while still in the love relationship.

The ones holding hands — the *mutuals* — have decided jointly to end the relationship. Notice how few of them there are! Many people ask them why they are ending the relationship if they are such good friends. They may be very unhappy *together,* and want to end the relationship for the benefit of both. They are good climbers because they do not keep tripping each other as often as the dumpers and dumpees do. Mutuals do not enjoy the game going on between dumpers and dumpees: "Keep-the-other-from-climbing-faster-than-me."

To get us started up this portion of the trail, here is an oversimplified summary of the chapter:

Dumpers are the partners who leave the relationship, and they often feel considerable guilt; dumpees are the partners who want to hang on to the relationship, and they often experience strong feelings of rejection.

Of course it is not really as simple as that! We will get into much more detail in the pages ahead, but that gives you an advance look at the topography of the area we are about to enter.

Rejection Really Hurts

Nearly everyone has been a *dumpee* in some relationship, and no one enjoys rejection. I find after being rejected I become very introspective, continually examining myself to see what fault causes people to reject me. Such a self-examination can help me see myself more clearly — perhaps I will want to change the way I relate to other people. In any case, to accept the fact that feeling rejected is an expected part of the ending of a relationship — particularly a love relationship — is helpful in itself.

One step toward overcoming those feelings of rejection is to learn that the breakup of the love relationship perhaps is not my fault. As we've explored on earlier stages of the climb, everyone brings much of the past into a love relationship, and the past often determines the course of events in the relationship. Because the love relationship ended does not necessarily mean that I am inadequate or inferior or that there is something wrong with me. Relationships do end. Maybe that ending is not an indication of inadequacy at all!

The goal is to say, "If we have a problem, it's not because there is something terribly wrong with me. If we can't work it out, then he (she) has as much to lose as I have — maybe more." Feeling that good about yourself is a difficult goal to reach emotionally. Don't be discouraged if it takes quite a period of time to admit that the responsibility is mutual, not yours or your ex-partner's alone.

You are a worthwhile person, capable of loving and being loved. You have something special to offer to others, and that is your own unique individual self. You really ought to believe that. You could even get to feeling so good about yourself that you might believe that anyone who dumps such a neat person must have a problem!

A Little Guilt Goes a Long Way

Let us look now at guilt. It may sound strange, but I think the ideal may well be to have "the right amount of guilt in your personality." If you feel no guilt at all, nothing other than being caught deters you from doing harmful things to yourself or to others. A sense of guilt is helpful in making decisions about the way one chooses to live. Unfortunately, many people experience so much guilt that they become very inhibited and controlled, unable to do the productive things which can bring happiness. The happy balance is "just enough" guilt to help maintain a sense of direction without severely restricting one's options.

Ending a love relationship tends to make one deal realistically with guilt feelings. The dumper especially, feels a large amount of guilt and says, "I'm feeling very bad about hurting somebody I love, or used to love, and I wish I could meet my needs without feeling so guilty." Guilt — or the tendency to feel it — appears to be deeply ingrained in the personality and it is difficult to overcome. The best solution appears to be rational thinking about the breakup: Listen to your head right now, not your heart (and its guilt feelings!). To end a love relationship may be *appropriate* because it has been destructive for *both* people. Under those conditions, instead of sitting around feeling guilty, those involved may be able to say, "This is probably the best decision for both of us."

One way to resolve guilt is to be punished. Once when I was teaching, I marched a misbehaving seventh-grade boy to the hall and gave him such a lecture that he began crying. I then felt somewhat mean and hurtful. After school that day, much to my surprise, he came to my room and acted as though I was his long lost friend. I realized that by punishing him, I helped him overcome his guilt, and he appreciated that. When we are feeling guilty, we often seek ways of punishing ourselves to relieve the guilt. If you see you are trying to punish yourself by setting yourself up to experience pain in relationships, maybe you should look for feelings of guilt which may be motivating your behavior.

Guilt is usually a result of not living up to some standard of behavior. If the standard is one you have freely chosen for yourself, and if it is a *possible* one, it is probably healthy to feel some guilt about falling short. But if the standard is someone else's, or society's, or the church's, and not one you have adopted for your own, your guilt feelings are not productive. Give yourself a break! It is tough enough to live up to your own standards, you can't expect to please everyone.

"But," you tell me ruefully, "staying married *is* one of my standards. I feel guilty because I didn't make the marriage work, so I failed one of my own standards. " I hear you, and I understand that feeling. What I hope for you is that you can come to accept your own humanness. Nobody is perfect! Maybe you could take another look at that feeling of guilt, and consider a more useful response to the situation.

Try this one on for size: "My love partner and I aren't able to make our love relationship meet our needs and provide us happiness. It appears that, somehow or another, we didn't learn enough about loving and communicating with another person."

Remember in school, taking a test you hadn't prepared for? You probably did poorly on the test, and felt pretty bad. But you didn't fail the whole course! As an adult, you feel bad because your love relationship didn't work. Maybe you can learn from this experience so you can do better the next time. You might even help your ex learn something positive. Maybe, if you can accept your guilt as appropriate for this situation, you can change yourself into a better person who could build a productive, meaningful relationship in the future.

Let's compare two types of guilt: *appropriate guilt,* and the large reservoir of *free-floating guilt* that seems to reside within our feelings and personalities. Appropriate guilt is when we do something wrong or do something to hurt somebody, and we feel bad about it. When a love relationship ends, it's very appropriate for us to feel bad about hurting somebody else or hurting ourselves. Appropriate guilt is a current process that we will work through.

Some of us, however, carry long-standing guilt, usually from childhood: a large reservoir of guilty feelings waiting to be released. Some event will come along and tap this reservoir of guilt. We suddenly experience so much guilt that we feel anxious, afraid, and fearful. The guilt is overwhelming because it does not seem to be attached to anything or related to anything. It just feels huge and enormous.

If you have this sort of free-floating guilt within you, you may need help from therapy to cut down and minimize the guilt and get it under control. Again, maybe the crisis of divorce will motivate you to work on something you have needed to do for a long time.

Acceptance is an important aspect of dealing with rejection and guilt. In my divorce seminars, the emotional atmosphere values acceptance of one's own feelings, and strong mutual support among the members. Being with people who help us feel accepted and supported heals feelings of rejection rapidly. If you can find warm, supportive, accepting friends, you will be able to heal feelings of rejection also.

Rejection and guilt are also closely tied to feelings of self-worth and self-love, which we will discuss further up the trail. You will find that as you improve your feelings of self-worth and self-love, you will be less devastated by life's inevitable rejections.

"Wicheryoo?"

In my classes, approximately half of the people state that they were dumpees, a third state they were dumpers, and the rest believe it was a mutual decision. I have no way of knowing if this is true of the general population. Theoretically, there would be an equal number of dumpers and dumpees in society. However, in some situations, one person feels like a dumpee, and the other person feels it was a mutual decision.

The divorce process is different in many ways for dumpers and dumpees. My research with the *Fisher Divorce Adjustment Scale* indicates that dumpees experience more emotional pain at the point of separation, especially in the areas of letting go and anger. However, if dumpers' pain could be measured while they were still in the love relationship, I am certain they would show more emotional pain than the dumpees. The dumpers began to let go before they left the relationship, so they have been able to back off from being lovers to being friends with the dumpees. The dumpee, however, is usually still deeply in love with the dumper when the relationship ends. (Mutuals tend to score like dumpers, but they experience less grief.)

Occasionally there are persons who have a strong negative reaction to the words "dumper" and "dumpee." They fail to see any humor in the words. They usually have not been able to accept their divorces, and definitely have not been able to accept the idea of being a dumper or a dumpee. Despite such strong reactions, I consider it good to use the terms because we each need to accept the reality of a dumper and a dumpee in nearly every dissolution. You can climb the mountain of rebuilding more rapidly if you accept your role.

You may not know if you are a dumper or a dumpee. First of all, you may not have thought about it. Second, the roles may switch back and forth. For example, George and Margaret were childhood sweethearts who married soon after graduating from high school. During the courtship and marriage, George was continually stepping out with other women, leaving home for short periods of time, and acting like a dumper wanting out of the relationship. Finally, Margaret reached her "martyr's tolerance limit" and filed for divorce. Immediately George's behavior and vocabulary became those of a dumpee. Margaret and George had switched roles.

It may occur to you to ask if the person who files for dissolution in court is the dumper. The person who files may or may not be the dumper; filing is not the deciding factor. And you may ask if there are more male or female dumpers. Of course I have no way of knowing about the general population, but in my classes there is exactly the same percentage of male and female dumpers!

The Language of Dumping

Language is an important clue to whether you are a dumper or dumpee. When I talk to an audience, I frequently can identify someone as a dumper or dumpee just by the question he or she asks. Questioners are surprised and wonder if I am a mind reader, until I explain that there are dumper and dumpee vocabularies.

Dumper vocabulary goes like this: "I need some time and space to get my head on straight. I need to be out of this relationship in order to get this time and space. I care for you, but don't love you enough to live with you. Don't ask me why I don't love you — I just know that I need out. I feel bad for hurting you, but there is nothing I can do about that because staying with you would also hurt you. Can we be friends?"

Dumpee vocabulary goes like this: "Please don't leave me! Why don't you love me? Tell me what is wrong with me and I will change. There must be something wrong with me, and I don't know what it is. Please tell me what I did wrong. I thought we had a good love relationship and I don't see why you want to leave. Please give me some more time before you leave. I want to be friends but I love you. Please don't leave me."

The dumper may reply: "I have been trying for a long time to tell you that I was unhappy in the relationship and that we needed to change. You just wouldn't listen. I have tried everything. I don't have any more time. You keep hanging onto me and I just want to be friends."

Dumpees at this point are likely to be hurt and to cry. They become introspective and try to understand what went wrong: "Why am I unlovable?" and "Why did our relationship have to end?" Often there is denial of feelings while the dumpee gains time to recover from the shock. The emotional pain is great for the dumpee at this point.

The vocabulary seems universal; almost all dumpers and dumpees use the same words. The problem of timing is evident. The dumper claims to have been trying for "months and years" to do something about the problem, during much of that time thinking about leaving. The dumpee has not heard this dissatisfaction, perhaps because he or she had started using denial long before the dumper actually left. But when the dumper makes the announcement, the dumpee really starts denying and refusing to believe there is anything wrong. "We had such a good relationship!"

Notice the difference in priorities. The dumper wants to work on personal growth: "I have to get my head on straight." The dumpee wants to work on the relationship: "I need more time and feedback about what I need to change." Listen carefully to the words the dumpee is saying to reflect the hurt. Can you hear the anger beneath the words? But the dumpee does not express these words because the divorce is still in its honeymoon period.

During this period, the dumper is feeling much guilt, acting super nice, willing to give the dumpee anything. The dumpee is feeling rejected, anxious for the dumper to come back, and afraid to express anger for fear it will drive the dumper even further away. The dumpee is acting super nice also. Eventually anger replaces the feelings of guilt in the dumper and the feelings of rejection in the dumpee. Then the honeymoon period ends. This phase often begins around three months after the separation, but the timing may vary a great deal. "Good court settlements" are often negotiated while dumpers feel so guilty they will give up everything, and while dumpees will settle for anything in hopes of getting the dumper back. Dumpers: "I want out so badly that I don't care about property or money. " Dumpees: "I won't ask for anything because all I want is for her (him) to come back. "

There is a strategy to change the honeymoon period in case you are interested. Both parties feel better and can speed up the adjustment process when the dumpee can express anger quicker. Dumpers feel less guilty when dumpees express anger because the anger helps them deal with guilt. And dumpees feel less depression by expressing anger quicker because some depression is the result of unexpressed anger. But it is not always possible to shortcut the process because the dumper may have a need to feel guilty for a while, and the dumpee may have a need to feel rejected and depressed for a while. Working through feelings takes time.

There is an exercise that will help you understand this dumper-dumpee concept better. Find a friend to role-play with you — one of you as dumper, the other as dumpee. Begin in the middle of a room, then have the *dumper* walk out of the room saying dumper vocabulary. The dumpee should follow after, trying to keep the dumper from leaving the room by using dumpee vocabulary and behavior. Change roles so you can experience being both a dumper and a dumpee.

The symbolism of the exercise is good. The dumper is looking toward the door and trying to get out. The dumpee is looking at the back of the dumper and trying to figure out a way to prevent the leaving. (I have known dumpees who follow the partner out of the room, out to the car, and then hang on the car as the dumper drives off.)

How does it feel to be a dumper in the exercise? Did you feel guilty? Did you feel the other person was hanging onto you to keep you from leaving? Did you feel reluctant to look back at the other person? Did you try to keep looking at the door? Did you feel like walking faster or maybe even running?

How does it feel to be a dumpee in the exercise? Did you want the other person to look at you? Did you feel the desire to physically grab the other person? Did you want to cry and plead with him/her not to leave? Did you feel rejection and loneliness as the other person left the room? Did you feel anger?

Good News, Bad News

At the risk of confusing this discussion further, I want to introduce a further breakdown in the dumper-dumpee categories. The words I am going to use are strong and somewhat judgmental, but they are helpful in understanding better the dumper-dumpee concept. There are *good-dumpers* and *bad-dumpers*, and *good-dumpees* and *bad-dumpees*.

The good-dumper is a person who has tried to work on the love relationship in order to make it last. A good-dumper was willing to make changes, invest emotionally in trying to change, and go for marriage counseling if appropriate. But finally the dumper realized that the relationship was destructive to both people, and that it is better to end an unhealthy relationship than to continue to destroy each other. This person has the courage and strength to end the relationship, and it often takes a great deal of courage and strength.

Bad-dumpers are very similar to runaway kids. They believe the grass is greener on the other side of the fence, and all that is needed for happiness is to get out of the relationship. There is often another love relationship waiting in the wings. The bad-dumper avoids dealing with feelings and avoids looking inside at attitudes that might need to be changed. Bad-dumpers often leave quickly without even a "goodbye" conversation or explanation of their intent to end the partnership.

Good-dumpees are open, honest, willing to work on the relationship, and willing to go for counseling if appropriate. They seldom have had an affair, and have likely worked hard on communicating. They are not "innocent victims" in the sense that they too have done things to hurt the relationship. They are basically at the wrong time and place when the internal explosion and the need to be out of the relationship take place in the dumper.

Bad-dumpees are people who want out of the relationship but do not have the courage and strength to be a dumper. They make it miserable for the other person who then is forced into being the dumper.

There are few who fit perfectly into these four categories. Most of us are a combination of both good and bad dumpers or dumpees.

"Maybe I'll Come Back After All"

Another important phenomenon in the dumper-dumpee relationship is the "pain cycle." The dumper is not hurting as much when the relationship ends, but the dumpee's pain is great and motivates rapid growth and adjustment. When the dumpee is reaching a good emotional adjustment, the dumper frequently comes back and begins talking about reconciliation. This really blows the dumpee away. Gordon exclaimed, "I devoted all my emotional energy to learning to accept the ending of the relationship and I'd given up completely the hope that Juanita would come back. And then she called me!"

There are many different ways to interpret this phenomenon: Perhaps the dumper, in contrast to the sense of euphoria when she/he first left, has found it so scary out there in the single world that the security of the old love relationship looks good. "There ain't nothing out there but turkeys, and the old lover looks better all the time." Another interpretation is illustrated by dumpee anger, "She made me the dumpee. Now she wants to make me the dumper, to share the guilt!" Perhaps the best explanation comes from observing that the dumper comes back around the time the dumpee is "making it" successfully. Maybe when Juanita no longer felt the guilt and responsibility of having Gordon cling with dependency, she felt free to come back into a more equal relationship.

The typical dumpee reaction is not to take the dumper back. Dumpees find that they can make it on their own, that being single has advantages, and that it feels good to experience the personal growth they have been experiencing. If you get a dumpee to talk long enough, you will learn what was wrong with the relationship. It is only during the first period of denial that the dumpee maintains there was nothing wrong with the relationship. "Now I can see what was happening all those years! Besides, I don't see that much change and personal growth in Juanita, so why should I want the old relationship back?" At this point the dumper usually gets dumped!

Down in the Dumps

It is no wonder that dumpers and dumpees have trouble working together! The timing is different, with the dumper often starting the adjustment process while still in the relationship. The feelings are different, with the dumper tending to feel more guilt and the dumpee tending to feel more rejection (although you may experience both, whether you were a dumper or a dumpee). The attitudes are different for the two people because the dumper feels pressure to leave the relationship (wanting "personal growth" of some sort), and the dumpee fears the relationship ending. The dumper has already let go much more than the dumpee, causing problems in communicating and interacting. These different attitudes and behaviors add to the trauma of adjusting to the ending of a love relationship.

One last note on the terms *dumper* and *dumpee*. Despite differences in timing and attitudes, the two people are not that much different. Both have contributed fairly equally to the relationship not working. Even differences in their attitudes are not major. Once a dumpee begins talking about the love relationship, he or she will say almost the same things about the problems that the dumper was saying, using dumpee vocabulary of course. *Timing* remains the essential element that separates the dumper from the dumpee.

I hope this discussion of dumpers and dumpees will enable you to see that feelings of guilt and rejection are part of the process. Intellectual understanding is often the first step of awareness that leads to emotional understanding. Feelings of guilt and rejection are normal and typical during the ending of a love relationship — in fact you may have been experiencing these feelings before. But the ending of a love relationship tends to magnify and emphasize feelings, so you can be more aware of them and thus learn to deal with them more adequately.

Don't Dump On Your Children

The concept of dumper and dumpee has interesting implications for the children of divorce. Often the children are very angry at the parent who decided to leave, and they have a great deal of difficulty maintaining a relationship with that person. They blame the breakup on the dumper, so they take out their pain and frustration on that person. They probably fail to see that there is not that much difference between the dumper and dumpee, since both of them contributed to the ending of the relationship, only in different ways.

Almost always, the children of divorce could be looked upon as dumpees. They had very little to do with the decision, thus may feel the same frustration and anger that dumpees do. Kids, however, are not like dumpees in the sense that they often recognize that the marriage is ending — sometimes before the parents do!

Kids have a definite problem with rejection and guilt. I mentioned in chapter one that kids may have problems with guilt when they feel they are responsible for their parents' marriage not working out. The youngsters may need help in seeing that it is not their fault, that divorce is a grown-up problem.

Kids frequently feel a tremendous amount of rejection because it seems one parent is leaving and rejecting the child. The rejection a child feels is often long-lasting and can even persist into adulthood. Adults who have never fully accepted their parents' divorce find that their own love relationships can be adversely affected.

Children must be assured that they are not guilty, they are not responsible for their parents' divorce, and they are not being rejected. If the parents can maintain a quality relationship with the children after their separation and divorce, the children will be able to deal with these feelings.

How Are You Doing?

I suggest we rest from our climb for a while. You may want to think about the differences between dumpers and dumpees, and try to understand the feelings and attitudes on both sides of the issue. Maybe you have changed your mind about whether you are a dumper or a dumpee after reading this chapter. In any case, take time now to consider the different perspectives partners get of *what happened* during a dissolution. I hope this chapter has helped you gain a better view of the end of your own relationship. After completing the check list below and treating yourself to some time to think about these ideas, I hope you are then ready to move on up the mountain!

1. *I am no longer overwhelmed by feelings of guilt and/or rejection.*
2. *I can accept that I was a dumper or a dumpee or that we made a mutual decision.*
3. *I have thought about whether I was a good/bad dumper/dumpee.*
4. *I can accept that being a dumper may not necessarily mean one should feel guilty.*
5. *I can accept that being a dumpee may not necessarily mean one should feel rejected and unlovable.*
6. *I am aware of the differences in feelings and behavior between dumpers and dumpees.*
7. *I realize that both dumpers and dumpees feel emotional pain even though it may differ in timing and intensity.*
8. *I understand that in some areas I was a dumper and in other areas I was a dumpee, since this is typical of most relationships.*
9. *I understand the concept of dumper/dumpee is most meaningful at the point of separation; as I grow it becomes less and less important.*
10. *I have looked at my life patterns to see if rejection or guilt feelings have controlled much of my behavior.*
11. *I am working to overcome the influence of rejection and guilt in my life.*

GRIEF
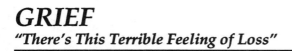
"There's This Terrible Feeling of Loss"

Grief is an important part of your divorce process. You need to work through grief's emotions in order to let go of the dead love relationship. An intellectual grasp of the stages of grief can help you become emotionally aware of grief. Then you can do the grieving that you may have been afraid of before.

Chapter 8

Weekends are...
All the lonely hours poured into remembering,
All the lonely thoughts poured into trying to forget,
The harder we try to forget, the easier it is to remember.
The past can't die and the future can't live,
But the present exists.

If silence is deafening, then what is quiet?
Quiet is weekends and weekends are hell.
Wake up and face reality — why?
Weekends enforce reality, weekdays subdue it.

Saturday — it's a world of two plus two,
Where one has no meaning and no value.
Sunday — the body rests,
But where's the "off button" for the mind?
                                        — "Honey"

We are now entering one of the most difficult and emotionally draining parts of the climb. All along the path sit people who are crying mournfully. Some will stop crying for a while, then suddenly start in again. Other people are trying to comfort them, but seem uncomfortable and not quite sure what to do. What is happening?

These people are experiencing grief. Whenever there is a loss of something important in our lives, we suffer grief. Perhaps you — like many of the people participating in the divorce seminar — had not been aware that grieving is a part of the divorce process. For death, there is a set ritual with a funeral, casket, and acceptance that grieving is important. For divorce, there is no prescribed ritual other than the court hearing, and grief is often not acknowledged or accepted. But, the death of a love relationship is cause for us to grieve!

The Many Faces of Grief

Many forms of loss occur when we end a love relationship. Most obvious, of course, is the loss of the love partner, which many people do grieve. There are other losses: the future plans as a pair; the love relationship; the role of *husband* or *wife* or *lover;* and the status associated with being a *couple.* Many changes occur as one progresses from being married through the transition to being single. For some people the loss of the relationship is as important as the loss of the partner.

There is the loss of the future. Married "till death do us part," there were plans, goals, joint careers, and a house that had become a home. Now all of these future parts of your life are no longer there. The future is a very difficult loss to accept, and many will need to grieve that loss for a long time.

The pain of ending a love relationship often forces us to look at past pain. Many people have not properly grieved a loss in the past, such as the death of a loved one. Re-experiencing a past pain intensifies the grieving process. For those who carry an unresolved loss from the past, divorce grief will be especially painful and difficult.

Similarly, a history of unfulfilled emotional needs — perhaps childhood deprivations — may become prominent during divorce grief. Dan reported that he dreamed frequently about childhood experiences on the farm while he was working through his divorce. As we talked about grief in the seminar, he realized that he was grieving the unhappiness he experienced during his lonely childhood.

Many divorced people are forced to move from the house they lived in while in the love relationship, and they may have to grieve the loss of that house. Single parents may have to grieve the loss of children when they are with the other parent. And the children must also grieve the loss of a house, a parent, a family — which are all part of their divorce process.

A Fable of Grief: The Check Mark

A favorite device of mine, useful in understanding grief, is known as the "check mark" theory. It goes like this:

Once upon a time, there was a little creature called Jot, living a good life, oblivious to the Black Cloud hovering over it. Suddenly, the Black Cloud let loose, and Jot's lover went away. In the anguish of its lost love, Jot tumbled down a huge slide, so long that Jot could not see the bottom of it. There were no handles to hold on the way down the scary slide, and the ride was painful, but Jot finally landed on a soft rainbow. Looking around, Jot spied stairs that led up into the sunlight again. The stairs were very difficult to climb at first, but became easier and more exciting as Jot neared the sunshine and began to feel completely renewed.

You might like to know what Jot's trip was like, since you will have to take the grief trip someday.

Descending (left) side of the check mark:

I hurt.
Why me?
I'm so lonely.
I'm so unlovable.
Won't someone hold me?
Sadness is my only friend.
I sigh a lot.
I don't want to eat.
I think about her (him) all the time.
He (she) better be hurting too!
Damn the S.O.B.!

Ascending (right) side of the check mark:

This looks like a tough climb!
Wow, it's a long way up, but I'm gaining strength.
Maybe I'll slow down to catch my breath.
It's great to have a few friends to help out.
I'm going to make it.
Look at the new me.
I'm OK — you're OK.
Two steps up, sometimes one step back.
Look at my new friends.
I'm beginning to like myself again.
It's great to be alive!
I'm renewed!

Some of Jot's friends see a mean Giant Dragon with fangs who's breathing fire at the top of the slide. The dragon frightens them right past the slide. Instead, they bury their heads, and imagine they read on the Dragon's T-shirt such things as: "Don't go down the slide — you must control your emotions — don't cry or show weakness — you aren't strong enough to take any more pain — you may end up crazy!" They stay in this self-chosen hell until they somehow muster the courage to confront the Giant Dragon, only to discover that the sayings on the Dragon's T-shirt are only myths. At last Jot's friends risk the slide and they too discover the steps leading to the warm sunshine.

Are you like Jot? Do you see a Dragon? What do you see on the T-shirt? Are you willing to risk the slide into pain, in order to gain access to freedom?

This check mark offers a good overview of the divorce grief process, and illustrates many of our fears about grieving. An intellectual understanding of the grief process may help us to emotionally understand our feelings as well. Eventually, however, each of us must allow ourselves to experience grief, not just talk about it.

Symptoms of Grief

Let's see what we can learn from a head trip. As a beginning, a list of the grief symptoms commonly felt during divorce will help you see that your feelings are much like those of others.

Many people talk continuously about their situation until they drive away their friends, and they need to seek new ones (the *verbal diarrhea* stage). The grieving person needs to stop talking about irrelevancies and begin to express the genuine feelings of grief. (If you find — or friends tell you — that you continually repeat yourself, this is a likely indication of a need to *express* your feelings rather than talking *about* them.) Later in this chapter you'll find some help with this.

Grief has a *push-pull effect*. Having been hurt, you have a big, empty feeling in your gut; and you expect friends to help you fill it. You try to talk with friends and get close to them, but at the same time this empty feeling — like a big wound — is very vulnerable to being hurt again. When people get too close, you tend to push them away to prevent further emotional pain. Thus, you pull people toward you emotionally, but push them away when they get too close. Quite a mixed message for your friends!

With grief, *feeling emotionally drained* and *not sleeping* are frequent problems. Many people in grief have trouble falling asleep at night without using drugs or alcohol. Often they wake up very early in the morning, unable to go back to sleep, yet too tired to get up. At a time when sleep is needed most, they have difficulty sleeping, and the hard emotional work has them tired all day long. Grief is hard work, and you will likely feel tired continuously until you have finished your grief process.

Eating is a problem during grief. You may have a feeling of tightness in your throat and find swallowing difficult. Sometimes your mouth will be very dry, also making eating difficult. You may not even have any appetite and may have to force yourself to eat. An empty feeling may occur in your stomach as though you were hungry, but you do not feel hungry. For these and other reasons, most people lose a great deal of body weight during grief. Although a few people do gain appetite and weight during grief, this is a small percentage compared to those who lose weight. During a break in one of my divorce seminars, several participants were comparing their loss of body weight during divorce grief. Of the six people present, all had lost at least 40 pounds! While the amount may not always be so dramatic, the unanimity is not surprising.

One of the most useful questions in the *Fisher Divorce Adjustment Scale* asks about *sighing often*. People are often not aware that they are sighing, but it is an indication to others that the person is grieving a great deal. Not only does the sigh itself release body tension, but also the deep breathing of the sigh seems to "carry feelings from the gut" that need release.

Rapid mood changes are typical during divorce grief. You have moved from the black pits of grief and finally feel good. Then, without apparent reason, you are out of control emotionally, unable to keep from crying. The whole sudden mood swing may have been triggered by a conversation with a friend or acquaintance who said something to you or did something for you. You were feeling fine and in control until then. Your change to the depths of grief again leaves that person confused and sad, not understanding what he or she did to upset you. For your part, the downer is made even worse because you feel bad about feeling so out of control. The incident is a clear sign that you have not completed your grief work yet.

There may be a sense of *loss of reality*, of being in a daze, in an unreal world. You observe the environment as though watching a movie, remote and detached from the events happening around you. You are unable to wake up from this dream to the real world.

You may experience a period of *lack of contact with your emotions.* You are afraid to trust your feelings because of your inability to control them. The emotional pain is so great, you have to protect yourself from feeling too much by deadening your emotions. You may sense an emotional "numbness."

Many people experience quite a bit of *fantasizing* during grief. You may fantasize that you see the former love partner, or that you hear his/her voice. You may fantasize that a part of your body is missing, as though your heart were removed, symbolizing the loss of the other person. This fantasizing may be frightening if you do not recognize it as a normal part of grief.

Loneliness, lack of concentration, weakness and helplessness, depression, guilt, lack of interest in sex, and perhaps even the *feeling of impotence or frigidity* may accompany grief. *Self-criticism* — a need to continually question your errors and how you would relive the past differently — persists.

Anger is a part of grief that results from the apparent unfairness of the loss. Anger directed toward the former love partner may approach rage in its intensity. We will look at it in detail in the next chapter.

Suicidal feelings are common during divorce grief. Approximately three-fourths of the participants in the divorce seminars admit to having experienced some suicidal thoughts during their grief periods. Research indicates a much higher than normal rate of actual suicides occurs among persons engaged in the divorce process.

All of these feelings can be overwhelming. *Uncontrollable mood swings, loss of reality, fantasies, depression, suicidal feelings...*one may wonder fearfully, "Am I going crazy?" For most people this is a difficult fear to discuss. And holding that fear inside makes it even scarier, even more crazy-feeling. The "craziness" is a real feeling, but is related to the situation rather than to a permanent psychological diagnosis. You may well be experiencing a normal grief reaction if you feel you are going crazy.

These grief symptoms may be handled by acknowledging them, accepting that they indicate grief work to be done, allowing yourself to feel the pain without denial. Crying, shouting, and writhing are other nondestructive actions to express your grief. Make a decision to manage the grief by deciding on an appropriate time and place to do grief work. On the job, for example, is not the time to cry and grieve. At work you must put the grief aside — "on the shelf," so to speak — and concentrate on your job. Because you have set aside time to grieve, your emotions become easier to control at other times, and you do not become caught in the grieving. But be sure you do grieve during the time you have set aside for grieving! If you do not manage the grief, it will manage you.

If you do not do your grief work, your body may express the repressed feelings of grief in psychosomatic symptoms of illness. You may have simple ailments like headaches, or you may develop ulcerative colitis, arthritis, asthma, or ulcers. Unresolved grief puts a great deal of stress upon your body, and may increase your medical and hospital bills.

Often people are reluctant to take the divorce class because they do not want to experience the pain and crying of grief again. I have learned to translate this reluctance into their need to complete grief work. Somewhere deep inside, you will know when the grief work is completed because of the feeling of letting go that you experience. You cannot be pulled down into the grief pits again!

Stages of Grief: The Work of Elizabeth Kubler-Ross
In this part of the climb it will be helpful to identify the five stages of grief. An intellectual overview will help us to work through the

five stages emotionally. We are all greatly indebted to Dr. Elisabeth Kubler-Ross for her fine work in helping to clarify the stages of the grief process.

Stage 1. The first reaction to the sense of loss is *denial:* "This isn't happening to me. If I just wait a while, everything will be okay and my lover will come back." There is often a state of emotional shock, numbness, and denial of any feelings. One may enter into a robot-like phase, acting as though nothing is happening, repressing anger and becoming depressed. Best manners are extended toward the former love partner, in the hope that it is all a bad dream and that person will not really leave! No one wants to tell friends and neighbors that our love relationship is ending. Indeed, we don't want to tell ourselves!

Stage 2. As one gradually begins to accept the ending of a love relationship a feeling of *anger* develops. The anger that has been turned inward, contributing to depression, is now turned toward others. Expressing the anger feels good, but there is also concern that the other person will not return because of the anger, thus some guilt and ambivalence. The frustrations that have existed in the relationship for years begin to come out. Friends may wonder how you have tolerated that person when you have been so emotionally upset in the love relationship for so long. In turn, you may go to great lengths to convince others how terrible your former partner was, resulting in a "Catch-22" situation: you lose both ways. If you talk about how good that person is, how do you stay angry? But if you say how terrible that person is, then the question becomes why you chose to love such a terrible person in the first place! You have started working through the grief process when you admit and express the grief anger.

Stage 3. Beginning to face the fact that the love relationship is ending, yet reluctant to really let go, one may start *bargaining:* "I'll do anything if you'll just come back. I'll change my ways, and put up with anything. Just take me back!" This stage is dangerous for the divorce process because many people do get back together, for the wrong reasons — to avoid the loneliness and unhappiness of ending the love relationship. They are not choosing to live successfully with the former love partner, but rather choosing the "lesser of two evils."

Stage 4. Stage four of grief is a final *letting go* of the love relationship, and is, in a sense, the darkness before the dawn. Depression is typical during this stage, but the depression is different from that of stage one. This depression is a "blahs" feeling: "Is this all there is to life?" There is much internal dialogue about the meaning of life: "Why am I here on earth? What is the purpose of my life?" This is a stage of personal growth to build a stronger identity, to find a deeper purpose for living, and to make life more meaningful.

A number of people feel suicidal during this stage: "I've tried so long and worked so hard, and here I am down in the pits again. I don't want to let go!" Because the stage sometimes comes so long after the actual separation, people are surprised to feel so depressed again. It is discouraging to have worked so hard but feel so little progress. I have found that people who are aware of this stage get through it much easier. They are comforted to realize that there is a purpose for the depression they are feeling, that it will not last long, and that it is different from that of early-stage grief.

Stage 5. This is the stage of *acceptance* of the loss of the love relationship. The person has begun to feel free from the emotional pain of grief and to feel no need to invest emotionally in the past relationship. Now one can begin to move on up the mountain toward fuller personal freedom and independence.

It is critically important to work through these five stages of grief before one enters into another love relationship.

Allow the Children To Grieve

Children, too, must grieve an important loss, although sometimes it is difficult for us as parents to let them do the grieving they need to do. We see them starting to cry because they miss their noncustodial parent, and we want to take away that pain and reassure them, "Now don't cry, it's okay. Your father (mother) will be back. You will get to see him (her) in the future." Reassurance is not necessarily what kids need, rather they need some sort of acceptance: "You feel very sad to have your father missing. You feel very sad living away from your father whom you love so much." It is easy for us to get our own emotions and guilt involved instead of allowing the child to express his or her feelings and emotions. Children will tend to cry and grieve more naturally than adults, I think, until we take away the permission and start interfering with the process.

The same may be true with the anger part of grief. The child may be very angry about being separated from a parent and having a lifestyle change. When children start expressing their anger, adults often try to take that anger away by saying, "Well, you just need to grow up and understand. Someday you'll see that what we did was normal, natural, and healthy." *Allow* the children to just be angry; try saying, "You feel very angry toward your father for being gone."

Children will go through the five stages of grief described earlier. They will start out by denying that their parents are separated and believing the parents will get back together again. As they proceed through the stages of anger, bargaining, and so on, children need to be *allowed* to work through all five stages of grief. The exercises described above, plus the check list at the end of this chapter, can be very helpful for children as well as for their parents.

Obviously, there is a difference in the children's loss because parents do not divorce the children. The relationship between child and parent will persist, it is hoped, although in many cases the child does not see the noncustodial parent.

As with all other feelings, a parent who shows the child how to grieve is far more influential than the parent who *tells* children about grieving. Children will emulate a grieving parent, and will gain much from experiencing that healthy and needed release.

I hope you are helping your children of divorce to grieve, rather than hindering them by not giving permission or not showing them it is OK. Try to allow your children to work through the process described in this chapter.

Working Through Your Grief

There is a process of grief. Many people are afraid of grieving because it could show weakness, or maybe even signs of "going crazy." It is reassuring to find that other people experience many of the same feelings and symptoms of grief. We may emotionally work through the grief stages effectively, overcome our fear of grief, and feel safer in our grief work. This process gives us permission to grieve with a minimum of fear and anxiety.

Take time now to get out your handkerchief and see if you can let go of some more grief while you rest on the trail. Now that you understand the grieving process and have permission to grieve as a mentally healthy activity, you may feel freer to do some needed grieving (maybe including some past loss also). I suggest you call upon a trusted friend, family member, clergyperson, or counselor to provide support (without interference) while you allow yourself to express the depths of your grief.

In our seminars we have an important, experiential homework assignment that I think you would find helpful also. It is to write a letter of "goodbye" to one of the areas of grief mentioned earlier in the chapter. It may be goodbye to your home, to the relationship, or to a past loss.

The letter is intended to help you actually do the emotional grieving and letting go. It is a difficult assignment, so I suggest you start with one of the more superficial losses. Eventually, you can write a letter of goodbye to the major loss. The letter may or may not be mailed to another person. It is really for your own benefit. In most cases, you will not want to share the letter with the person you are grieving about.

On the following two pages is an excerpt from a letter of goodbye that a woman in the divorce class wrote. It will give you insight into her thoughts and feelings, and maybe it will help stimulate you to write your own letter of goodbye. I urge you to read it thoughtfully, then begin work on your own letter(s).

goodbye

goodbye to the New House that I spent endless afternoons and weekends looking for ~ making sure that it met all the rigid requirements. I'll probably never find another house like that again. It was so much more than a house~ it represented an end to looking, an achievement of a goal; a new beginning; a readiness for our family to begin. And now I'm back at the beginning of the beginning. So very far away from that place I'd worked so hard to get to. God, I was so tired of searching and so grateful to have found it, and now I've lost it all.

goodbye to the home we were making for our future. goodbye to the tulips we planted in the Fall but that we never saw together in the Spring when it came time for them to bloom. goodbye to the plans we made for the nursery and fixing up the old cradle for the baby we never had.

goodbye to all that potential our new beginning was bringing us.

goodbye to the confidence and satisfaction I felt as "your mate" ~ the well-defined role; knowing what was expected of me.

goodbye

I've wanted so badly to say goodbye. To let go of you.
To push you swiftly and completely from my life
        as you have done with me

What is it that I'm holding onto?
        Promises
            the good old 'as-soon-as-we" promises...
                degrees...
                travel...
                jobs...
                honeymoon...
                money...
            funny how they changed to "as-soon-as-I" promises

I loved you because you were the other half of a marriage that
        I needed very badly in order to feel whole
    because you were the future father of our family
    because I needed someone to care for, to nurture, to parent;
        you made me feel needed.

I guess I've already said goodbye in more ways than I would have thought possible. You've been gone for a year and a half. Somehow I'm still here; all here; and no where, not even on the final decree, does it say that I am now only half a person with only 50% of the purpose, of the value that I once had. I am not trying to say goodbye to my self-worth or dignity ~ I've not really lost that ~ but rather I am trying to say goodbye to my need for your credibility stamp on those feelings in order to make them valid.

The last goodbyes are the positive ones. For they are goodbyes to the negatives.
    goodbye to the feelings of enslavement
    goodbye to your picky little dislikes
        onions, mushrooms, olives and
        my flannel nightgown and
        getting up early and
        Joni Mitchell and
        my friend Alice and
        going to the zoo.
    goodbye to your lack of direction and
        your lack of creativity and
        your lack of appreciation and
        your lack of sensitivity
    goodbye to your indecisiveness and
        your stifled, dried-up emotions and
        your humorless sense of humor

    goodbye to feeling ashamed of getting angry and showing it,
        feeling embarrassed for being silly
        feeling guilty when I knew the answer and you did not.

                                goodbye
                                Trisch

Now, dry your eyes and read through the check list for grief work. As before, please be sure you have dealt thoroughly with this rebuilding block before you go on. Grief is a tough and painful stage. Do not just bury it! And do not try to get through it in the time it took you just to read this chapter. Use your lifeline friends (see chapter six) for help as you work through your grief. The mountain will still be yours to climb when you are ready.

How Are You Doing?"

Here again is a checklist for your review. Take a few minutes to answer these questions honestly, and to consider how much grief work you may have to complete before you move on up the mountain.

1. *I have given myself permission to grieve if I need to.*
2. *I am not burying the grief sadness but am trying to express it.*
3. *I now have physical and emotional energy from morning until night.*
4. *I have stopped feeling depressed most of the time.*
5. *I have no trouble concentrating.*
6. *I no longer feel like crying most of the time.*
7. *I have overcome the feeling that I am in a daze.*
8. *My emotions and moods are back in my control.*
9. *I have no trouble going to sleep and sleeping all night.*
10. *I rarely sigh now.*
11. *I notice my body weight has stabilized.*
12. *My appetite is good.*
13. *I no longer feel mechanical in my daily living habits.*
14. *I have outgrown the feeling that I am losing my mind*
15. *I have stopped talking continuously about my crisis.*
16. *I have no thoughts of attempting suicide.*
17. *I have no more lump in my throat.*
18. *My stomach feels relaxed and at ease.*
19. *I am beginning to be emotionally close to people again.*
20. *If feel emotionally alive rather than emotionally dead.*
21. *I understand the grief process.*
22. *I have identified which of the five stages of grief I am in.*

23. *I have identified any past grief that I have not experienced and worked through.*
24. *I have identified what I need to grieve (person, relationship, future).*
25. *I am comfortable talking about my feelings of grief with a friend.*
26. *I have written a letter of goodbye to the loss I am experiencing now.*

ANGER

"Damn the S.O.B.!"

You'll feel a powerful rage when your love relationship ends. Feeling anger is a natural, healthy part of being human. But anger is different than aggression, which is a destructive form of expressing anger. It's not healthy to keep your anger inside, nor to express it aggressively. You can learn to express both your divorce anger and your "everyday" anger constructively.

Chapter 9

I don't know what came over me. I saw his car in the parking lot and I knew he had met his girl friend and left in her car. I went over and let the air out of all four tires. Then I went behind the building and waited until they returned so I could watch them find his car with the tires flat. I watched them trying to solve their problem and I felt so good. I've never done anything like that before in my life. Guess I didn't know how angry I could get.

— Jean

We're approaching a point in the trail where we are in danger of being consumed by the fire of anger. The possibility of fire is great during the divorce process, and if we do not deal with it adequately, the fire of anger can spread to the other rebuilding blocks and keep us from making progress.

Divorce anger is an extreme rage, vindictiveness, and over-powering bitterness that is felt when a love relationship is ending. It is a special kind of anger that usually hasn't been experienced before. Married friends don't understand it unless they too have ended a love relationship.

You may try to keep this anger inside and not express it. As a result, you may become more depressed. Many therapists, and I'm among them, believe that anger not expressed is an important cause of depression. The divorce process can be pretty depressing anyway, and people who fail to express their anger during the early stages of divorce often become even more depressed.

Dumpers don't express anger because they feel so guilty, and dumpees don't express it because they fear the other person won't come back if they do. Both are "nice" for a while, and both feel a lot of depression.

Anger may be expressed in violent ways, of course. Given the opportunity while they are angriest, some people do commit acts of violence during the divorce process. We are lucky if we are able to restrain ourselves and find more suitable methods of expressing these feelings of rage and vindictiveness.

There are more constructive uses for anger than destroying ourselves with depression and psychosomatic problems (headaches, body tension, ulcers, and the like). Also, since the fires of anger can spread to other rebuilding blocks, working through this block will result in much less trouble on other parts of the trail.

Three Phases of Anger

The anger rebuilding block fits rather naturally into three phases. The first phase is learning to accept that *it's okay to feel angry* — it's part of being human. There are many myths in our society that say that to be angry is to be weak, childish, destructive, and sacrilegious. (We are supposed to "turn the other cheek." But Christ became angry and drove the money changers out of the temple! Why can't we be angry like that?)

Most of us learned that it's not permissible to feel angry. Now we have to relearn that it is okay after all. This may be easy to do intellectually, but it is much more difficult emotionally. The strong emotional reactions of others when you've become angry may make you very reluctant to accept your angry feelings now. Just remember there is a difference between your *feeling* of anger and the way you act to *express* it!

The second phase, after acknowledging that you're human and can feel anger, is to *learn as many positive ways of expressing anger as possible* — ways that will not be destructive to yourself or to those around you. It can be done with humor, physical exercise, and other ways that we will explore in this chapter.

Let me add a caution here: One of the most destructive things that happens to many people during the divorce process is the use of children as a vehicle for expressing anger at the former spouse.

Corinne makes the children into spies when they come back from visitation. Annette will not allow Russ to see the kids until he pays child support; Russ will not pay child support until Annette allows visitation. We forget about what's best for the children because we are so intent on getting that other person. Getting back through the kids is hitting below the belt.

For the sake of the children, if for no other reason, learn constructive methods of expressing anger.

The third stage of anger is to *learn forgiveness.* Those of you in the first two stages may react emotionally with a big outburst now — "I will never forgive! " Well, it's not just forgiving the other person but learning to forgive yourself as well. When we take it down to the final line, we are usually angry at ourselves.

You are responsible for that anger because it is your feeling, not someone else's. Although projecting blame for anger onto someone else may be a part of the process — the part that allows us to get out the anger that may have been causing depression — when you get further along, you must learn to take responsibility for that anger yourself.

There is a powerful anger item in my *Fisher Divorce Adjustment Scale*: "I blame my former love partner for the ending of our love relationship." People who have not yet dealt with their anger will answer "Yes" to that question. Those who have worked on their rebuilding enough to have dealt with the anger begin to realize that failure, blame, and responsibility are two-way streets. What happened was part of a complicated interaction that did not work, rather than the fault of one person.

Taking responsibility for anger takes a long time for some of us. It requires a great deal of maturity and strength to do that. It is so much easier to blame the other person! The stage of forgiveness is actually learning to forgive ourselves, and letting go of our anger.

Appropriate Anger — and the Other Kinds

Have you thought about how appropriate it is to feel very angry when your love relationship ends? "What," you may ask, "is *appropriate* anger?" Anger that is related to the present situation is appropriate. Harry is frustrated because someone ran into his new car (one of the participants in the seminar ran into her ex's new car when he came to pick up the son); Jan feels angry because someone has said something mean to hurt her; Sharon may become angry when she is unable to accomplish a simple task such as threading a needle. Appropriate anger is realistic for the situation; the feeling fits the event.

Aggressive anger does not fit the event. Bea is driving and the light turns red; she also turns red. A chance remark is made and Bart starts a fist fight. The response is out of proportion to the event. Often this person is bringing up past anger that was buried, sometimes way back in childhood.

What about childhood and its relationship to anger? We start our lives in the womb, truly the center of our own universe. All of our needs are met while we remain completely passive. The first big trauma is birth, when we are thrust into the "cold, cruel world. " We suddenly have to start bawling and screaming to get fed and changed. During the process of maturing we become more and more responsible for meeting our own needs, often a frustrating experience. Thus maturity is reached, in part, through a process of frustration and anger.

If you were taught as a child to express your angry feelings freely and in constructive ways, you're not likely to accumulate and "sandbag" anger. But if you weren't allowed to express anger in constructive ways (such as those I'll describe later in this chapter), or if you grew up among very angry people or others who greatly increased your normal frustration to abnormal levels, you probably accumulated what might be called *childhood rage.*

Anger which accumulates in childhood becomes like layers around the gut, and any small event may trigger off inappropriate behavior. You won't have to think very long to imagine someone you know whose anger expression is always out of proportion. Look out for such people during the divorce process. They sometimes do violent things, like running over people with cars!

Beneficial Anger

A few pages back I said it was appropriate to feel angry when your love relationship ends. In fact, it is not only appropriate but it is beneficial and productive. "What?" you say, "Anger is beneficial?" Yes, because anger helps us to let go and become emotionally distant from the former love partner. People who are unable to express anger will prolong the letting go process. They often experience a great deal of depression, stay stuck, and are unable to end the strong feelings they have for that former love partner.

The next point contains both good news and bad news. Because people who divorce usually had trouble expressing anger in their marriages, they have a lot of unexpressed anger. When the divorce anger adds to the flame, that reservoir of anger explodes; and thus we have both the appropriate anger of the present and the no-longer-relevant anger of the past. That's the bad news. The good news is that expressing divorce anger often frees the person to express other anger from the past as well.

Victor posed a question in the seminar, "Why do we have to go through a divorce to talk about the problems that occurred five or ten years ago?" The answer is because it took the divorce anger to get those buried problems out in the open.

"I Messages" and Other Fair Fighting Methods

Because anger expression is such a common problem in marriages, divorces, and remarriages, one of the important topics in my "Relationships After Divorce" seminars is to help the participants learn to express anger constructively through the techniques of fair fighting. This is a group of positive ways of expressing anger with your love partner first developed by psychotherapist George Bach. Many professionals who work extensively with couples have contributed to the technique.

One fair-fight tool is use of "I messages" — communications that allow you to get the angry feelings out of the way so that closeness, intimacy, and love may come into the relationship. "I messages" were first introduced as a part of the Parent Effectiveness Training programs of psychologist Thomas Gordon.

"I messages" start with the word "I," and place the responsibility for your feelings on you, rather than making the other person the source of your anger. "I messages" also help you identify what it is you are feeling, rather than covering up your feelings by blaming the other person. Maybe the most important part of an "I message" is that it communicates to someone else what you are feeling.

Learning to use "I messages" will help you communicate with all of the loved ones around you — lovers, children, friends, relatives. I suggest you start practicing "I messages" as a way of improving your interactions with others, and as a way of expressing anger constructively. A simple example: instead of "You *make* me mad! " try "I *get so mad* when you....! "

I used to think that all a couple needed to do to make their love relationship work was to learn to love and be loved. As I matured in my professionalism and my own personal growth, I learned that expressing anger constructively is probably equally important in making a love relationship productive and keeping it clear of all the garbage that accumulates. (Another cause of divorce — how many is that now?) Anger left unexpressed will grow like a volcano until it erupts. Talking out anger is the relief valve that keeps the pressure cooker (marriage) from exploding. And talking out anger usually leads to intimacy and good sex. It is worth it!

Assertive Anger Expression

Anger is like a fire that must be burned up into the ashes of forgiveness. If we are passive, it is like throwing more logs on the fire and we never get to the ashes of forgiveness. You may need to learn methods of direct — but not aggressive — assertiveness in order to get your divorce anger fire to go out.

Many people find logs blocking the trail in this section that keep them from learning about anger with its many positive uses. I have encountered these people in counseling and have learned the feelings behind these roadblocks. Theresa had been very abused as a child and had accumulated childhood rage. We were trying to help her express her anger and I asked her what would happen if she expressed it with me. Theresa was silent for a long while, and then admitted that she felt I would hurt her. The fear of retaliation keeps many of us from expressing anger.

Anthony came into my office with a "Buddha smile" on his face. His son was flunking out of school by doing nothing, and his daughter was running away. I have learned that the smiling Buddha face is a mask for anger. Anthony, a self-ordained minister, was unable to express his anger because he had an image to maintain: "ministers don't act angry." But his anger came out with his children through physical abuse. His children reacted with appropriate angry *feelings*, but their *behavior* was harmful and not constructive . The children needed to learn positive ways of expressing anger, but emotionally they were learning instead to abuse their future children.

It is clear that we often learn to express anger the same way our parents did. We may learn to express it in *passive* ways (non-assertive), aggressive or hostile ways, or direct-but-non-hostile (assertive) ways. Sometimes it is a reaction to our parents' anger that we learn. Jim saw his father throwing temper tantrums and acting childish, and he decided that he would never be like his father by acting childish around his children. So when he felt angry he became the stoic who put on the stone-face mask, like Anthony's "Buddha." His face would look like granite, but he would never admit that he was feeling angry.

Scapegoats, Martyrs and Other Anger Targets

Poor Jeannette — she was the *scapegoat* in her family. Some families have an unhealthy interaction style, whereby they need someone to blame for everything that goes wrong. They find a scapeboat and dump all of the blame upon him/her. When I was a probation officer, some of these families came to me for help. It was a temptation at first to remove the scapegoat from the home for placement in a foster home. But as I became more experienced, I learned that if you remove the scapegoat there are two possible reactions: either the caseworker becomes the scapegoat, or another member of the family becomes the scapegoat. There will always be a scapegoat until the members of the family learn to take responsibility for their own feelings rather than projecting their unhappiness onto another.

A person who has been a scapegoat in his or her family (were you?) will have great difficulty expressing anger. Anger is appropriate because this type of situation leaves a person with a great deal of childhood rage. There is a scapegoat in almost every divorce seminar, because the scapegoat is prone to divorce. Scapegoats have to do a great deal of emotional relearning before they can overcome the feeling that they are so worthless that they do not have the right to be angry. Being the scapegoat is so destructive that one may need to seek professional counseling to escape this destructive role.

And, oh! We must not forget the *martyr*. Almost every class I have taught has had someone in it who was either a martyr or the victim of a martyr. Martyrs try to live through other persons. They completely sacrifice themselves to "helping" others. Martyrs will give to others, seemingly without limit, at great personal cost to themselves. The feeling behind martyrdom may well be genuine, but the giver does things whether he or she feels like giving or not. *There is* the deep, subtle process going on. The giver is not giving because he or she cares, but from the fear of losing the other person or because it is a way of interacting that the martyr learned at an early age. This giving, for what turn out to be selfish reasons when we look closely, will cause resentment in the other person. But the other person will find it very difficult to express this resentment and anger because the martyr's self-denying style generates a nurturing response.

The principle operating underneath this relationship is that martyrs do not have identities of their own. They try to find their identities through other people. Living through others is what makes the martyr relationship so destructive and harmful to both people. In chapter twelve you will find an exercise which may help clarify the martyr role.

How do you escape being a martyr if you are one yourself? Or how do you help another person to escape being a martyr? The martyr who does not have an identity of his or her own needs to work at finding that identity; to stop exclusively giving; to learn to accept from others as well; to feel good about himself or herself; to find an identity through relationships, activities, interests, goals; and to escape the martyr role.

Some of us have been on the receiving end of martyrdom, and we have learned so much guilt that we have difficulty expressing our anger. Quite possibly if you have been on the brunt end of the martyr relationship, you have already begun to express your anger toward that other person. But, many people who have been on the brunt end have kept their anger turned in and have become martyrs themselves to the people around them. In many cases, we learn how to be martyrs by living with a martyr parent.

For some of us, learning about martyrs may be an emotionally heavy situation. Trudy watched and learned about martyrs in the seminar one evening. She went home, did not sleep all night, and called a friend to talk to the next day because it overwhelmed her to see that she had been a martyr in her marriage and had controlled her husband by making him feel guilty. So find a friend or a therapist to talk to if you need to work through feeling guilty for being a martyr.

It can also be helpful to observe that anger may be a secondary feeling that is covering up and disguising another feeling, such as frustration, rejection, inferior feelings, hurt, or feeling unlovable. It can be difficult to get in touch with these feelings. Anger just seems to come more easily for many of us, even though we feel bad about it. It is important to work hard at finding out if there may be other feelings confused with your anger.

Push-Button Anger

I have found it helpful in the seminars to have people list their pet peeves. What really gets you angry when someone pushes a button? Elaine, so angry about Steve's efforts to gain custody of the children in court, may be feeling doubts about her abilities to parent. Charles may be so angry about Marie leaving the marriage because he is reexperiencing feelings of rejection from the past when his mother died. What are some of your pet peeves? And what are some of the feelings underneath that push your buttons and make you angry? It is worth a break on the trail to think about it for a time.

Earlier I mentioned that dumpees tend to feel more anger than dumpers. That may be easier to understand if we look for other feelings underneath the anger. Consider, for example, the frustration of being out of control. Most of the power is in the hands of the dumpers. They hold the cards, and the dumpees have to take whatever hand is dealt. It is frustrating to feel out of control, and frustration can lead to anger.

How about rejection? Dumpees usually are still in love, and the people they love are suddenly saying they do not love them anymore. That is deep rejection and often leads to anger.

How about the future? The dumpee may have thought the future was all planned. Then suddenly he/she has to face being alone (and lonely), and has to develop a new life plan. This may be accompanied by fear of making it financially, which is difficult and frustrating. The dumpee feels afraid — often *really* afraid. Anger can seem to be a beautiful way to fight being afraid, and may be one way to get the adrenaline going to overcome the fear. Dumpees thus tend to feel more anger, and their scores on the *Fisher Divorce Adjustment Scale* tend to reflect that. Again, each person is an individual, and there are some dumpers who feel a great deal of anger because of their unique situations.

Venting Divorce Anger

I would like at this point to discuss positive ways to express anger; ways that will not be harmful to you or to others.

Let me reemphasize the important difference between the special *divorce anger* you may feel about your dissolution, and your anger in connection with other life situations. First I'll present some methods for constructively expressing the divorce anger, then some ways for you to express your anger *whenever* it occurs in your relationships.

Divorce anger needs to be *vented* and *released* in nondestructive ways. Anger in future relationships — friends, family, lovers, children — needs to be *expressed directly, firmly, honestly,* but in a constructive way to encourage communication and a deeper relationship.

Another point that I feel very strongly about: Our temptation and desires are to take our anger out on our former spouses directly. We want to call them up and hurt them, get back at them, be vindictive, and vent our anger directly at them. I do not believe that this is helpful in most cases. When you throw a few logs on the divorce anger fire, your ex may throw a few logs back in retaliation. Pretty soon the fire is consuming both of you. I suggest that you express your anger in other ways, such as those suggested here, rather than taking it out on your former spouse. This recommendation to avoid direct display of anger applies only to this special case of divorce anger at your ex. Usually, I encourage the direct approach.

There are a few couples who have learned to express anger to each other in their relationships and are able to continue to express this anger as they go through the divorce process. However, if you — like most of us — were not able to express anger in your marriage, how do you expect to express it constructively now? Later in this chapter I will offer some tools for dealing more effectively with your anger in the future. For now, concentrate on releasing the *old* anger that has built up toward your ex!

Humor is a very effective way of expelling angry feelings. Harriet was the comedian of one class. She would come to the group and say, "I don't know what to tell people when they ask me where my ex is. I don't want to tell them that he's off with another woman." One week she arrived with a big smile, "I finally decided that the next time a person asks me, I'll tell them that he croaked!" She laughs and the whole class laughs, and everybody has vented angry feelings through laughter. A sense of humor is always valuable in life, but it is especially valuable in dealing with anger.

One of the most effective ways of expressing anger is to *call a friend* and say, "I need to talk about this anger that I'm feeling toward my former spouse. I know I may not make sense sometimes. I know that I may become very emotional. And I know that some of the things that I say may not be what I'm really feeling all of the time. But right now I'm feeling really angry, and I need you to listen to me talk about my anger." A life-line support friend who will help you through these times is one of your best tools for dealing with anger.

Many people who experience divorce anger are able to use

fantasies to help them express it. Sandy was an expert at this. She would fantasize the following incident: "I would go to the garden store and buy a sack of hot lawn fertilizer. Then in the middle of the night I would go over to my ex's house and write obscene four-letter words with the fertilizer in front of his house. Then he would read them every time he had to mow his lawn all summer long!" We have to keep remembering these are fantasies and that we should not act them out! If you do not have much self-control, possibly you should not use fantasies because you may tend to act on them, which is likely to be destructive in most cases.

Physical exercise of any sort is usually helpful. Physical games, jogging, house cleaning, beating on a rug, or anything like that is especially helpful. Anger is a source of energy and it's important to use up the energy. Physical activity is a good way.

You can be more effective in expelling anger through physical exercise if you use other techniques along with it. For example, when you play a game of golf or tennis, you can fantasize that the ball is that person's head. In addition, if you can do some grunting and groaning, using your vocal cords along with physical exercise, that would be more effective. When you go jogging, with each step you can mentally picture his or her face on the ground in front of you, and you can add grunts and groans.

If you feel comfortable using *cuss words*, this can be an effective way to vent angry feelings. Using your vocal cords provides a vehicle for getting your gut feelings to literally come out your throat and mouth and be expelled from your body.

Try getting your feelings out by *screaming*. Many of us would not be comfortable screaming with people around, but maybe you can find a place to go and scream alone. Charlene was able to do this by driving her car to a private place. Then she could park for a while and do the screaming, crying, and yelling that she found so helpful to get out her anger. Her kids became aware of it and when Mother was getting upset they would say, "Mom's about ready to go to her screaming place again!"

Tears are another way which helps some people to express anger. Crying is a positive, honest expression of feelings. Many people, especially males, have difficulty crying. You need to "give yourself permission to cry" — it will help you feel better. Crying is a natural body function for expressing sadness or anger.

Another effective way of getting anger out is to *write a letter* saying all of the things that you would like to say to that former lover. Write it in really big letters; maybe use a piece of crayon and write it with lots of anger. But after you have written the letter, do not mail it. Instead, take the letter to the fireplace and burn it up. You have both expressed and symbolically burned up your anger.

You can use the *"empty chair,"* an effective Gestalt therapy technique. Imagine that the person sitting in a vacant chair is your former love partner, and say everything that you would like to say to that person. If you are good enough at imagining, you can even switch chairs and say the things that person would say back to you. Then go back to your chair and say the things that you would like to say again.

Another simple and effective way of venting anger is to take an old garden hose and cut off a three-foot piece. Careful now! Use this piece of hose only to *beat on something that will not be damaged* by it. The accompanying loud "smacks" add to the satisfaction of the pounding. (Please remember that such a device is only for non-destructive noisy release. Do not hurt yourself or anyone else!)

So you see there are many ways for you to vent your divorce anger. You will not find all of these ways helpful to you — in fact, you may have a great deal of resistance to some and be completely unable to use them. But you are only limited by your own creativity, ingenuity, and inhibition in finding ways for anger expression.

Incidentally, some people are not able to express anger because of a need to keep it. It is like a companion. If you let go of that anger, you will not have it as a tool for punishing the other person. So you may have some sort of payoff or reward for keeping the anger. The question for you to think about is: What kind of person would you like to be? Do you like being an angry person, or would you like to let go of the anger?

Only You Can Prevent Block Fires

Anger is one of the most important rebuilding blocks because it spreads to the feelings in the other rebuilding blocks. If the fires are burning out of control in you, then you will have trouble working up the trail until you get them under control.

A great sense of relief will result from working through your anger until there is nothing but ashes left. It will free you to have energy for other areas in your life. You can forgive yourself and the other person for the love relationship not working out. You have stopped blaming yourself; you have stopped feeling like a failure; you have found the internal peace that comes from letting go of everything that was painful. You find that you can talk to the former love partner in a calm and rational manner without becoming emotionally upset. Now you can deal with friends — either your partner's or yours — without becoming irritated. You suddenly wake up and find there is sunshine in your life instead of the stormy cloud of anger. You realize that things just happened the way they happened, and that there is no point in blaming somebody.

Zack, a fellow in the divorce class, picked up a slogan that is very useful when you work through the divorce process: "It just doesn't matter." So many things that seemed important to us before just are not anymore. Once you have reached the stage of forgiveness, you no longer need to punish or be vindictive toward the other person.

Beyond Divorce: Expressing Your Everyday Anger

I hope the preceding material has helped you learn to express your divorce anger. Now, I am going to discuss everyday, "garden variety" anger — the kind we all experience in response to the ups and downs of daily life.

First, notice that how we act (our behavior) is not the same as how we feel (our emotions). Feelings and behavior are really two different parts of who we are.

Anger is a *feeling*. Assertion and aggression are types of *behavior*.

Remember Jean at the beginning of this chapter? She's the one who let the air out of her ex's tires. Jean was feeling such strong anger that her behavior was definitely aggressive. It would have been possible for her to express her anger in other ways as well. For instance, she could have been even more aggressive and acted in some violent way toward her ex himself — maybe by physically attacking him. Or she could have taken an assertive approach to expressing her anger by confronting him directly and telling him exactly how she felt: "I'm so mad at you I feel like letting the air out of your tires! You've been unfair and unreasonable. . .!" Of course, that is the special situation I have advised against, but you get the idea: angry feelings can be expressed in different *behaviors*.

Put yourself in the following situations:

You have been waiting in line for concert tickets for two hours. Two "friends" of the man in front of you walk up and say, "Hey, Joe, how about letting us in here?"

The child support check is two weeks late, and you really need the money to buy clothes for the kids before school starts next week. When you call your ex, the answer is, "Well, I had a lot of expenses from my trip to Hawaii, and I won't be able to pay you until next month."

You read in the newspaper that your state legislature has just voted itself a 20 percent raise — and voted to cut support for education by 10 percent.

Angry? Well, you should be! These situations and a thousand other examples of unfairness, abuse, thoughtlessness, and other mistreatment are good cause for anger. Never mind what you were told as a child — anger is natural, normal, healthy, and human! We all feel it at times. (If you think you *never* get angry, maybe you have already forgotten the difference between feelings and behavior. Go back and reread the paragraphs above!)

The question now is, "What *do* I do about my anger?" We have already discussed some ideas for releasing the strong feelings of divorce anger — humor, fantasies, exercise, screaming, crying, and others. These ways are helpful while you are getting rid of that powerful anger toward your former partner. But they do not give you much help for dealing with your anger in everyday situations because they are designed to release pent up anger in a situation you are no longer in. We need methods to use in situations involving on-going relationships.

Psychologists Bob Alberti and Michael Emmons, who wrote the assertiveness training bestseller, *Your Perfect Right,* offer us a system for learning to express anger toward another person in positive, constructive, assertive (not aggressive) ways. I agree with most of what they have to say, and encourage you to try it in your own life. Like all the changes we have discussed in this book, it will take some effort, but you will find your relationships — and your own well-being — will benefit! The following excerpt, reprinted from *Your Perfect Right* with permission, deals with anger:

"Our view of a healthy approach to dealing with anger is this:
(1) Recognize and allow yourself to believe that anger is a natural, normal, healthy, non-evil human feeling. Everyone feels it, we just don't all express it. You needn't fear your anger.
(2) Remember you are responsible for your own feelings. You got angry at what happened; the other person didn't "make" you angry.
(3) Remember that anger and aggression are not the same thing! Anger can be expressed assertively.
(4) Get to know yourself, so you recognize those events and behaviors which trigger your anger. As some say, "find your own buttons, so you'll know when they're pushed!"
(5) Learn to relax. If you have developed the skill of relaxing yourself, learn to apply this response when your anger is triggered.
(6) Develop assertive methods for expressing your anger, following the principles described in this book: be spontaneous; don't wait and let it build up resentment; state it directly; avoid sarcasm and innuendo; use honest, expressive language; avoid name-calling, putdowns, and physical attacks.
(7) Keep your life clear! Deal with issues when they arise, when you feel the feelings — not after hours/days/weeks of "stewing" about it.... Go ahead! Get angry! But develop a

positive, assertive style for expressing it. You, and those around you, will appreciate it."

Righteous Anger

Before I end this chapter, a brief word is in order about the religious beliefs that prevent many people from showing anger. Many believe that we should "turn the other cheek," and that expressing anger is somewhat "sinful." I personally believe that expressing anger in a positive manner and freeing myself from that anger is the most spiritual thing I can do. I do not believe that God wants us to be controlled by anger any more than by any other strong emotion.

"Smoke Gets In Your Eyes"

Don't stop climbing when you feel the fires of anger starting within you. This chapter has given you permission to feel angry, offered you ways of expressing anger positively and constructively, so you have nothing left but ashes. The fire may smoulder for a long time, but it is better to let it burn out so that you can be free. Take your time in this part of the trail, with forest fires raging around you, and be careful. It is important that you get through without destroying the people in your environment or destroying yourself. Uncontrolled anger can be very destructive.

My research indicates that the average person going through the divorce process stays angry at ther ex-spouse for three years. How long will you choose to be angry at your former partner?

Children Get Angry Too!

Children of divorce experience the same type of extreme divorce anger that parents do. I remember the daughter of one divorced parent who became uncontrollably angry at her father in the swimming pool one day. The anger was far stronger than the situation warranted, and was apparently a direct result of a feeling of abandonment, for which she blamed her father.

It is very easy for divorced parents not to allow their children to be angry. The custodial mother will many times try to establish a good relationship between her children and their father, even though he has not kept visitation appointments and appears to be involved in something other than the children much of the time. The mother may try to help the children to accept their father without being angry. But it is appropriate for children to be angry at the noncustodial parent who lets them down.

It is also easy for us to withdraw love when our children express anger. We may be so emotionally uptight ourselves that when children get angry, we immediately become unaccepting: "Go to your room until you can learn to behave properly! " We need to find that extra energy to listen to and accept our children's anger. But we also need to see that they do not become aggressive, have temper tantrums, or break things. Allow the children to express their anger in the same positive, constructive ways explained in this chapter. When they say that they are very angry at their father (mother) for not coming, just accept that and say, "I think it's right for you to feel angry in this situation. "

Most of us learned our emotional blocks for expressing anger through some interaction with our parents. We were punished for being angry, or we were not allowed to be angry, or we were sent to our rooms and had feelings of rejection and loss of love. It is far better for children to learn that anger is part of being human and that it is okay to express anger in a positive way.

How Are You Doing?

Check yourself with these statements before you go on. Remember to be honest with yourself!

1. *I can communicate with my former love partner in a calm and rational manner.*
2. *I am comfortable seeing and talking to my former love partner.*
3. *I no longer feel like unloading my feelings of anger and hurt on my former love partner.*
4. *I have stopped hoping that my former love partner is feeling as much emotional pain as I am.*
5. *I no longer feel so angry at my former love partner.*

6. *It is not important any more that my family, friends, and associates be on my side rather than on my former love partner's side.*

7. *I have outgrown the need to get even with my former love partner for hurting me.*

8. *I no longer blame my former love partner for the failure of our love relationship.*

9. *I have stopped trying to hurt my former love partner by letting him/her know how much I hurt emotionally.*

10. *I have overcome my anger and have begun to accept the things my former love partner has been doing.*

11. *I am expressing my anger in a positive manner that is not destructive to me or to those around me.*

12. *I am able to admit it when I feel angry rather than denying my angry feelings.*

13. *I understand the emotional blocks that have kept me from expressing anger in a positive manner.*

14. *I am able to express my anger constructively rather than venting it inappropriately.*

15. *I am reaching a stage of forgiveness rather than remaining angry.*

LETTING GO
"Disentangling Is Hard To Do"

You need to stop investing emotionally in your dead love relationship. It is easier to let go if your own life-bucket is full rather than empty. Dumpers tend to let go more quickly, often because they have let go even before they left. Failure to let go may be a symptom that you are not facing some painful feelings within yourself.

Chapter 10

Stella: *"Harry left me four years ago and he immediately remarried."*

Counselor: *"I notice you are still wearing a wedding ring."*

Stella: *"Yes, it's very important to me."*

Counselor: *"And you wrote me a check for the therapy with Harry's name still on the bank account!"*

Stella: *"I guess I just can't let go."*

Some days I get a song in my brain that I keep humming over and over. How many songs can you think of that have to do with letting go? Here are a few to get you started:

Whatcha Going to Do When She Says Goodbye?
Breaking Up Is Hard To Do
One Less Bell To Answer
I Will Survive
I'm Gonna Wash That Man Right Outta My Hair!
I'll Be Loving You, Always (for us old-timers)

I have had surprising difficulty finding information of any importance concerning how to disentangle. Yet most of us have ended a love relationship at one time or another in our lives, even if it was when we were teenagers and dating. It is interesting that this common phenomenon has been researched so little. We have to depend upon the poets and song writers to teach us about ending a love relationship.

What Is This Thing Called "Disentanglement"?

First we need a definition of just what letting go is. Imagine your hands clasped together with the fingers intertwined, and then imagine pulling those hands apart while you continue to clasp. That gives you a graphic description of what I mean by "disentanglement." It involves the painful letting go of all the strong emotional feelings for that other person.

The feeling of being in love is not the only thing that is hard to give up. There are also anger, bitterness and feelings of vindictiveness. Whenever a person still talks about the former love partner a great deal, whether in endearing or angry terms, I know that person has not let go of strong feelings for the ex.

It's common for people to claim that they want to continue being friends during the "honeymoon period" of the divorce process. Then when the dumper guilt and dumpee anger set in, the desire to stay friends begins to disappear. But many people strive so hard to remain friends that they fail to let go — and fail to allow the anger to come and help them do it. As a result, I find it advisable not to maintain the friendship during that early stage; wait until after you have disentangled. Trying to be friends may prolong the process and even endanger the possibility of being friends later on.

Another aspect that needs to be mentioned is the runaway syndrome. Most divorced people at some time in the process have a strong urge to run away. They want to get into a new community, away from where the former spouse is living. This will avoid the pain of running into the former spouse or his/her friends.

Coleen had been married to a college professor who left her when he became involved with a young student. Driving her car down the street, Coleen saw him in his car with the younger woman. Before she could stop her car, she vomited. It is very painful to see that former love partner with a new mate.

If you are running toward something, such as a new job, a former home with a support system of family or friends, or anything that is an advancement in your life, maybe the move is advisable. If you are running away from dealing with the unpleasant situation, you should reconsider. You are already under a stressful situation, and a major move will only add to the stress.

There may be advantages to staying in the present community and dealing with the painful feelings of seeing your former spouse and his or her friends. ("So you were married to the president of the Chamber of Commerce? I know him well.") People who move may just be burying and denying the process of letting go. Those who stay will likely be able to see and talk with the former spouse sooner without becoming emotionally upset. They will have dealt with the disentanglement rebuilding block more effectively by confronting it.

There appears to be a connection between three key rebuilding blocks: *denying* that the love relationship is ending; *grieving* the loss; and *letting go of* the dead relationship. As we climb the trail, we may be working on all three interconnected blocks at the same time.

Don't Drag It Out

(I want to talk to you dumpers for a moment; you dumpees may listen in if you want, because we will be talking about you.)

The dumper may want to "be kind" to the dumpee to avoid feeling guilty, but this only prolongs the process. If you are going to be a dumper, do it with strength, courage, and firmness. It is far kinder than being timid about dumping.

Richard thought he would be a kind dumper, and made it a point to take Barbara (the dumpee) out to dinner every week, supposedly to make her feel better. But each time he did it, it was like throwing a few crumbs to a hungry cat. It kept the cat from finding other places to eat, and it kept the cat at a starvation level. Barbara failed to let go as long as there seemed to be some hope of reconciliation. Bluntness may be far kinder than "kindness" to the dumpee. Richard was being "kind" only to himself — easing his guilt feelings.

There are other situations that prolong letting go. Lengthy court hearings will drag things out. Children and pets that have to be exchanged at regular intervals may prolong the process, as may continuing to live close to each other. A joint business that forces you to keep dealing with each other is another delaying factor. (Business matters often do make disentanglement more difficult; weigh carefully any decisions in this area. You'll want advice from your attorney and tax advisor.)

Another problem in letting go has to do with in-law relationships. Divorce usually includes separation from the ex-partner's family as well. While in most cases the ties with in-laws are broken or much loosened at the time of divorce, the breakup may have the opposite effect. In some situations, the in-laws' emotional ties remain closer to their son- or daughter-in-law than to their own son or daughter.

The Colorado State Supreme Court has ruled that grandparents have visitation rights with their grandchildren regardless of who has custody. This landmark ruling has established both a legal precedent and a custom which for many will result in maintaining the bonds of one's "family by a former marriage."

Disentangling Is Hard Work

With or without all of these complications, the big question remains — HOW do you let go? For many of us, "How do I stop loving that person?" is the tough issue. It is much easier to let go, of course, if you have other things going for you. A good job, a good support system, friends and relatives who are helpful and supportive, some sort of internal fullness rather than emptiness — all of these will help fill the void created when the beloved person is removed.

There are some specific things you can do to help yourself let go. Start by going through the house and removing all of those things that tend to keep you thinking about your former love partner. Pictures, wedding gifts, birthday gifts, and similar mementos can be removed so that they are not a constant reminder. You may need to rearrange the furniture in the house, perhaps even to make the house look as different as possible from the way it was when you were living there as a married couple. The marriage bed is often an especially important symbol. You may need to put the bed in another room or sell it, or at least move it to a new spot in the bedroom.

You may want to make a collection of all those reminders of your former love relationship and store them in a box in the garage or basement. Some weekend you may choose to do some implosive grieving, whereby you bring out all of these mementos and set aside a period of time to grieve as heavily as possible. This heavy grief period will probably be very depressing, and I suggest you have another person around for support. Becoming as much out of control as possible in your grieving may help you to let go more rapidly. By increasing the intensity of the grief, this implosive grieving may shorten the number of weeks or months it takes you to let go fully.

Another area that is a problem for many people is dealing with all the phone calls, letters, and visits from the former love partner. If it is evident that he or she is hanging on, you may feel irritated. But the fact that you keep allowing it to happen may indicate that you have not let go either! It takes two to keep this game going. If you simply refuse to play the game, it will be easier on everyone in the long run. You will have to become assertive, or perhaps even to start hanging up the phone or returning letters unanswered and unopened.

You also can make a decision to control your thinking and fantasizing about the former love partner. Whenever you find yourself weeping about that person, think about something painful or something unpleasant in the love relationship. That will lead you to stop thinking about the person. As an alternative, you may simply choose another image or subject to concentrate on, instead of focusing on the past love.

Letting Go of Your Fears

There is a more abstract answer to the problem of letting go. Often a pattern of behavior has at its core a specific feeling — such as fear of rejection, guilt, fear that one is not lovable, or low self-worth and lack of confidence. It is surprising how often we set up our lives to feel the feeling we are most afraid of! If we fear rejection, we either consciously or unconsciously set it up to be rejected. If we have a need to feel guilty, we set up situations that make us feel guilty.

When Teresa and Patrick came to see me for marriage counseling, his pattern of behavior was to seek rejection, and hers was to feel guilty. Their neurotic needs fit together perfectly! They went through years of marriage with her feeling guilty because he felt rejected. She set up reasons to feel guilty, thus feeding his feelings of rejection.

When love relationships end, we tend to respond with the feeling which is at the root of our behavior. If it is rejection, we feel rejected; if guilt, we feel that. Unfortunately, such a feeling may be so great that one is not strong enough to endure it and let go at the same time.

If you are having a difficult time letting go, ask yourself, "What feeling would I feel the strongest if I did let go of my ex-love?" Maybe your reluctance to let go is actually covering up your inability to face the primary feeling that is underneath. For instance, you may be afraid to let go because it will force you to deal directly with your feelings of rejection. So, you avoid feeling rejected by not letting go. You will probably have to face that feeling directly before you will be able to let go. Get help from a life-line friend or a counselor if you feel the need for support.

Invest in Yourself

The goal of working through this rebuilding block is to emotionally invest in your own personal growth instead of investing in the dead relationship. There is no return on the investment in the relationship's emotional corpse. In contrast, the greatest possible return comes from investment in yourself.

Helping the Children To Let Go

Children of divorce deal with letting go by letting go of the old concept of the two-parent family. Suddenly it is a one-parent family, with a custodial and a noncustodial parent. Even if there is joint custody, the children still have to deal with different lifestyles. It is hoped that the children will not have to let go of a quality relationship with both parents.

The child may have difficulty, however, in dealing with the parents' ability to let go or not. This may become an important rebuilding block for children if they continually hear from one parent about all of the good things (or bad things) the other parent is doing.

If the parents have not let go of the relationship, the children will tend to get caught in either the positive or negative feelings between the parents. This will prolong the adjustment process for the children.

How Are You Doing?

Take time on the trail now to stand still and shake off those feelings from the past that keep you investing in the dead relationship. Jump up and down to feel strong inside, shake off the heavy burden you have been carrying, and find the free feeling that comes from not carrying that dead love relationship on your back.

Finally, check yourself out on the items listed below. Have you really let go?

1. *I think of my former love partner only occasionally now.*
2. *I rarely fantasize about being with my former love partner.*
3. *I no longer become emotionally upset when I think about my former love partner.*
4. *I have stopped trying to please my former love partner.*
5. *I have accepted that my former love partner and I will not get back together.*
6. *I have stopped finding excuses to talk to my former love partner.*
7. *I rarely talk about my former love partner with friends.*
8. *I have outgrown any feelings of romantic love for my former love partner.*
9. *I no longer wish to continue a sexual relationship with my former love partner.*
10. *I have given up my emotional commitment to my former love partner.*
11. *I can accept my former love partner having a love relationship with another person.*
12. *I feel like a single person rather than a person in a committed love relationship with my former love partner.*
13. *I am no longer angry at my former love partner.*

SELF-WORTH
"Maybe I'm Not So Bad After All!"

It is okay to feel good about yourself. You can learn to feel better about yourself, and thus gain strength to help you adjust better to a crisis. As you successfully adjust to a crisis, you will feel even better about yourself! If you are experiencing a personal identity/rebellion crisis, you may be seriously straining your love relationship.

Chapter 11

When I was a child, my father continually warned me about getting a "big head" and becoming "stuck on myself." Then I went to church and learned that I had been born sinful. At school it was the jocks and the brains that got all the attention. Finally I married so there would be someone who thought I was worthwhile. It made me feel good that someone cared. But then she became a pro at pointing out my faults. I finally reached a point where I began to believe I was truly worthless. It was then that I decided to leave the marriage.　　— Carl

Wow! This self-concept portion of the trail is crowded with people who appear unable to continue the climb. Some sit on rocks, dejected, without energy left to climb. Some are lying on the ground like door mats, expecting everyone to walk on them. The faces of some show the effects of criticism and feelings of worthlessness. Some seem almost invisible, as if a shield surrounds them, blending them into the background.

Notice those people who are followed everywhere by a black cloud! Rain falls on them, but not on those around them. That woman over there seems to have misplaced her black cloud for a while. She is anxiously peering over her shoulder, stumbling over rocks — can she be searching for the lost cloud? Sure enough, the cloud has caught up with her and is raining on her again, and she actually seems more content now.

The Importance of Self-Worth

In this portion of the climb, learning more about self-worth and ways to improve it are our main concerns. Self-worth — also referred to as "self-concept" and "self-esteem" — is the skeleton that supports personality. We're talking about the way each of us sees ourselves — our core beliefs about our value as human beings. Heavy stuff. When self-worth becomes fractured, the whole personality begins to fragment.

When I was growing up I thought I alone suffered from an affliction called "inferiority complex." I never realized that the term was used so often because many others were feeling inferior also! I have often asked the participants in seminars to raise their hands if they want to improve their self-esteem — usually *all* hands go up! Do you see how important this rebuilding block is?

Have you ever wondered whether self-concept exists at birth or if it is learned later? Apparently we learn much of how we feel about ourselves at an early age from the significant people around us, including parents and siblings, teachers, ministers, and relatives. This basic level of self-concept is later influenced strongly by peers — especially during the teen years. As an adult, the love partner becomes a primary source of validation and feedback, and greatly affects one's feelings of self-worth.

Many marriages that end in divorce developed a pattern of interaction destructive to the self-concept of the parties involved. In fact, some become so destructive that the parties may not be able to end the marriage due to feelings of worthlessness. For example, the battered wife often thinks that she *deserves* the emotional and physical abuse. She is unable to leave the marriage because she's convinced she would not be able to make it on her own. Many people suffer serious erosion of their self-esteem in bad marriages before finally seeking relief in divorce.

But when the physical separation comes and the love relationship ends, self-concept hits an all time low. So much of a person's identity is involved in the love relationship that when the marriage fails, the identity suffers. I administered the *Tennessee Self-Concept Scale* (a paper-and-pencil psychological test designed to measure feelings of self-worth) to recently-separated people. It would be hard to find another group of people whose average score was as low as theirs. Ending a love relationship can be devastating to self-concept. In fact, feelings of self-worth at this time may be the lowest ever experienced. A low self-concept immobilizes some people emotionally, making them unable to function in their jobs, in their parenting of children, or in their interaction with others.

Further study of the self-concept scores of this same group of people showed that people with a good self-concept were better able to adjust to the ending of their love relationship. The research confirms what our common sense tells us: a good self-concept makes adjustment to a life crisis easier.

Obviously feelings of self-worth are very important to the way we live. Since ending a love relationship is usually detrimental to self-concept, most of us need to improve our feelings about ourselves after experiencing a major life crisis such as this. It is reassuring to know that self-concept can be enhanced. That is an exciting and optimistic viewpoint — we can relearn, grow, and change! We do not have to be saddled with old feelings of low self-worth.

Eleven Steps to Greater Self-Esteem

In the divorce and personal growth seminars which I have taught continuously since 1974, changes in self-worth are among the most significant outcomes for participants during the ten weeks. What techniques are used? How do people make such big changes? Let me share with you some tools you may use to improve your own self-esteem.

Step one seems obvious, but is often overlooked. You must *make a decision to change.* A few years ago, I discovered several clients who were being followed by little black clouds — like those people we met earlier on the trail. When there was progress in therapy, they would become uncomfortable, look for the cloud, and expect rain to fall!

Frustrated, I decided to take a solitary walk in the mountains. I hiked up the Big Thompson Canyon in the Rocky Mountains. Near the top of the trail is a little sign pointing out a Douglas fir tree uprooted by the wind. The tree had been lying on the ground long enough for the end of the trunk to bend around and continue growing toward the sunlight. The new growth was pointing toward the sky for about 20 feet. Because the old trunk's roots stick mostly out of the ground, one wonders how the tree could grow for so many years! Besides the trunk, several branches also reach from the upper side of the trunk to the sky. One of these branches is about 30 feet high.

I thought to myself, as I studied this tree, that it was uprooted in its life just as a person's life is uprooted by a crisis such as a divorce. The tree sought its own fullest potential, continuing to grow and reach for the sky. I was greatly moved by the sight of this tree. I realized that there is a force within each of us that will help us to reach our full potential after a crisis has uprooted our lives. The tree's continuing reach for the sky led me to develop my belief in changing self-concept.

We need to find and listen to that inner source of emotional energy which encourages the development of our potential. If we get in touch with that source — whether it be called a religious soul, a psychological ego, or the life force — we will be capable of making the changes that we desire. I suggest that you look within yourself for this source of strength and use it to become the person you would like to be.

If you make a decision to improve your self-concept, almost everything in your life will be affected: your work; your relationships with other people; the way you parent your children; your choice of a partner in a future love relationship; and, most of all, the way you feel about yourself. Enormous changes may occur in your personality and your life if you proceed to improve your self-concept. The decision is the first and perhaps the most difficult step. If your commitment is firm, the steps which follow will come much more easily.

Step two is to *change the way you look at yourself.* Most people can easily list 20 things they do not like about themselves. Why not make a list of 20 positive things you *do* like about yourself? When I give this assignment in my seminars, there are groans and comments such as, "How about two instead of 20?" I once received a phone call late at night from one of the class participants. He started the call with, "Damn you! I came home from teaching school and started the list of things I like about myself. It took me an hour to come up with the first one. It took almost that long for the second one. Now it is 11 p.m. and I only have five things on my list!" That was the most important homework for him in the whole ten weeks.

This is an important task; take time to do it. Be sure to write the list down so you can do the next step.

Step three: *Say positive things about yourself aloud to others.* Good things may be easier to write to ourselves than to say out loud. All the old messages inside us start screaming, "Don't act stuck up and conceited!" Ignore those messages; take your list and share the comments with a friend. Get your courage up and break the negative pattern. It is *okay* to make good comments about yourself. It does take courage to say them out loud. Remember, changing your self-concept is *not* easy!

Those voices that scream inside us are especially loud if a critical person influenced us when we were growing up. In class Charlie said that he could not do step three because his parents had told him so often "not to get a big head." He was a good athlete in high school, and the exercises could have helped him to build confidence in himself. But the parent voices were louder, and he had learned to be "humble." As an adult he could not say good things out loud about himself because he still felt his parents would be unhappy! That statement may sound ridiculous to you, but not to Charlie. He was finally able to read his list aloud in the seminar, although with a look of pain on his face. When he finished, everyone applauded; and he said, "Boy, I feel good!"

Step four is a tough one: *re-examine your relationships with others, and make changes which will help you break destructive patterns and develop the "new you."*

Much of your self-concept is validated by feedback that you get from others. Take a hard look at your relationships. Which are constructive for your self-concept? Which are really more harm than good? If you see that some of your relationships with other people are destructive to your self-concept, choose either to end those relationships or to make them more productive and positive for you. Old and established patterns of interaction are hard to change. Nevertheless, to remain in a comfortable relationship which reinforces a poor self-concept is to choose to keep a major obstacle in your own path of growth.

As a probation officer, I often heard people say that a certain juvenile in trouble "only needed to find a new peer group" to solve all the problems. I found that, for juveniles, it is generally necessary to make changes in both their peer group and their feelings about themselves. They tend to seek feedback from others that basically agrees with their own self-concept. Peer group relationships powerfully reinforce the present level of self-concept. This happens partly because the group was chosen as a reflection of the self-concept: "I really feel at home with these people."

Changing your relationships may be very difficult due to your tendency to follow the old patterns and find relationships that reinforce your present level of self-esteem. But I believe that if you sincerely want to feel better about yourself, you will need to invest in positive relationships — those which help you feel good about being you!

Step five: *Get rid of the negative self-thoughts in your head.* We all hear messages playing in our heads — "parent tapes" in Transactional Analysis vocabulary. These parent tapes may have originated from parents or from teachers, ministers, or other significant adults: "Be careful and don't let this success go to your head. Remember that it is sinful to be conceited and selfish. You think you're smart, don't you?" Such messages are destructive, and prevent you from improving your self-concept. They were originally designed to discipline and control. Unfortunately, they turn out to be neither helpful nor productive to us.

As adults, we choose whether we want to continue to listen to those messages or not. Say your own "tapes" out loud and write them down. Think about whether they are appropriate. The transactional analysts suggest you take these messages from your parent or child ego state and analyze them with your adult ego state to see if they are rational and appropriate messages at this time in your life. Then rid yourself of those that prevent progress toward feeling better about yourself.

You may need to express these feelings of not being okay in a counseling session, with life-line friends, or perhaps in self-therapy. Write these messages down or tape record them. You need to somehow "carry out the emotional garbage of the past," so you can stop letting it control and burden you now. Allow yourself to air, ventilate, express, and verbalize those old not okay messages. Move them out of your path toward improving your self-concept.

Step six may sound like a silly activity, but it worked for Trudy, a member of one divorce seminar. I suggest that you *write positive notes to yourself and pin them up around the house in prominent places:* on a mirror or on the refrigerator, for example. These notes might be compliments such as, "You have a pretty smile." The notes could come from the list of 20 positive things that you like about yourself. Trudy came to a weekend seminar and was like an emotional corpse. She had a great deal of difficulty paying attention, but somehow this exercise rang a bell for her. She reported the next week that she had written about 100 notes to herself, even placing one on the toilet! She became a different person, her self-concept improved almost miraculously! Writing notes to herself appeared to make the big difference. Such a dramatic change is rare, but shows the potential power of *active effort*.

Step seven: *Open yourself up to hearing positive comments from others*. People tend to hear only what they want to hear. If you have a low sense of self-worth, you will hear only the negative comments that other people make. When somebody praises you, you deny it, ignore it, or rationalize it by saying, "Oh, they're just saying that. They don't really mean it." Some people protect themselves from hearing anything positive because their basic self-concept says that those positive comments do not fit. The next time a person praises you or compliments you, try to let that compliment soak in, rather than defending yourself against hearing it. This may be hard for you to do. But it is very important to break your negative pattern of hearing. When you can hear positive comments, then you will feel better about yourself.

Step eight: *Make a specific change in your behavior*. Determine a part of your personality which you want to change. Maybe you would like to say "hello" to more people, or to be on time to work or school, or to stop putting off small jobs, like making your bed each morning. Decide to change that behavior every day this next week. Make the change easy so that you can accomplish it and feel successful. Do not set yourself up for failure by deciding to make an impossibly big change the first week.

Perhaps you will want to mark a check on the calendar to reward yourself a little each day. At the end of the week you can look back and say, "I accomplished it! I've changed something! I'm different *in this particular area* of my personality." After you have accomplished this first step, then during the following week take a second step — another small change — and begin! If you do this for several weeks in a row, you will notice that you can make significant changes in your personality, which will in turn improve your self-esteem.

Step nine is one of the most fun. *Give and get more hugs!* There has been almost a fear in our society about touching other persons to show affection, probably related to the undue emphasis upon sex and the Victorian attitudes toward sex. Many people are not aware of the difference between affectionate and sexual touching. Some are afraid that any touching will lead to sexual involvement. Many of us avoid touching and hugging altogether. Many other societies appear to have overcome this hang-up and are more comfortable with touching.

A warm and meaningful hug from a friend reinforces far more than spoken words can. A hug heals us and improves our self-concept more rapidly than any other methods. It frees us, warms us inside, improves our feelings of self-worth. "I am worthwhile enough to be hugged!" may be the warmest message we can hear. If you can overcome your fear of touching and even ask for a hug (if you are not getting enough), you will make a big step toward improving your regard for yourself — and you will enjoy the process!

Step ten suggests you *work hard at meaningful communication with another person.* Some of the most significant growth I was able to experience after my divorce was accomplished while communicating with friends. Ask for and give honest feedback about each other. Say things that you never said to anyone before. Call it as you see it! Such a dialogue provides a mirror for you to see yourself as others see you.

Step eleven has to do with therapy. You may *choose to enter into a therapy relationship* in order to enhance your self-concept. It is a safe place to talk about anything you want to. Guidance from a professional may shorten the time it takes to change your self-concept. Therapy does not have the stigma that it once did. Most therapy now is personal-growth oriented, or aimed at resolving specific life issues, such as stress. To the average person, therapy no longer means "mental illness."

If you work diligently at these exercises, you may be able to make some of the same changes that participants in the seminar are able to make. All you have to lose is your poor view of yourself! Make this part of the trail an important part of your growth. This rebuilding block will probably affect more aspects of your total life than any of the others.

Children: The Most Fragile Self-Concepts

Be aware that divorce can be very damaging to a child's self-concept also. Suddenly life has been uprooted. Children feel rejected, lonely, alienated, and perhaps guilty, questioning what they did wrong that contributed to their parents' divorce.

Children's adjustment to divorce may be complicated if they are also going through certain growth stages which are, of themselves, threatening to self-concept. As a prime example, there is some evidence that the junior high years are the most difficult years in growth and development for most children. I have listened to many adults talk about the painful difficulties of their junior high years. Puberty means dramatic changes in the body: height; weight; sexual characteristics; body hair; and voice. Suddenly, their identity — or who they *thought* they were — is also changing. They are experiencing new attitudes and feelings, such as attraction to the opposite sex. Relationships with peers have become much more important. This rapid period of change is a real strain upon a teenager's self-concept, even under the best of conditions. So youngsters who are going through these extreme changes in themselves are also faced with the stress of their parents' divorce, the children's self concepts are more likely to be affected.

The exercises in this chapter are helpful to share with your children. In fact, doing the exercises together is a good way to increase family communication. I suggest that you parents of divorced children take these eleven steps toward improving your own self-concept, and assist your children in following the same steps.

How Are You Doing?

Here is your check list for this portion of the trail. Once again, allow yourself adequate time to deal with this important area. When you are comfortable with most of these items, you are probably ready to resume the climb. Take care!

1. *I am willing to work hard to improve my self-concept.*
2. *I want to improve my self-concept even though I understand that it will change many aspects of my life.*

3. *I like being the person I am.*
4. *I feel I am an attractive person.*
5. *I like my body.*
6. *I feel attractive and sexually desirable.*
7. *I feel confident most of the time.*
8. *I know and understand myself.*
9. *I feel good being a woman or a man.*
10. *I no longer feel like a failure because my love relationship ended.*
11. *I feel capable of building deep and meaningful relationships.*
12. *I am the type of person I would like to have for a friend.*
13. *I'm attempting to improve my self-concept by using the 11 steps listed in this chapter.*
14. *I feel what I have to say is important to others.*
15. *I feel I have an identity of my own.*
16. *I have hope and faith that I can improve my self-concept.*
17. *I am confident that I can solve the problems facing me.*
18. *I am confident that I can adjust to this crisis.*
19. *I can listen to criticism without becoming angry and defensive.*

TRANSITION
"I'm Waking Up and Putting Away My Leftovers"

Early experiences are extremely influential in our lives. The attitudes and feelings you developed in childhood, and in relationships with family, friends, and lovers, are bound to carry over into new relationships. Some of these attitudes and feelings are helpful, others are not. Other common leftovers which cause problems for adults, include an unresolved need to rebel against prior constraints (such as parental rules), and power struggles over control. Recognize the valuable leftovers, so you can keep and nourish them; work at changing those which get in the way.

Chapter 12

"When I was a child, I spoke as a child, I understood as a child, I thought as a child; but when I became a man, I put away childish things."   —St. Paul (I Cor. 13:11)

We're well over halfway up the mountain now, and it's time to make a careful inspection of our packs, before we proceed to the top. Many of us may be carrying extra, unneeded weight. I am reminded of a story told to me by a friend who, on his first backpacking trip, carried a quart of water to the campsite at 11,000 feet in the Sierra Nevada Mountains. When he arrived at the top, he realized that he had been carrying an extra two pounds of water while climbing through five miles of snow!

Are you lugging an unnecessary load of leftovers from earlier days? You may have extra weight from your past marriage, or perhaps from relationships with parents, school friends, or others while you grew up. It's time now to put away those unneeded burdens! In this chapter, we'll take a look at the most common leftovers, where they come from, and how to deal with them.

After teaching the Rebuilding class for many years, I have been impressed with how few participants understood the importance and power of four key leftovers from their pasts: their *family of origin issues*, the influences of their *childhood experiences*, the confusing period of *rebellion*, and the frustration and hopelessness of the *power* the primary love relationship. And there aren't many self-help books in bookstores helping people understand these influences.

These four influences overlap and are difficult to separate from each other. I arbitrarily define the events that happened in your parental family before you were born as *family of origin* influences. The events that happened from the time you were born until you moved away from your parental home as *childhood* influences (these include events happening outside of the home such as school, church, and society), and the attempt to find an individual identity separate from the expectations of family and society as the period of *rebellion*. The *power struggle* is a combination of all the unresolved issues from all areas including the above three.

(This chapter extends the work we did in Chapter Two, and is designed to help you further understand why your relationship died. If you want to learn how to make a love relationship work, I suggest you read my follow-up book, *Loving Choices: A Growing Experience*. Also, if it is available in your community, you will find it helpful to enroll in the ten-week class I call, "Reconnecting."

Family of Origin Influences

Your *family of origin* is the family in which you grew up. Your parents, siblings, grandparents, aunts and uncles, all were important influences shaping your view of "how a family should be." Most of the ideas you gained during those years were probably healthy, some were not.

Now think about the beginning of your own love relationship. If you could imagine the bride's "significant parent" married to the groom's "significant parent," you would have an idea of what your marriage would be like in later years. (In my own case it would be my father married to her grandmother. They never met but if they had, it would have been disastrous!) There is hope: we can grow beyond our family of origin patterns of interaction. But many of you can see that it was your parents in you and your partner who were divorcing each other.

I've asked audiences from many different countries the following question. "How many of you would like to have a marriage basically like your parents' marriage? Raise your hand." Less than five per cent of the people raise their hand. If we don't want a marriage like our parents, what kind of marriage do we want?

Some of the family of origin influences are easy to see and understand. We tend to belong to the same political party as our parents, to join the same religious organization, to live in the same community. Some of us rebel, striking out on our own and choosing a completely separate path. Even in rebellion, however, the family of origin is an important element.

There are many other subtle influences. My love partner comes from a family of powerful females. I come from a family of powerful males. One of our family of origin issues was to make a compromise as to which gender was going to be the boss. (She says I won and I say she won.)

Another issue is how you handle money. My mother came from a family where the males were very irresponsible in handling money. She learned to be the saver and controller of money. She, of course, lived out her family of origin influences by marrying a man who was, like the men she grew up with, under-responsible in handling money. Many people married thinking they were escaping the family influences only to discover they had perpetuated them.

"That doesn't seem to fit," you observe. "If your father was the dominant and stronger personality, why was your mother the one who controlled the money?" The answer shows up in sociological studies of families, and may have been true in your house as well. The "woman of the house" often was more powerful than it appeared but *she exercised her power in a subtle and indirect manner.* Dad appeared to be in charge, but Mom held the purse strings.

It is confusing, when you thought you were marrying the father or mother you didn't have, to end up *being* a father or mother. Do you recall the explanation in our discussion of adaptive behavior patterns in Chapter Two? Most of us learned to adapt when we didn't get all of our needs met in the childhood formative years. Often the adaptive behavior was to become a "father" or "mother," which resulted in giving to others what we were hoping to get.

Skeptical about family of origin influences? Here's an exercise you'll find helpful: make a list of how your most significant parent(s) dealt with the various human emotions: anger, guilt, rejection, loneliness, fear, intimacy. Then make a similar list for yourself. When you compare the lists, you'll have a better idea of just how independent you are from the influence of your significant parent. Until we question and grow beyond the influence of our families of origin, we tend to deal with emotions in much the same way as our most significant parents.

Incidentally, when people who've made such a list are asked to identify their "most significant parent." those who are in the process of divorce quite frequently list an adult other than mother and father. When one parent was not there physically or emotionally, many of us found another "pseudo-parent" to compensate for the loss.

Those of us who didn't receive enough good parenting tend to make our partners responsible for making it up to us. There is a part in each one of us that wants our love partner to provide the parenting we didn't receive from our mothers and fathers. For some this part is large, for others it is small. When this happens in a love relationship, it often contributes to the demise of the relationship. Few love partners are happy to change diapers and nurse and make up for the parenting we didn't receive when we were little.

Family of origin issues, of course, are extremely complex and pervasive in our lives. A full discussion is beyond the scope of this book. Such issues as birth order, scapegoating, boundaries, family triangles, rituals and traditions, secrets, substance abuse, and many others are powerful influences on who we are, and how we relate to our love partners. For now, let's agree that we all need to wake up to the important effects of these family of origin leftovers, and to learn how to deal with them in our future relationships.

Healing the Influences of the Family of Origin

Linda offers one typical example of an unresolved family of origin issue. When she began to realize she married Noah because he was like the parent she had not finished making peace with, it was the beginning of the end of the relationship. This concept can be expressed in one of two ways. Linda might have married someone like her disliked parent because that relationship was comfortable and familiar, even though it was stressful and painful. Or perhaps she did *not* marry someone *like* the parent, but when she began the process of healing that parental relationship, she put Noah on the stage so she could work through the unfinished business. She told him, "you're always telling me what to do, just like my father did." It may not be true but her old anger at father for being so domineering makes it *seem* as if Noah is bossy also.

When one or both partners begins waking up and realizes the marriage is much like their parents' marriages, they have a problem. Either they have to accept their parents' marriages (instead of disdaining them), or they have to change their own marriage into what they want it to be. Without one or the other they'll probably feel their marriage is a failure. (Actually the *marriage* didn't fail; the process of healing family of origin influences was not successful.)

Childhood Influences

In the first years of life, we adopt many beliefs about ourselves, about the world, and about relationships. We learn how we feel about ourselves and our self-worth. We learn whether the world is safe, and if we can trust the people around us. We learn to feel loved and, when we don't feel loved enough, we learn to adapt. We may develop fears of rejection and abandonment. We learn if we are "OK" or "not OK."

Have you ever tried to compliment a not-OK person, one with low self-esteem? It usually goes like this: "I like your hair." "*Oh, I just washed it and can't do a thing with it.*" "Such a pretty dress you have on tonight." "*What, this old thing? I found it at the Goodwill store.*" Complimenting such a person causes them discomfort because their inner-child does not agree! They've adopted, at an early age, a belief that they are "not OK."

Any part of your growth and development that you didn't complete during your formative years, you are at some level attempting to grow through in your adult relationships. People who learned low self-worth at an early age want to improve their feelings of self-worth in their marriages. But they prevent learning what they want to learn because they don't believe the partner's compliments. "You tell me you like my hair, but you are just saying that to make me feel good."

It takes more than a few compliments to change a person's inner-child beliefs. If low self-esteem is the central belief of your inner child, I hope you paid special attention to Chapter Ten. You may want to go back to that point in the trail and read it again. (And I urge you to carry out the homework assignments.)

Another example of a lasting childhood influence is the emotional bonding that ideally takes place in the first year of a person's life. Parents who are comfortable being intimate and who are able continually to hold their babies closely and look them in the eyes, help their children learn to be intimate. Those who didn't learn early to bond emotionally often are attempting to finish the process with adult love partners. But they may not even be aware of what emotional bonding is and may actually emotionally distance partners who attempt to become intimate. They want intimacy but "check out" — one way or another — when they begin to experience it.

Healing the Influences of Childhood.

There are many examples of attempts to heal negative childhood influences. A man who has remained childlike and under-responsible may resent his partner's parental behavior; he finds another relationship or starts having an affair. But when you look at it closely, he has found another mother figure to serve his need for the mothering he didn't receive as a child. The third-party relationship may not be the problem. The inability to heal the unmet needs in the inner-child is where the person needs to heal.

If you'd like to learn more about how family of origin issues and early childhood experiences influence the adults we become, I strongly recommend Virginia Satir's classic book, *Peoplemaking* (see the Bibliography).

Rebellion: The Rocky Road to Adulthood

One of the most common leftovers we carry from our earlier experiences is the unresolved need to establish ourselves as independent persons by rebelling against our parents and their rules for us. If you or your partner carried that particular burden into your love relationship, it may have seriously jeopardized your chances of success.

There is a period of rebellion in each teenager's growth when the not-quite-adult is seeking an individual identity. Although it is a necessary part of young adult development, it causes a tremendous strain in the family relationship. Let's take a look at these key developmental stages we all must grow through on our journey toward independent adulthood. I call them the *shell* stage, the *rebel stage (external and internal)*, and the *love* stage.

The Shell stage occurs when we are young, conforming and trying to please our parents. During these years, children have the same moral and political values, belong to the same church, and more or less behave in ways expected of them by their parents. The shell stage child is basically a reflection of the parents, similar to the egg that is laid by a chicken, with no identity of his/her own. Vocabulary of people in the shell stage is full of inhibitions: "What will people think? I must be careful to do what I'm supposed to do. I should follow the rules and regulations of society. I must conform to what society expects from me."

In the teen years, or sometimes later, a person begins a period of rebellion, breaking out of the shell. This two-stage process includes changed behavior, doing what one "should not" do, pushing against the limits, and trying to find out how far one can go. It is very experimental at this stage, and the person is trying out different kinds of behavior. The little chicken inside is growing, beginning a life of its own, and starting to pick its way out of the shell. Vocabulary of the rebel stage is: "I've got to do it on my own. I don't need your help. If it weren't for you, I would be able to be the person I want to be. Please leave me alone!" The rebellion occurs in two stages: *external rebellion* and *internal rebellion*.

Rebel stage — external: The rebellion identity crisis usually begins when the person starts being overwhelmed with feelings of internal pressure and stress — the point where the burden of carrying around the "shoulds" from family of origin, childhood, and society become too great. Having learned such behavior as over-responsibility, perfection, people pleasing, or avoiding feelings, the person is like Atlas who carried the world on his shoulders: tired of the whole situation. The rebellious partner wants to run away and may begin to act like a rebellious teenager, searching for an identity separate from the identity given by parents and society.

The behavior of people in rebellion is predictable. (Isn't it interesting that non-conforming rebellion is so predictable and conforming?) The following behaviors are typical of external rebellion.

1) These people feel unhappy, stressed, smothered, and caged in. They believe their partners are responsible for their unhappiness and they project by saying things like, "As soon as you change, I will be happy." They project their unhappiness upon others and especially their love partner.

2) They like doing all the things they didn't feel comfortable doing before. They start having fun and don't understand why people don't appreciate the things they are doing because it feels so good to be doing it. Their partners say, "This isn't the same person that I married."

3) They like being under-responsible after feeling so over-responsible for all of their lives. They take a less responsible job or quit work if possible. One partner of a person in rebellion said, "I have four kids and I'm married to the oldest one."

4) They find someone they can talk to. They tell their partners, "I could never talk to you. But I found this person who understands me and really listens to me." Such people are usually younger and potential love partners. It looks like an affair but persons in rebellion will usually deny having an affair. Often everyone believes they have a sexual relationship but quite often it is platonic.

5) The vocabulary of external rebellion often goes like this:
"I care for you but I don't love you. I thought I knew what love was but now I don't know. I'm not sure I ever did love you."

"*I need to be out of this relationship so I can find myself. I need emotional space away from you. I need to find my own world and I don't want to continue to be sucked into your world. I want to be me.*"

"*You remind me of my parent and I don't want to be around anyone who is parental. I can smell a parent a mile away.*"

If all of this behavior is happening in a love-relationship, is it any wonder that the relationship ends? The partner usually buys into each one of the rebellious behaviors above, takes it personally, and gets bent out of shape emotionally and psychologically. Instead what they need to do is sit back and watch the show and become aware of how much growth and change can be taking place in their rebel partners. They need to realize it is an internal process going on with a person in rebellion and has very little to do with themselves. The rebels are trying to get rid of people and relationships from the past, but often dump their love partners in the process.

Rebel stage — internal: When people in the process of rebelling gain enough courage and insight to look at themselves, they may be able to evolve into internal rebellion. This is when they realize the battle is within themselves and is basically a battle between their "should" part and their "want" part. They realize they are trying to separate from the expectations of their family of origin and society, and the battle is within themselves rather than against their love partners and other parental figures.

Love stage: Eventually rebels begin to gain individual identity. This often leads to being able to make choices about life based upon love instead of being based on doing the "shoulds." They feel more self-love and love for others — especially their parents.

The vocabulary of the love stage are words of acceptance and understanding. "My parents did the best they could. They made mistakes and many times I was angry and upset with them, but they've tried and they've done the best they could. I understand and accept them for who they are." I call this adult period the love stage because the person has an independent identity, and is capable of loving another person as an adult rather than because of childish expectations.

In the shell stage, one does what one *should do;* in the rebel stage, what one *should not do;* and in the love stage, what one *wants to do.* Many times behavior in the love stage will be similar to behavior in the shell stage, but the motivation behind it is entirely different. Instead of trying to please somebody else, the person is trying to please her- or himself.

The partner needs to be involved. The partner of someone in rebellion often decides to wait until the rebel comes "back to sanity" again, believing that the relationship will then work. The partner considers the rebel to be the "patient," and doesn't accept any responsibility for finding a solution to the difficulty.

On the other hand, partners of rebels often become emotionally drained and bent out of shape. They have bought into the behavior of their rebellious partners, assigning them all the blame. They don't recognize that the love partnership is a system, and that they share responsibility for its problems. People who adopt this attitude toward the love relationship usually don't have the courage and emotional strength to do the personal work they need to do.

Rebellion is not an accident. The partner of a person in rebellion is usually parental. The partner has, at some level — maybe unconsciously — found a partner who needs parenting. "I know what's best for my partner, if he would only listen!" Their need for control makes it difficult for these folks to accept the rebel when he or she seems "out of control."

Instead of waiting for the storm to blow over, the partner of a person in rebellion needs to take the opportunity to look inward, and to experience as much personal growth as possible.

Shell, Rebel, Love: A Summary

I've prepared a chart summary of the progression through these three stages, Figure 1 on page 173. The chart shows some typical characteristics of the stages: vocabulary, behavior, and growth steps one may find helpful. Please recognize that these are highly individual. Although some patterns exist, each individual will be unique!

Figure 10-1. "BECOMING AN ADULT" IN THREE NOT-SO-EASY STAGES

	SHELL	REBEL	LOVE
VOCABULARY	"What should I do?" "I'll do whatever you want." "Take care of me." "You're everything to me." "I only want you to be happy."	"If it weren't for you..." "I don't need your help!" "Leave me alone!" "I'll do it anyway." "If it feels good, do it!"	"I've considered the alternatives." "I'll take responsibility for my choice." "It may not work, but I want to try." "You and I can both enjoy ourselves."
BEHAVIOR	Compliant, obedient. Caregiving [obliged]. Consistent, predictable. Careful, non-risking. Obligations, not choices.	Self-centered, selfish. Irresponsible, blames others. Erratic, unpredictable, careless. Childish, "plays" with young folk. Sports cars, flashy clothes, sex.	Self-enhancing, respects others. Responsible, flexible, open. Willing to risk, learns from mistakes. Makes choices based on facts.
GROWTH STEPS — self	Begin to trust self. Begin to take risks. Begin to communicate openly. Begin to accept responsibility. Begin to try new behavior.	Try positive growth activities: classes, recreation, exercise, friendships, hobbies, community. Enter therapy [with spouse?]. Talk to spouse, friend, therapist. Maintain moral, ethical balance.	Work at self-awareness. Work at self-acceptance. Work at open, honest communication. Develop close, non-romantic friends. Express anger assertively. Maintain balance of independence and interdependence in close relationships.
GROWTH STEPS — partner	Encourage partner's growth. Lessen dependence on partner. Cooperate in therapy if needed. Prepare for turbulence when "rebellion" starts!	Maintain stability, patience. Allow partner to grow up. Be available to talk with partner. Encourage joint therapy. Recognize rebellion is against shell, not you!	

Members of my divorce classes over the years have provided many examples of the shell/rebel/love phenomenon.

Eloise came to class very angry one night because her ex, Larry, was going through the rebel stage and causing her a lot of unhappiness. Larry had been a school principal when he was in the shell stage; but because he was looking for less administrative responsibility, he returned to full-time teaching. He developed a relationship with a woman involving "a lot of communication," helping him to find out "who he was. " Larry was, of course, very excited about this new relationship. After his young son came to visit, Larry sent him home with a suitcase full of clothes and a note explaining to Eloise how great his new relationship was. Needless to say, this made her extremely angry! As it happened, we were discussing the rebel stage that week in the seminar. Eloise began to understand what was happening with Larry and his attempt to grow up and leave some of the old leftovers. She was able to let go of some of her anger as she gained an understanding of what was happening.

Gretchen became very excited as I explained this theory in class. Her husband had been a college professor and had proceeded to run off with one of his students while he was in the rebel stage. The whole thing seemed insane to her, until she heard the shell/rebel/love theory of growth and development. When she recognized that Charles was trying to get free from past expectations and become a person of his own identity, Gretchen was able to see that there was some sanity in what had appeared to be insanity.

Bill told the group that three years ago his marriage suffered a crisis while his wife was going through the rebel stage. When he and Charlotte went for marriage counseling, the therapist put a damper on the rebel stage and pushed Charlotte to "behave as she should" — in effect telling her to remain in the shell stage. Bill said he felt this was a mistake at the time. The marriage lasted another three years until suddenly Charlotte's growth pressures and need to rebel surfaced again, and she became "completely irresponsible," leaving the marriage and the home without even taking any clothes! Bill did not hear from Charlotte for three weeks. Looking back on those painful events, Bill observed that maybe people need to be concerned about what stage of growth and development their *therapists* are in!

Many people ask, if so many marriages end when one person is going through the rebel stage, is there any way to have the relationship *last* when a person is going through the rebel stage? The rebel who can focus inward and realize the internal interaction going on between him- or herself and the parental figures of the past can deal directly with the *shoulds*, the *oughts*, and the expectations. To talk about one's rebellion rather than acting it out will be much less destructive to those near and dear at the present!

I believe it is possible for a person to find the emotional space *within* a marriage to rebel, perhaps by becoming involved in therapy, college classes, community service, recreational or sports programs, or other creative activities. The rebel needs opportunities to experiment with behavior, to try new styles of relating, and to interact with people other than the spouse. If the couple can understand directly what is happening — that the rebel is working on an internal conflict which has little to do with the spouse — it can free the work of growth and development to be done within the person, rather than strain the love-relationship.

Healing the Relationship with Rebellion Present

It is necessary for both partners to participate actively in the process if the relationship is to have any chance of healing. Rebelling love partners need to accept that their process of rebellion is an internal one and not the responsibility of other people. Their partners need to work on healing their own "inner-child," because their parenting and controlling behavior patterns result from unmet needs.

"That's all nice theory, " you may be saying, "but what does it have to do with *rebuilding?*" Well, as it happens, many marriages are built on a foundation of immaturity, with one partner stuck in the shell stage, spending his or her whole life trying to please and do what others want. Eventually, the shell partner gets fed up with this role. The pressures of inevitable personal growth become so great that the person's behavior changes, sometimes radically, like a volcanic eruption. This major shift by the formerly compliant partner puts a tremendous strain on the relationship. The shell stage partner has broken out of the shell, into the rebel stage, by rebelling against the love-partner.

The Stormy Seas of the Power Struggle

Many couples find themselves arguing over the correct way to squeeze the toothpaste tube and which way to unroll the toilet paper. And the issues they argue over never become resolved even if they think they are. Each person feels he or she has no power or control in the relationship. Both feel hopeless and helpless, and tired of fighting. The war may be a hot war with a lot of shouting, anger, and verbal abuse. Or it may be a cold war with the silent treatment, walking out, pouting, and other such passive ways of attempting to gain control and power.

The two people involved have stopped talking about or sharing feelings. They talk using "you" messages at each other. They have given up on finding any intimacy other than the pseudo intimacy they feel while fighting. Neither wants to lose, so both use any method they can to win the war.

The power struggle is like a pot of stew boiling over on the stove. The ingredients in the stew are all of the unresolved issues within each partner that are projected out into the relationship. The heat under the stew is a belief that someone else is responsible for my happiness or unhappiness. They married with the belief that they would live happily ever after. It worked fine as long as the honeymoon lasted and they were happy. But when the honeymoon was over and they sometimes were less than happy, the person who was responsible for their happiness is now responsible for their unhappiness. They gave away their power when they began to believe someone else was responsible for their happiness or unhappiness.

Calming the Rough Seas of the Power Struggle

The power struggle changes into growing-pains when each person takes ownership for the unresolved problems within them. It may be concerned with the three stumbling blocks listed above, but the unresolved issues can come from anywhere in their lives or their personality. It is truly an internal power struggle projected out upon the relationship. The problems each person is unable to face and overcome become projected out into the relationship and the pot keeps boiling over.

The power-struggle is diminished when:
- each person learns to talk about feelings,
- each person starts using "I" messages instead of "you" messages,
- each person takes ownership for their unresolved problems,
- each person looks at the other person as their relationship teacher trying to help them learn more about themselves instead of projecting the hurt and blame upon the other person.

Leaving Leftovers Behind

As with any life transition, this stage of the climb is very uneven and quite difficult. Waking up and understanding why your past relationship died is usually not an easy process. It may even be quite painful: it is much easier to see the splinter in your eye than it is to see the log in mine.

When I was a juvenile probation officer, I typically referred a family a week for family counseling. When each person was going to counseling to discover what they could learn and change about *themselves*, the counseling was usually helpful and successful. But when each person in the family was going for counseling because *the other person* needed to change, family counseling was usually unsuccessful.

Next time you see a person on the trail acting like a teenager, rebelling and always angry at parental, authoritative figures, you can be understanding. You know that rebel is trying to grow up emotionally, to gain an independent identity, and to become free from past expectations and controls. Even though you may want to become parental and tell the rebel how to behave, maybe you need to back off, remain adult yourself, and say, "I think that's probably the best thing for where he or she is right now." Indeed, perhaps you are still in the shell stage yourself, needing to start some rebellion of your own to improve your sense of self-worth and to find a better identity!

Do you notice that you are really making progress in the climb up the mountain? The fact that you are able to face and deal with leftovers is an indication that you are getting a much broader perspective of life and yourself. You probably could not have done much about carrying out the leftovers when you were at the bottom of the mountain trying to survive emotionally.

Children and Transition

As with their parents, most children will have some difficulty with their parents' leftovers: family of origin issues, childhood experiences, rebellion, and power struggles. A child's view of the actions of others is based on only a few years of life experience, and a limited repertoire of behaviors.

A very strong influence on children during this process is the feeling of internal pain. The growing child will interact with other significant adults as he or she learned to do with the parents, until some healing learning takes place. (Children are, after all, going through their own family of origin and childhood experiences.) If a new stepparent comes into the picture, for example, the child will tend to have the same problems with that stepparent as he/she had with his/her natural parent. This will change only when the child learns — perhaps with loving support from understanding adults — how to deal effectively with those old emotions (e.g., without destructive adaptive behaviors), and how to develop new ways of relating to adults.

Homework to Ease Your Transition

• Describe what a relationship between your partner's most significant parent and your most significant parent would be like. Would your past relationship be anything like that imaginary relationship?

• How did your family of origin influences affect the ending of your love relationship?

• Make a list of the ways your family of origin reacted to anger, love, fear, guilt, rejection, intimacy, and conflict. Make a list of the way you react to these same emotions.

• Do you perceive your former love-partner to be like one of your parents? Did your marriage begin to resemble your parent's marriage? Are you wanting a marriage that is different from your parent's marriage? How would you go about creating such a marriage?

• Do you believe you emotionally bonded with your parents in your childhood? Are you comfortable being intimate with another? Did you learn good feelings of self-worth in your childhood? Did you have a good relationship with both of your parents? Is your relationship with your love-partner anything like the relationship with one or both of your parents?

• This chapter identified the stages of rebellion as 1) Shell stage, 2) Rebel stage (External and Internal), and 3) Love stage. In which of these stages are your parents? Your former love partner? You?

• Did the process of rebellion have anything to do with your love relationship ending?

• If the person in rebellion is able to find an individual identity, and the partner is able to let go of being parental and controlling, there is a chance for the two people to carve out a new relationship. Do you think there is any possibility of the two of you at some future point being able to carve out a new relationship?

• Were you and your partner in a power-struggle when you ended the relationship? Did you believe that when you became married, you would live happily ever after? Do you believe someone else is responsible for your happiness and/or unhappiness? Have you identified any of the unresolved issues within you that contributed to you and your partner having a power-struggle? Example: You as a woman started standing up to your husband like you wished you had stood up to your father? You as a male started being responsible for yourself instead of letting your wife smother-mother do everything for you.

• What did you learn in this chapter that you need to work on before you can create a healthy relationship in the future?

How Are You Doing?

After you make sure you are ready by responding to the check list below, go on to the next part of the journey. After a discussion of the importance of open and honest communication, we will take a look at that elusive but ever-present phenomenon, love.

1. *I am aware of the leftovers I am carrying from past relationships.*
2. *I am working on my leftovers rather than blaming others for them.*
3. *I am building relationships that will help me eliminate my leftovers.*
4. *I understand that I will have to change attitudes and awareness within me in order to rid myself of leftovers.*
5. *I am avoiding becoming emotionally involved with stray cats.*
6. *I have identified whether I am in the shell, rebel, or love stage in my growth and development.*
7. *I have thought about my spouse's growth and development in terms of the shell, rebel, and love stages.*
8. *I have thought about my parents' development in terms of the shell, rebel, and love stages.*
9. *I have identified positive ways of rebelling in contrast to more negative, destructive forms of rebelling.*
10. *I can understand and accept those elements of my spouse's behavior which were related to the rebel stage.*
11. *I realize the shell, rebel, and love stages are something that may happen several times in my life.*
12. *I am attempting to do the self-care needed to remain strong and stable.*
13. *I will attempt to get rid of as many leftovers as possible before I get into another long-term, committed love relationship.*

OPENNESS
"I've Been Hiding Behind a Mask"

A mask is a false face — a feeling projected to others that's different from what you're really feeling. Some masks are appropriate; others are inappropriate. Masks may protect you from emotional pain you feel or fear, but wearing masks takes a great deal of emotional energy. Masks distance you emotionally from others, keeping you from building intimate relationships. When you remove your masks appropriately, you find intimacy rather than emotional pain.

Chapter 13

After my divorce, looking for ways to meet new people, I took a small part in a little theater production. One night at rehearsal I suddenly realized that's what I'd been doing in my marriage — reciting lines. I wasn't myself, I was a character in a romantic comedy-tragedy.

— Scott

At this point in our climb most of us have learned a lot about ourselves and our former love relationships. You probably have a good idea of what happened, and I hope you're starting to think about how you'll avoid similar mistakes in the future.

One key element in successful love relationships is *openness*. Were you really honest with your partner? Are you really even honest with yourself? Or do you often hide behind a mask of "everything is okay"?

Masks and Openness

All of us wear masks at times. Sometimes you just don't want others to know what you're feeling, and a "mask" is a convenient way to hide what's going on inside—a protective shield. So the mask projects a different attitude or feeling on the surface, protecting you from the pain underneath. The pain may be fear of rejection, fear of somebody not liking you, fear of feeling inadequate, or maybe just a feeling that nobody really cares.

Young children don't wear masks as adults do — that's one of the reasons it's enjoyable and delightful to be with younger children. We develop our masks as we mature and become "socialized." It's not a conscious effort to deceive, the idea is simply that the masks will help us to interact with people more effectively.

However, some masks are not productive in helping us to interact with others. Instead, they keep us at a safe emotional distance from the other person. Openness, after all, can be pretty scary at times.

What Color Is Your Mask?

What are some examples of the masks I'm talking about?

There are some people who, as you become emotionally close to them, immediately start making jokes and cracking humor — I call this the *humor mask.*

A similar mask is the *"Barbie Doll* ™ *face" mask.* Whenever you start getting real with such a person and start talking about something important, you immediately see the happy, smiling, unchanging face that looks like a Barbie Doll ™.

Many people going through divorce put on the mask of *"I'm so strong."* They project an image that they are going to be in control at all times and never show any weakness. But underneath lies the real turmoil of confusion and helplessness.

Like nearly all divorced people, Connie had been close to the fire of emotional intimacy. When she was married to Chris, he made her feel really warm. Then she was burned by the fire, and she grew afraid to become emotionally close to warmth from another person again. Now she distances other people emotionally in all kinds of sophisticated ways. Her *"don't mess with me"* angry mask has a reputation for miles around; it's very effective in keeping others at arm's length.

Who's Masking What from Whom?

Some masks are not very productive. In wearing them, we fight against the very things we long for: closeness, intimacy, a feeling of being safe with another person. But because we've been hurt, we're also afraid of that same intimacy and closeness.

Marian projected a mask and thought she was fooling people, that they didn't know what she was really feeling. She learned, however, that not only did others see through the mask, they saw her more clearly than she saw herself. That's one of the strange things about masks: we often fool ourselves more than we fool other people. The mask Marian thought nobody could see through allowed others to know — better than she knew herself — the pain she was feeling underneath.

A mask may keep you from getting to know yourself, rather than keeping somebody else from getting to know you. You are actually denying your own hurt from yourself. It's kind of like the ostrich: with his head in the sand he thinks no one can see him, just because he can't see them.

Masks Can Be a Burden!

Sometimes we invest a great deal of emotional energy in wearing our masks.

You're carrying around a great big burden all the time by trying to act the way you think you "should" act, rather than just being yourself. Emotional energy that is put into carrying a mask is sometimes almost overwhelming. You spend more energy carrying the mask than you do in learning about yourself, achieving personal growth or doing anything more productive.

Think about how lonely it is behind a really big, thick mask. A person is more or less living in his or her own world, and there is no one else who really knows and understands this lonely person down inside the big mask. And often the more lonely you feel the more mask you create around that loneliness. There seems to be a direct connection between the amount of loneliness you feel and the thickness of the mask you are wearing.

Anybody who has been carrying around a really heavy mask and then takes it off, either in counseling or in sharing and talking with a friend, discovers a great feeling of freedom after unloading the burden. It leaves a lot more energy to do other things in life.

Jeff started wearing a mask as a child. He learned early that he had to exhibit certain "acceptable" behavior in order to get the love or the strokes or the attention that he needed. He learned to take care of other people when he really wanted to be taken care of himself. He learned to excel in school, even though he really didn't care whether he got A's or not. He learned to keep all his feelings inside rather than open up and share himself with others. Jeff grew up with the idea that love was not related to being himself. It came to him when he wore his "good boy" mask. He sure learned well not to value openness.

It appears to me that we develop most masks because we have not felt loved unconditionally just for being ourselves.

"Let's Do Lunch: My Mask Will Call Your Mask"

Imagine somebody trying to kiss you when you have a mask on. That's a good image for how hard it is to get close to another person when either of you is wearing a mask. It gives an idea of what a mask does for the communication between you and another person. Think of all the indirect and devious messages that are sent because of our masks! So much for openness!

There are appropriate masks and inappropriate masks, of course. An appropriate mask is one that you wear at work while dealing with other people. You project the feeling of efficiency, of competence, of "I'm here to serve you" — an evenness and a calmness that makes your work with other people more effective. But when you get off work and go home to be with a friend or a loved one, the same mask becomes inappropriate. It emotionally distances you from your partner, prevents straight communication, kills openness, and doesn't allow either of you to be yourselves. That could be appropriate when you need time just for yourself, but it's tough on intimacy!

A Matter of Choice

It appears to me that a mask that you *choose* to wear is probably an appropriate mask, but the mask that chooses you is probably inappropriate. It chooses you because you are not free to expose the feelings that are underneath. And in that sense the mask controls you. Many times you are not aware that you're wearing a mask that controls you.

Are You Ready To Take Off Your Mask?

How does one decide to take off a mask?

Some time along in the divorce process it becomes appropriate to take down some of the masks you've been wearing — to try openness instead. Is that time now?

What would happen if you took your mask off? Try it with some safe friends. Take off a mask and see how many times you find acceptance from those friends, rather than the rejection you expected. See how many times you become closer to somebody rather than being hurt. See how many times you feel freer than you felt before.

Here's an example of how to take off a mask with a friend you can trust. You might say something like, "You know I've not been very honest with you at times in the past; when you come close to me, I become a joker. The 'joker mask' is a defense I use to protect me from getting hurt. When I'm afraid or feel that I'm about to get hurt, I start making jokes. When I make jokes at inappropriate times it keeps me from knowing you and you from knowing me. I want you to know about my mask. When I tell you, it destroys some of the power of the mask. I've removed the mask somewhat already, just by sharing this with you."

Some friends may hurt you when you take the mask off. Those people are not able to handle the feelings you've been covering up with the mask. But, if you had your choice, which would you choose? To continue to wear the mask and not get to know that person? Or take off the mask, be open, and risk being hurt or rejected? If you are at a point emotionally where you can think ahead to a possible love-relationship in the future, what kind of a relationship would you like to have? One that would include openness, intimacy and trust? Or one where both of you wear masks of one kind or another? You *do* have the choice!

If you are wearing a mask because of the pain underneath, then part of removing the mask must be to deal with that pain. As a counselor, I prefer to help my clients try to get in touch with the pain behind the mask and to express and verbalize it. While she was going through divorce, Sharon was trying to be the strong person, always in control. I encouraged her to talk about the pain and confusion she was feeling underneath. As she did so, hesitantly, I pointed out to her that maybe it is appropriate to be confused when one is going through a confusing situation, and that taking down the mask and dealing with that confusion is productive. It took her several sessions in therapy to fully acknowledge her pain, and to build some constructive coping strategies which allowed her to keep the mask off.

Many people who have been hurt by the ending of a love relationship tend to put on more masks than they were wearing before. Part of climbing the divorce process mountain is learning to take off some of the masks you may have put on to cover the pain of ending your love relationship.

Your Self Behind the Mask

We all have a little "S" inside of us — the "Self" — the real person down inside. We all develop our personalities — the face we show to the rest of the world — around this essence of Self. We communicate outward from that Self down inside, through the personality, to the people around us. Ideally, the communication is two-way, from one Self to another.

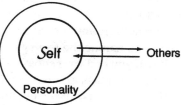

When you develop a thick shell or facade or mask to "protect" your inner Self, your communication is blocked by the mask. Instead of Self-to-other-to-Self, your messages go from mask-to-other-to-mask.

In this situation, your Self is not really involved in the communication. If you keep the mask up, your inner Self becomes starved and never sees the sunshine and never finds anything that will help it grow. Your inner Self becomes smaller — or at least less influential — until it is such a small S that you may not even be able to find your own identity. Meanwhile the shell around you grows thicker and harder all the time.

There's another variation on this theme: you may mask certain areas of your personality but not others. In the example below, there are thick spots in parts of your personality that prevent communication through them, but there are other parts of your personality through which you do communicate to other people.

As a probation officer I found some juveniles very easy to work with, while others felt very defensive around me. After a while I began to see a pattern: the juvenile who was easy to work with usually had a good relationship with his father. He was able to communicate well with me because as a probation officer I was somewhat of a father figure. A young man who felt uncomfortable relating to me probably also had been uncomfortable with his father. He had grown a powerful protective mask which prevented communication between his inner Self and adult males in authority. This same juvenile might find it easier to work with a female probation officer, particularly if he had learned to relate well with his mother.

Who Are You?

Do you know yourself? Are you pretty sure of your own identity? Many people use masks because they lack a sense of identity. They can't be open because they don't know who they are or what they're really feeling. They start wearing masks, and the masks begin to get thicker and thicker and the Self inside gets even harder to identify. Pretty soon these people have lost touch with their identities completely. They have to wear a mask because there is no way for the scared little Self down inside to communicate.

If you're a person who has never developed a clear sense of your identity, you'll find it difficult to take off the mask until you start to develop this identity. How does one do this? Start by taking off a portion of the mask whenever possible with somebody you can trust, and entering into an open, meaningful communication with that other person. Allow your little Self to reach the warmth, sunlight, support and encouragement that it needs in order to grow.

If you want to take down the masks, then you need to get as many things into the open area as possible. When you share things about yourself that you have not shared with anybody before, you are actually taking down a mask. And when you ask for feedback from other people, you often find out things about yourself that you did not know before, and this takes down some of the mask that you have used to keep you from knowing yourself.

To get rid of some of the inappropriate and unproductive masks that you are carrying around, begin to open yourself as much as possible to other people. Develop some relationships with other people that have a great deal of open, *meaningful* communication (not just talking about yourself endlessly!). These connections with others will help you to take off the masks, to allow your inner Self to grow, and to place all your relationships on a foundation of honesty and openness — with yourself and with those you care about.

I've found many people whose little boy or girl inside is extremely frightened and fearful of coming out. If you're experiencing that kind of fear, I think you'll find it helpful to enter into a professional counseling relationship. Counseling is a safe place to let your scared little boy or girl out — to get open with yourself.

Homework to Help You Move from Masks to Openness

• Sit down and write a list of all of the masks that you use. Look at these masks that you have listed and identify the few that are appropriate and those that are inappropriate. Identify the masks that you would like to take off because they are inappropriate.

• Become introspective and try to get in touch with your feelings, and find the feelings of pain that are underneath the masks that you wear. Why is it important that you wear inappropriate masks that keep you from feeling and becoming intimate with others? The feelings are probably fear of some sort. Look at those fears and see if they are rational or perhaps fears you have developed from interacting with other people in an unproductive way.

• Find a friend or a group of friends with whom you feel safe and whom you can trust. Explain this exercise to them and explain that you are going to try to share some of your masks with them, with the understanding that when you share a mask it will not have the same power over you as it has had in the past. Share with these friends some of the fearful feelings you have found that have kept you from being open and honest and intimate with others. Ask the other people to do the same thing with you. Open, meaningful communication between you and your friends will help you get free from the masks you've been carrying around, and will help you recover some of the emotional energy they've required.

The Masks of Children

How open and honest are you with your children? Have you shared the important things happening in your relationship that directly affect them? How did you tell your children when you were ready to separate? How consistent have you been with them? Can they depend upon you to do what you say you will? In short, can they trust you?

Some things the children have said in our Children of Divorce Workshop I will never forget. One thirteen-year-old girl, when asked what kind of an animal she felt like, said, "That's easy. When I am with dad, I am one person. When I am with mother, I'm another person. I try to please both of them so they won't be so upset. I'm a chameleon."

It is so hard for us to really listen to our children when we are caught up in our own pain. We can easily be hurt and upset by their comments. No wonder they walk around on thin ice, being careful what they say and do. They often feel so responsible for us, so sympathetic with us, so afraid they will upset us even more.

Children should be encouraged to speak their truth and their thoughts and feelings, even when it's hard for us to hear. If you can't listen without judgment or criticism or getting upset, help them to find another person — someone more detached and more objective — whom they can talk to.

Their whole world has been shattered. They wonder what will happen next. When they have open and honest communication with their parents — or at least with one understanding adult — they begin to feel a part of the solution, instead of being to blame.

How Are You Doing?

Before you go on to the next portion of the climb, answer the following self-evaluation review for yourself:

1. *I'm beginning to recognize the masks I've been wearing.*
2. *I'd like to be more open with the people I care about.*
3. *I'm willing to face the fears behind my masks, even though it's scary.*
4. *I've risked sharing with a trusted friend a fear I've been hiding.*

5. *I've asked a trusted friend for some honest feedback about myself.*
6. *I'm beginning to understand the value of openness in relationships.*
7. *Openness is becoming more natural for me.*
8. *I can choose to wear an appropriate mask when it's important.*
9. *My masks don't control me any more.*

LOVE
"Could Somebody Really Care for Me?"

Many people need to relearn how to love, in order to love more maturely. Your capacity to love others is closely related to your capacity to love yourself. And learning to love yourself is not selfish and conceited. In fact, it is the most mentally healthy thing you can do. There are a number of specific steps you can take to increase your self-love.

Chapter 14

Love is like bouquet of roses: you don't remember the work to get them; you only remember the love in her eyes when she received them.
Love is like sitting with my back to the fireplace. I can feel the warmth without ever seeing the fire.
Love is the greatest gift you can receive. But you have to give it to yourself.
—Ed

As we make our way up the mountain, we observe graffiti on the rocks, written by poets commenting about love. Most of what we learn about love is from the poets. Who had any homework in school concerning the nature of love? Would you take time right now to do some "homework?" In the space below write your definition of what love is. (I am talking about love between two people in a romantic relationship, not about parental love, spiritual love, or love for humankind.)

LOVE IS:

Okay, when you are finished, turn the page and let's continue up the trail.

195

I have asked hundreds of people to do this exercise in the divorce adjustment seminars. It is a very difficult assignment for divorced people — or for anyone, for that matter. A typical divorced person says, "I thought I knew what love is, but I guess I don't." Many people feel inadequate about the definition of love. Love is like a diamond. You can view it from many different directions, and there is no right or wrong way of defining it. There is only the way you feel about love.

In our society many people have stereotyped love to be something you do for somebody or to somebody. Very few people have learned that love is something that should be centered within you, and that the basis for loving others is the love you have for yourself. Most of us recall the instruction in the Bible to "Love thy neighbor as thyself." But what if you don't love yourself?

Here is a somewhat cynical definition upon which many relationships are based: "Love is the warm feeling that you get toward somebody who meets your neurotic needs." This is a definition of neediness rather than love. Because we are not whole and complete people, but have emotional deficiencies, we try to fill those emotional deficiencies by "loving" another person. What we lack in ourselves we hope to find in the other person. In other words, many of us are *half-people* trying to love someone in order to become whole. Love coming from a whole person is more mature, and more likely to be lasting.

"Falling in Love with Love"

Perhaps you have heard the expression "warm fuzzies with a fish hook in them." A *warm fuzzy* is a nice gesture that you give somebody — such as saying, "I love you." Unfortunately, many of us are still struggling to fulfill *ourselves*. If my own life bucket is empty when I say, "I love you," to another person, it probably means, "Please love me." The other person finds the warm fuzzy, swallows it, and is hooked. Saying "I love you" from an empty bucket tends to be manipulative, while love from a full bucket allows others to be themselves and to be free.

Another problem with love in our society is that falling in love is the most acceptable reason for getting married. However, *falling in love* may have more to do with loneliness than with warmth toward the other person. Falling in love to overcome loneliness is not actually love. It is rather a feeling of warmth which comes from breaking down the barriers that have kept us from being intimate with other people.

Sometimes one does not love the other person, but loves instead the idealized image of that person. When the difference is realized, one becomes disillusioned, falls out of love, and the relationship is dissolved. If a couple can grow past the stage of loving their idealized images of each other, there is a possibility that they will be able to love in a more mature manner. For some, this growth will occur in the love relationship, and their love for each other will mature. For others, maturity comes only after dissolution of an immature relationship.

I see many people loving with an immature love: Love equals doing something to somebody or for somebody; Love equals taking care of someone; Love equals achieving; Love equals always being in control; Love equals "never having to say you're sorry;" Love equals always being strong; Love equals being nice.

Shirley had believed that love equals being nice, and she was trying to improve an unhealthy love relationship. Ken asked her in class why it was not working for her to be nice. Shirley replied, "I guess I just wasn't nice enough."

Unconditional Love: "Warts and All"

Many (most?) of us, while growing up, have not received enough unconditional love — love that was given by parents or others just because we were, not because we earned it by being "good." We adopt immature forms of love toward others because we have not been loved unconditionally. That's a tough history to overcome. Nevertheless we can come to realize that mature love equals loving yourself for being what you are, and likewise loving another person for whom he or she is. When we can feel such unconditional no-matter-how-you-act love, we have learned what I call mature love. Mature love allows you fully to be yourself with the loved one.

For many people it is difficult to give up the immature forms of love. That is the way they have always received their strokes, attention, and good feelings. Yet, eventually they recognize that they had to keep striving harder in order to earn the love they were seeking. It is like settling for second best, taking whatever strokes we can, rather than going all the way to get really good strokes by learning to love ourselves.

The need to be loved unconditionally is not met very often. As a child, parents' love can be seen as unconditional. After all, most parents are able to provide the basics of food, clothing, shelter, care, and physical affection. The child's limited awareness makes this seem to be unconditional love. The child has no question that this love is infinite and omnipotent.

However, with age, maturity, and awareness, one recognizes that any human being may at any point stop loving another for any reason. Or the love may be ended by death. For adults it is difficult to emotionally accept *unconditional* love. Perhaps you can attack the problem from another direction: by learning to love yourself unconditionally. Sound like "pull yourself up by your bootstraps"? Actually it is simply an acceptance of yourself for what you are: a unique individual, with no one else like you. You can begin to feel that you are an *okay* person, and begin to feel love for yourself.

It is difficult to love yourself if you have not been loved as a child. This is where a spiritual relationship can become very important. If you can develop faith in a Supreme Being who gives the unconditional love that you have difficulty accepting within yourself, then you have experienced one of the greatest values of spiritual life. The omnipotent God loves us for what we are, not for what we do to or for somebody. The person who has developed a spiritual relationship with a Supreme Being, can in turn feel loved unconditionally. He or she will also have the potential to love others in the same way.

Many psychologists place a great deal of emphasis upon the diagnosis of "personalities." One way of looking at psychological diagnoses is that they are all trying to define different ways that people are compensating for the lack of unconditional love. If we could peel all of the psychological diagnoses down to the heart and core, we would find that the problem is basically that people have not learned to love and be loved.

We tend to teach our children the same concept of love that we learned ourselves. Thus, if you have developed an immature form of love, your children may tend to develop an immature form of love also. If you want to teach your children to love in a mature way and to make them feel loved unconditionally, you will have to learn to love yourself! Then you can develop the capacity to love your children so that they feel loved unconditionally.

I am emphasizing unconditional love so strongly because it is such a very vital quality for human growth. To know that I am valuable enough — just because I am me — to be loved regardless of how I act, is the greatest gift I can give myself and my children.

"... As You Love Yourself"

Look at the definition of love that you wrote at the beginning of this chapter. In my classes, most people include in their definition of love something that makes the love other-centered — centered in the other person rather than within themselves. Many people write that love is caring and giving and making that other person happy. Very few people include in their definition of love a mature idea of self-love.

Let's examine that. If the center of your love is in your partner and the relationship dissolves, the center is suddenly removed; as we considered earlier, this makes divorce even more painful. What might it be like if you had become a whole person and learned to love yourself? If divorce came, there would still be pain and trauma. But it would not be so devastating; you would still be a whole person.

Divorce is especially traumatic for those who have not centered their love within themselves and learned to love themselves. They end up feeling unlovable, or that they are incapable of loving another person. Many spend a great deal of time and energy trying to prove to themselves that they are lovable. They may search for another love relationship immediately, because that helps to heal the wound. They may become sexually promiscuous, developing all kinds of relationships with anybody who comes along. Many of these people have confused sex and love, feeling that if they go out and find sex, with it will come the love they have been missing and needing. I sometimes think it would be more appropriate for them to say, "I sex you," rather than, "I love you"!

As we discussed in Chapters Two and Six, it is wiser to go easy on the love relationships during this difficult time. Invest in friendships instead, until you have made good progress at learning to love yourself. More on this in Chapter Sixteen, also.

The Beatles' line, "All the lonely people — where do they all come from?" expresses well the vital needs of so many people who have never really learned to love and to be loved. Sometimes it seems easier to love others, and not allow oneself to be loved. By "wanting to love another person," you may really be hiding your own need to be loved.

I would like to share a personal experience that happened to me as I was working through the divorce process. I was taking part in a meditation exercise. We sat with our eyes closed and meditated to bring a flow of energy through the different levels of our bodies until it reached the tops of our heads. I was able to follow this meditation and feel a warm flow of energy within me, gradually rising higher in my body. When the guided fantasy had reached the level of our chests, the leader said, "Many of you at this point will be feeling that the flow of energy is leaking out the front of your chests. If you are feeling such a leak, then imagine a cover over the front of your chest so that the warm flow of energy will not leak out." She was describing exactly the way I felt! I was amazed!

After the guided fantasy was over, I asked, "How did you know how I was feeling when I was sitting there with my eyes closed, not talking?" She replied that many people have the feeling that the flow of energy is leaking out the front of their chests. She related it to be belief that love is doing something to somebody or for somebody, and that it is other-centered rather than centered within ourselves. Thus the flow of energy leaks out toward others. We emotionally drain ourselves by putting the love into others, rather than filling our own bucket of life.

I thought about this a great deal and decided that my goal was to learn to love myself in a more adequate manner. I decided that I would like to have my love be a warm glow, burning within me, warming me and the people with whom I came in contact. My friends would be warm without having to prove that they were lovable. They simply would feel warm by being close to my fire!

Since a special, committed love relationship involves being very close, that special person gets an extra flow of warmth from my fire.

How about you? Do you have a fire going within you? Or has your fire gone out? I think it is important for us to care for the fire within us and make sure that we have a glow that warms us and also allows the people around us to be warm.

Styles of Loving

Our lives express our definition of love. If we believe that love is translated as making money, then that is how we spend our time. We act out our definition of love in our behavior. How have you been acting out your definition of love? What has been the important priority in your life? Are you satisfied with the definition of love you act out by your behavior, or do you want to change? Think about it.

An interesting paradox exists about the way we love others. While each of us has a unique style of loving, each person tends to believe that his or her style is *the only way there is* of loving! It is difficult for us to see that there are styles other than our own.

When you enter into a love relationship it's important to be aware of your own style and that of the other person. Perhaps by examining some of these styles we can better understand ourselves and others. My own observation of love relationships over two decades parallels many of the findings of University of Toronto sociologist John Alan Lee, whose research came up with nine "types of love." Here is my contribution to our understanding of the many styles of loving:

The *romantic* style of loving has a lot of warmth, feeling, and emotion. It is the "electricity" type of love, sending all kinds of tingly feelings through your body when you see the beloved person (you actually do have physiological changes in your body, such as increases in heart beat and body temperature). This tends to be an idealistic type of love, leading you to search for and find the "one and only" person for whom you can feel it. Many of our popular songs refer to this style of love. The romantic lover tends to love deeply and to need a sexual relationship along with romantic love. Withholding sex from a romantic lover is sometimes compared to withholding food from a baby. It is an important part of this style of loving. Because it is so loaded with feeling and emotion, romantic love may not be as stable as some of the other styles of loving.

Friendship love is not as loaded with emotion and feeling. The relationship starts with a liking for each other, and then the liking "just sort of grows" into something more, which might be called love. It is cooler, lacking the passion of romantic love. Sex is not as important to the friendship lover, often developing long after the relationship has started. This is one of the most stable styles of loving, and it is not unusual for people who get into this style of loving to remain good friends even if they divorce. Their loving was based upon mutual respect and friendship rather than strong emotional feelings.

Game-playing love regards the love relationship as a game with certain rules to follow. Game players are not as interested in intimacy as romantic lovers. In fact, they may have several simultaneous love relationships in order to avoid closeness and intimacy. Game-playing love is like the popular song that says, "When the one you love is gone, love the one you're with." Game-playing lovers tend to make up their own special rules, and their sexual relationships will follow whatever rules are most convenient.

There is a *needy* style of loving that tends to be full of possessiveness and dependency. This style of loving is very emotional, and the need to be loved makes it very unstable. The people involved tend to have difficulty maintaining the relationship; and they feel a lot of jealousy, possessiveness, and insecurity. Many people who have been through the divorce trauma adopt this style of loving because it reflects the neediness resulting from the divorce pain. Especially typical of the first relationship after the separation: "I've got to have another love relationship in order to be happy." This is an immature style of dependent and possessive love.

The *practical* lover takes a realistic look at the love partner and decides, on a rational and intellectual basis, if this love is appropriate. This type of person will make sure that there is similarity in religious beliefs, political beliefs, ways of handling money, views on raising children.... The lover may look into deficiencies in the person's family by considering socioeconomic status, characteristics, and genetic makeup. The practical lover will choose to love someone whom it "makes good sense" to love.

There are *altruistic* lovers, who may be somewhat other-centered and very willing to meet the needs of the other person. Carried to the extreme, the altruistic lover may become a martyr, trying to meet his or her own "empty-bucket" needs. There is, however, an authentic altruistic lover: a person who has a full bucket and enough inner strength to be able to love another person in a very unselfish manner. Many altruistic lovers have strong religious beliefs, and find a relationship with a Supreme Being keeps their own buckets full.

A couple with whom I was doing marriage counseling had a great deal of difficulty because he was a friendship lover and she was a romantic lover. She felt that his cool love was not love, and he felt that her romantic love was unstable. His style of loving was to take care of her, provide for her needs, and stay with her in the marriage; and he felt that this was proof of his love for her. Her request was for him to say, "I love you," and to express different forms of romantic thoughts that would make her feel loved and romantic. His friendship love was not a good mix with her romantic love. They had difficulty in communicating and understanding each other's viewpoints because their basic beliefs about what love was were not compatible.

Each person obviously is a mixture of the styles, and there is no one style that fits anyone at all times. Understanding your own mixture of styles is very important when you get into a love relationship with another person.

Learning to Love Yourself

As I guide people up the trail in the divorce seminars, the question often arises, "How do we learn to love ourselves?" As we have seen, the answer is not easy. Here is a specific exercise that will *help* with learning to love yourself, however:

Think of a time in your life when you started to make changes. It may have been when you first had difficulties in your marriage, when you first separated from your beloved, or when you started reading this book. Make a list of the changes that you have made, the personal growth you have experienced since that time, and the things you have learned about yourself, others, and life. Consider the feeling of confidence you have gained by learning these things and getting more in control of your own life. That confidence is what gives you the good feelings. The length of your list may surprise you.

The late esteemed psychotherapist Virginia Satir devised another method of helping people learn to gain more self-love. Make a list of five adjectives that could describe you. After you have listed these five adjectives, go through and put a plus or minus sign after each word to indicate whether you think each is a positive or negative adjective. After you have done this, look at the minus adjectives and see if you can find anything positive about each particular adjective, quality, or aspect of your personality.

A woman in the class listed the adjective *bitchy*. When questioned about it, she stated that her husband constantly referred to her as bitchy. As she began to talk about it, she realized that what he called bitchiness, she recognized as *assertiveness* — a positive way to stick up for herself. Once she understood that difference of labels, she was able to accept that as a part of herself and to feel good about it.

After all, that's what self-love is: learning to accept ourselves for what we are. As famous psychologist Carl Rogers observed, when we learn to accept ourselves for what we are, that allows us permission to grow, change, and become something different. As long as you don't accept a part of who you are, you have trouble changing that part! Does that sound like a strange paradox?

We all need to discover that "it's okay to not be okay" in certain areas. We have all had traumatic experiences that have left us wounded someplace, incidents when we did not feel loved, and experiences that have left us less than whole. But those experiences are part of life and part of living. We are not perfect; we are human beings. And when we can learn to accept some of the non-okay things about us, then we feel more okay.

How does one learn to love another person? What causes the feelings of love for that other person to begin suddenly? Perhaps it was a kind and thoughtful deed he or she did; maybe by doing something that met your needs, she or he helped you feel good. What would happen if you did kind and thoughtful deeds to yourself? If you would set aside a period of time tomorrow to do something that really felt good and made you feel okay about yourself, that could be a way of learning to love yourself more fully and more completely. After all, it would be you that was capable of doing something kind and lovable for you!

Perhaps the most important method of learning to love yourself is to *give yourself permission* to love yourself. If you can decide that it is okay, and not selfish or self-centered to love yourself, maybe you can allow yourself to go ahead and have feelings of self-love!

The growth you have achieved is something that no one has done for you, so no one can take it away from you. Your life is in your control, through knowledge of yourself and others. To that extent, you are not at the mercy of others anymore. Let the good feelings of your growth soak into your body, and let yourself feel the warmth of what you have achieved. Let yourself just feel love for yourself for a while. It is okay to love yourself. No — it's more than okay — *it is the way life is meant to be!*

Let the Children Know They Are Loved

While everyone is concerned about what love is, children may feel somewhat unlovable because one parent has left. Many suffer from the fear of losing the other parent as well. At the very time children need a great deal of parental love, parents are undergoing their own trauma and often are incapable of giving as much love to the children as they would like. Awareness of this problem and special efforts to overcome it — especially through much honest conversation with youngsters about what is going on, and reassurance that they are much loved by both parents — are much needed at this crucial time.

A mother recently told me a delightful story, one of those little vignettes in life that seem to make everything worthwhile. Her three-year-old son came down one morning and sat on the davenport. He was sitting there thinking and meditating, and suddenly popped up with, "What do you know? It seems like everybody loves me. Isn't that nice!" Those are special moments in life. As parents, a major goal for us is to try to help children of divorce feel that same way, even though we are going through a period of feeling unlovable ourselves.

How Are You Doing?

Check out your own self-love before you proceed to the next chapter:

1. *I feel I am lovable.*
2. *I am not afraid of being loved.*
3. *I am not afraid of loving another.*
4. *I have an understanding of what I believe love is.*
5. *I am living a lifestyle that is congruent with my definition of love.*
6. *I feel comfortable meeting my own needs rather than feeling selfish.*
7. *I am able to accept love from others.*
8. *I am able to express love to others in a way that makes them feel loved.*
9. *I am able to love myself.*
10. *I have experienced a great deal of personal growth since my crisis began.*
11. *I am trying to develop my immature, needy, dependent parts of love into a more mature style of loving.*

TRUST
"My Love-Wound Is Beginning to Heal"

If you say, "You can't trust men (women)!" you are saying more about yourself than about the opposite sex. Love relationships after divorce often are attempts to heal your love-wound, so many of them will be transitional and short-term. In your new relationships with others, you may be reworking and improving the way you got along with your parents. By building a basic level of trust within yourself, you can experience satisfying emotionally close and intimate relationships.

Chapter 15

I was doing just fine and enjoying myself. Then he said, "I love you."
I panicked and told him to get up, put on his clothes, and go home.

— Ann

On this trust part of the trail, you will notice people who walk some distance away from members of the opposite sex. They are like wild animals that come close, hoping to get some food, yet run for cover the minute you move toward them. These people talk about relationships a great deal of the time, and they seem to want to date and be with the opposite sex. But as soon as someone makes a move toward them, they run and shout, "Stay away!" They wear T-shirts with a motto saying, "You can't trust men (women)!" They have severe *love-wounds.*

A love-wound is the internal pain felt after the end of a love relationship, but it may originate much earlier in life. Many of the teenagers I worked with as a juvenile probation officer suffered from love-wounds. They had learned that "love equals getting hurt." If they were put in a warm, loving foster home, they would run away. People who have painful love-wounds will hold others at a distance emotionally until the love-wound is healed. It may take months or even years for some people to heal — to be able to be emotionally close again.

There Are Relationships, and then There Are Relationships

Relationships are important to people after divorce. When I use a questionnaire in the seminars asking participants what topics they want to discuss, every class picks "relationships" as the most important topic.

(Have you ever noticed at a gathering of singles how often the word *relationship* is used? One woman suggested that the word be censored with a "bleep," she was so tired of hearing it! I use it a great deal in this book and in my seminars, simply because I do not know a better word with that meaning!)

It is often assumed that the only way to prove that you're okay is to become involved in another love relationship. In fact, some experts in the divorce field consider remarriage an indication of divorce adjustment. A research study using the *Fisher Divorce Adjustment Scale* demonstrated the inadequacy of that assumption. A large number of remarried people have not adjusted to the past divorce.

The idea that another relationship will "prove you are okay" leads many people to start immediately to find a new one-and-only. The healthiest early relationships after divorce have the goal of healing the love-wound. They are *transitional* — rather than long-term, committed — relationships. (More on this in Chapter Sixteen.)

You've probably seen the poster that says, "You have to kiss a lot of frogs before you find a prince." It seems to be healthier to conclude, "You have to kiss a lot of frogs before you *become* a prinz." (Prinz is a non-sexist word for prince and princess.) If you can make this transition in your thinking, you can free these early relationships from expectations, pressures, and a futuristic outlook. Don't let the all-important question be, "Can I live with this person for the rest of my life?" Try instead, "Can this person and I benefit from some time together?"

Allow your new relationships to flow in the present and to help heal your love-wound (and perhaps the other person's love-wound also). Sit back and enjoy the sunsets each day, stop to "smell the roses," let yourself heal, and realize that many of these early relationships will be short-term because they are built during a needy time in your life. Let these early transitional relationships help you clear the confusion. You have plenty of time later to rebuild another permanent relationship when you have rebuilt a good foundation within yourself.

The divorce adjustment process may be viewed in two major steps. The first is *learning to be a single person*, ready to face life alone, with the rubble of the past cleared away. The second step is *learning to love again* after you have rebuilt your strength to carry the burden of a long-term committed relationship. If you complete step one first, step two will be easier!

Styles of Relationship: A "Body-Sculpture" Exercise

Here is an exercise which will help you examine your own *style* in relationships. It is called *body sculpturing* and is derived from the work of family therapist Virginia Satir. You'll need a friend to help. The diagrams illustrate different body positions which show various types of love-relationships that people have. Let's look at the body sculptures and consider the feelings underneath each style:

1. A-Frame Dependency Relationship

In the dependency relationship, two people lean on each other. Dependency upon another person sometimes feels good, but it's somewhat confining. When one person wants to move, change, or grow, it upsets the other who is leaning on him/her. Try this sculpture with another person and then put into words some of the feelings that you have while you are assuming this position.

2. Smothering Relationship

Here is a position quite frequently seen in teenage relationships. The vocabulary for this relationship is, "I can't live without you. I want to spend the rest of my life with you. I will devote myself completely to making you happy. It feels so good to be close to you." Many lovers start out by smothering, then gradually release the strangle hold on each other to allow more room for growth. This smothering pattern may be particularly significant during the honeymoon stage of a new love. The smothering relationship feels good for a while, but eventually the partners begin to feel trapped.

3. Pedestal Relationship

This "worshipful" relationship says, "I love you not for who you are, but for who I think you are. I have an idealized image of you and I'd like to have you live up to that image." It is very precarious on top of the pedestal because there are so many expectations to live up to. You can see the problems of communication here. In love with the person's idealized image, the worshipper is looking up to and trying to communicate with that image instead of with the real person. There is a great deal of emotional distancing inherent in this relationship, and it is difficult for the two people to become close.

4. Master/Slave Relationship

The master acts and is treated according to these ideas: "I'm the head of this family. I'm the boss. I'll make the decisions around here." Do not assume that this relationship necessarily places the male as the boss and head of the family. There are many females who are masters, making all of the decisions for their families.

In most relationships one of the partners has a personality which is at least a little stronger than the other, and that is not necessarily bad. It is when a relationship becomes rigid and inflexible, and one person is set up to make virtually *all* of the decisions, that emotional distancing and inequality take place. Maintaining one person as master and the other as slave tends to take a great deal of emotional energy, and often results in a power struggle that interferes with the communication and intimacy of the relationship.

5. Boarding House: Back-to-Back Relationship

Linked by their elbows, these two have some sort of contract or agreement that they are going to live together. There is no communication in this relationship. The typical thing is for people to come home and sit down and watch TV while they are eating, then retire to their own living habits for the remainder of the evening. There is no expression of love toward each other. Notice as you try this position, that when one person moves forward, changes (i.e., grows and matures), the other person is linked to that change. Back to-back is a very confining relationship. Many persons recognize this as the pattern that existed just before their relationship ended.

6. Martyr Relationship

Here is the person who completely sacrifices by trying to serve others. Always doing things for other people, never taking time for self, the martyr goes about "asking" to be stepped on. But don't let the lowly posture fool you! The martyr position is very controlling. Note that when the person lying down moves, the other person — who has a foot on the martyr — is thrown off balance.

How does the martyr gain control? You guessed it — through guilt. How can you be angry at a person who is doing everything for you, who is taking care of you completely? The martyr is very efficient at controlling people. It is very difficult to live with a martyr because you feel too guilty to express your own needs and angry feelings. Perhaps you have a martyr parent, and can recognize ways of dealing with that parent by understanding the martyr relationship.

7. Healthy Love-Relationship

Two people who are whole and complete have happiness within themselves. Standing upright, not leaning on or tangled up with the other person, they are able to live their own lives. They have an abundance of life to share with the other person. They choose to stay together because they are free to be individuals who are sharing their lives together. They can come close together and choose the smothering position temporarily; they can walk hand-in-hand as they might do in parenting their children; they can move apart and have their own careers, their own lives, and their own friends. Their choice to stay together is out of love for each other rather than needing to stay together because of some unmet emotional needs. The healthy love-relationship gives both people the space to grow and become themselves.

Again, let me urge you to try these different body-sculpture exercises with a friend and see how you feel in each instance. Talk or write about the feelings you were experiencing while in each body position. Which of these positions describes your past love-relationship? Many people in the classes state that they think that their love-relationship went through almost all of the unhealthy body positions!

Did you learn more causes of divorce from the body sculpturing? The unhealthy relationships seem to suggest a half person looking for another half person. As you become more of a whole person (do we ever become completely whole?), your chances of developing a healthy, healing relationship are greatly increased.

Feelings Into Actions

We tend to act out our internal feelings in our relationships. If you are angry, you probably express anger in your relationships. If you are lonely, you tend to be possessive in the relationship in order to keep the other person from leaving you and making you lonely again. If you are in deep emotional pain, you'll likely have a relationship full of pain. If you have a love-wound, you will emotionally distance others to avoid bumping your love-wound.

Many of us seek relationships with persons who have qualities we are missing in ourselves. If you are introverted and want to be more comfortable around people, you may marry an extrovert. Lacking confidence, you marry a person who exudes confidence. To meet your need to feel guilty, you develop a relationship with someone who will make you feel guilty.

And of course, the coin also has a positive side. If you are happy, confident, and feel lovable, you marry to act out those feelings in your relationship. We can learn much about ourselves by looking at our relationships. What feelings are you expressing in your relationships? Is there a pattern? (Do you always bring home a stray cat?) Do your relationships reflect good feelings within, or do they reflect neediness?

Is Your History Repeating Itself?

Another major factor in our relationship styles is one I've mentioned before: the interaction we had with our parents. Each of us learned how to respond to love, anger, rejection, and intimacy from our own parents. If your parents fought, then you are likely to have a very tough time with fights. If your parents were cold and untouching, then you may find it difficult to touch and to handle warm emotions. Many a marriage is not satisfactory because the partners are interacting like their parents did.

Jeff told me, "Marriage may be like a pot of stew. If you don't make it right the first time, you keep doing it over until you get it right. In my first marriage, I was acting out the unproductive patterns I learned as a child. I didn't change internally after my divorce, so I continued to act out those patterns in my second marriage!"

If you can use each relationship to learn about yourself and how you are acting out your internal feelings in your relationships, you can then use each relationship to become more the person you want to be. I think it is possible to grow from each relationship, and that is a positive way of looking at more than one marriage.

After divorce, we often regress and interact the way we did earlier in life. This can be positive: becoming a healthy person emotionally is like climbing a slide in the playground. You progress up so far, then lose your grip and slide back down. Then the next time you are able to climb to a higher point. Although each relationship that ends may put you back down the slide, when you climb again, you know how to climb higher and become more healthy. In their relationships after divorce, many people are reworking the patterns of interaction they learned from their parents in order to make those patterns more productive.

I hope the body sculpturing and this discussion of various concepts of relationships are helping you carry out the rubble and make room to rebuild yourself. The problem of trust is largely internal rather than external, and understanding your past is helpful in understanding where you are now. The first step of growth is to become aware of ourselves, our patterns of interaction, and our methods of relating with others.

Enough of carrying out the rubble — let's start rebuilding!

"Where Do I Meet Someone?"

This is one of the questions formerly married people ask most frequently. The simple, almost absurd, answer is "Right where you are!" People go to bars, singles groups, and ceramics classes (amazing how many formerly-marrieds do that!) in their attempts to meet people.

I don't quarrel with going places where single people gather. But take care! The "bar scene," for example, typically includes many lonely people who can't relate until they are slightly under the influence. And the bar hoppers are often game-players out to practice and improve their games of interaction, frequently with sex being the goal of the game. Singles groups, too, may have a certain amount of desperation and loneliness, and usually consist predominantly of women.

The question, "Where do I meet someone?" often indicates that the asker is looking for a committed, long-term partner. Perhaps somewhat desperate and sending out desperate vibrations with body language, vocabulary, and "the look in their eyes," these persons tend to drive people away. Others fear that they will become sucked in by the neediness; some call the needy ones *vacuum cleaners!*

How often have you heard it said, "There ain't nothing but turkeys out there?" Of course, it is partly true. Many formerly married people are hurting, and are not especially attractive dates during the rough periods. But have you thought about what you would do if an eagle landed near you? You would probably run like mad! A person who is eligible and looks like a possible marriage partner scares the hell out of you if your love-wound is still very painful. Maybe you are *looking* for turkeys because they are safe? Maybe you are still hurting, and more or less a turkey yourself? Turkeys do tend to hang together, you know. Maybe, if there "ain't nothing but turkeys out there," you're still a turkey yourself, and haven't rebuilt yourself to the status of an eagle.

When you have blinders on and see only potential marriage partners, do you realize how many people you are not seeing out there? When you start becoming interested in getting to know the people around you, then you start making friends. And some of those friends might become lovers, but *looking* for lovers keeps both friends and lovers away! It bears repeating: Your goal (for now) is to get acquainted and develop friendships with the people around you. Pay no attention to whether or not they are "eligible singles"; notice only if they are interesting people you would like to get to know. Develop as many positive relationships with people of both sexes as you can — if some become lovers, it's frosting on the cake!

You can get to know these potential friends wherever you are. When you go to the grocery store and send out positive vibrations and act interested in others, you attract people like flies to honey. At parties, if you are not trying to find a bed partner or someone to go home with after the party, you might get to know a number of interesting people. If you've found happiness within and send out those vibrations, people will enjoy being with you.

I am fully aware of the difference in the numbers of formerly married males and females. The ratio is unfair because there are so many more females than males. Women live longer than men; for each year of life there are more females than males living. Also, there are many males who remarry someone much younger, often a woman not married before. (It may be small compensation to women, but it is true that women adjust to living alone much better than do men.)

Ginger posed another issue frequently discussed in my seminars, "Everytime I go to a singles gathering, it becomes a game of 'my place-or-yours?'" There are many singles who have not learned to deal with the opposite sex other than sexually, but that doesn't mean you have to narrow yourself the same way. Keep developing your personality and broadening yourself. The more interests you develop, the more interesting people you will find.

Rebuilding Trust
Some ideas have grown out of the divorce seminars which may help you overcome problems of trust.

Try this one: Be really honest the next time you go out. If you are hurting, and have a painful love-wound, explain to the person that you want to be with him/her, but you fear you'll be a wet blanket. Don't try to put on the mask of cool and sophisticated, when in reality you're scared to death. When you explain your fears to others, you might be surprised to learn they were feeling the same way! After all, we're *all* human. And you'll both be relieved to be able to be yourselves instead of the "Joe Cool" you thought you had to be.

Have you thought about learning to trust with friends rather than lovers? If you find someone of the opposite sex with whom you can be a friend, that person is much safer for you than a lover. When you add romance to the ingredients of a friendship, it adds instability to the relationship, and makes it harder to take risks and learn to trust.

We project our lack of trust upon others. I have often counseled parents who said their teenager was not to be trusted. Valerie's parents, for example, feared their daughter would become pregnant and would not allow her to date, even though she was a junior in high school. I discovered that the mother had become pregnant as a teenager, and was projecting her lack of trust in herself upon Valerie.

A similar event often occurs in marriage counseling. Tess told me that her husband Andre kept checking on her to make sure she was not having an affair. Then she discovered that Andre was having the affair and projecting his lack of trust upon her! Like so many other feelings, lack of trust may become a self-fulfilling prophecy. Valerie told me she felt she should become pregnant because that was what her parents seemed to believe was going to happen. And Tess felt she might as well have an affair if that was what Andre suspected anyway!

A severe love-wound leads to fear of trusting. As appealing as the warmth may be, to become close is to risk being burned again. Relationships after divorce are controlled by this lack of trust. The purpose of these relationships ought to be to learn trust again and to heal the love-wound. Thus many of the relationships are short-term. Trying to make them into something long-term often does nothing but increase the love-wound and prolong the adjustment process.

We have all learned how to interact from our love-relationships and from our parents. As adults, we may choose to improve the styles of interaction that we learned. Becoming aware of one's style is an important first step. It may also take several friendships and love-relationships to help one develop healthier styles.

We have to take risks to learn to trust. Risks may backfire and lead to rejection or misunderstanding, but risks are necessary if one is to become close and experience intimacy again. The rewards are worth the risk.

Trust and the Children

The problem of trust is especially difficult for those children who did not know what was going on with their parents' divorce, so the children are now adjusting to a parent's absence with little or no direct communication with that parent. If the father, for example, suddenly leaves the family, and doesn't communicate why he is leaving or the problems that the parents are having, the child may feel deserted, and have trouble trusting that absent, noncustodial parent.

Kids really are tougher than you think, and can handle an awful lot of direct communication and reality if parents will just take the time to communicate with them. Parents who hide their heads and feel they cannot share the reality of their situation with their children often create a great deal of mistrust in the children, and lose a potentially valuable source of love and support for themselves! It is a very unusual — or very young — child who does not know that the parents are going to get a divorce before the parents tell him/her. The more you can communicate and level with your children, the more they will trust what you have to say.

How Are You Doing?

Here are some items to see how you are doing and if you are ready to continue the climb. We are nearing the top, so take care not to rush here — this rebuilding block must be securely in place before you proceed.

1. *I can trust members of the opposite sex.*
2. *I have begun to understand that men and women are much more alike than different in their responses to feelings such as love, hate, intimacy, and fear.*
3. *I can trust myself and my feelings.*
4. *I trust my feelings enough to act on them.*
5. *I am not afraid of becoming emotionally close to a potential love-partner.*
6. *I am aware of the ways that I distance people.*
7. *I am building relationships that will help me to heal my love-wound.*
8. *I am building healing and trusting relationships with friends of both sexes.*
9. *I communicate with others where I am emotionally rather than giving mixed messages.*
10. *I understand that not everyone is capable of being trusted.*
11. *I am capable of trusting someone when it is appropriate.*
12. *I want to heal my love-wound and experience intimacy.*
13. *I am trying to live in the present in my relationships.*
14. *I realize that many of the early relationships after divorce may be short-term.*
15. *I am taking risks in my relationships by exposing my true feelings and thoughts.*
16. *I am truly interested in the friends around me rather than desperately looking for another love-relationship.*

RELATEDNESS
"Growing Relationships Help Me Rebuild"

It's okay to have an important relationship after your primary relationship has ended. We often need support, companionship, and feedback from others to help us rebuild. These relationships are often short-term, so we need to learn how to have "healthy termination." We need to take credit for creating these relationships as part of our growing process. And we need to become aware of how we can make these relationships as growing and healing as possible.

Chapter 16

Have I had a growing relationship? Not one, but four. Each seemed healthier than the one before. I guess I learned something from each one.   — Susan

I had one with a woman who had a great built-in 'crap-detector.' When I was sorting through my stuff, I could bounce off her and she would tell me what parts of me were authentic and what parts of me were crap. I think I found the perfect partner to have a growing relationship with.   — David

Many people climbing the mountain decide to pair off, to help support each other in the difficult climb. They appear to enjoy each other's company very much for a while, but often they part ways and continue the climb alone.

It helps to have another person's support for a while, but sooner or later one or both of them eventually realize they need to make this climb alone. When they part, one or both of them feel very sad for a while. They often have to rework some of the blocks they had already gone through, such as grief and anger. Both appear to make rapid progress while they are together, but when this new relationship ends, their progress slows down considerably.

What Is a Growing Relationship?

I call these unions *growing relationships*. Other professionals have variously labeled them "transitional relationships," "rebound relationships," "experimental relationships," and "healing relationships." Psychiatrist Martin Blinder for example, in his book *Choosing Lovers*, describes the various types in some detail, and asserts that each type is unique, meeting particular needs of the partners. Later in this chapter, I'll discuss a couple of the more common types I have observed.

Growing relationships, because they help folks manage the climb better for a while, can be very healthy for both partners. But it's not enough just to let them "happen." We need to understand them and how they work, so we can make them more growth-enhancing, longer lasting, and — just maybe — hurt less when they end.

Among the typical characteristics of growing relationships:

• They often occur after a marriage or love relationship has ended, but they can occur at any time.

• They often are with a potential love partner, but they can be with a friend, a family member, a therapist, or even with your primary love partner.

• They usually are temporary, but they can become a more permanent, long-lasting relationship. They are usually very healing, but they can be destructive.

• They usually occur when you are in a personal growth or transformation period in your life.

• They are an attempt to find new ways of creating and building relationships with yourself and with others.

• They can end with a "healthy termination," rather than the painful, destructive endings you may have experienced in the past.

• They typically involve good communication. Usually the two people spend a great deal of time talking with each other about important topics such as personal growth and the meaning of life.

• These relationships are based upon honesty and openness — with each other if not with their primary love partners — and the people often share themselves in ways they have never shared before. Instead of "dressing up and putting on good clothes" — to put on their best facade for the new partner (as most of us did in the old "courting" system) — these people strip to the bare emotional essentials, so they can present their true essence in ways that allow them to feel excited about their new behavior.

- They are growth-oriented, not stagnant. I want to differentiate this type of healing relationship from the one that is simply a summer re-run of old shows. The male who needs mothering is often married to an enabler/over-responsible person. He often leaves that relationship and marries another enabler/over-responsible person (often with the same or a similar first name!). The female who needs to take care of someone may marry another "stray-cat" so she can continue her old pattern. In contrast, the growing relationship is dedicated to developing a new and different relationship — a laboratory for personal growth — not to perpetuating old patterns.

Are We Talking Affairs Here?

Sometimes a person in a primary love relationship has a third-party relationship and calls it a growing relationship. Such a union can take the form of an affair. I've worked with clients who have been able to make their third-party relationships into healing experiences, using them to enrich their primary relationships and make them stronger. That usually is possible only if the new pairing is a friendship, rather than a romantic affair. Romantic third-party involvements typically have long-term consequences, and make it difficult for the people involved to heal the pain of the affair.

My old childhood parent-tapes about sex and marriage come back and say to me, "When you talk about relationships outside of marriage that may include sex, aren't you encouraging affairs or promiscuity?" No, I don't think so. These relationships don't have to be romantic or sexual. If your religious and moral values are such that you don't want a relationship that is sexual outside of marriage, I think you can still learn and heal tremendously by having a non-sexual friendship.

A growing relationship must fit your moral values while it focuses in on the learning and the lessons that you need to learn.

Why Are Some People More Likely to Create Growing Relationships?

There are some groups of people who are more likely to have growing relationships:

• Dumpers after a divorce will tend to get into other relationships quicker than dumpees.

• Males will tend to get into other relationships quicker after a divorce than will females.

• Females are more likely than males to create a growing relationship with a friend.

• Extraverts are more likely than introverts to use the growing relationship to heal. From research with the *Myers-Briggs Type Indicator*, a psychological test which describes people by personality types, we learn that extraverts heal better with other people, introverts heal better by themselves.

• People who are able to be emotionally open and vulnerable will more likely create a healing growing relationship than emotionally closed-down people who can't talk about feelings.

• People in rebellion will usually have a growing relationship. (See Chapter Twelve on Transition for more on rebellion).

• Younger people are more inclined to develop growing relationships than older people.

• People who are involved in divorce recovery classes or seminars will almost automatically develop growing relationships with the other participants in the class. This is one of the great "side benefits" of participation in a class. The friendships you make in such a class will probably last for a long time, maybe for the rest of your life. And the friendships will be more healthy and growing than many of the relationships you have had in the past. Remember that you can create the same kind of relationships outside of class that you have created with other class participants.

• Many people will not want to start such a relationship because it could become more than they can handle. They want something safe that won't become long term. It's important to be clear and communicate your intentions, needs and desires directly and openly with a potential partner. You can decide how to control your future involvement and not let the relationship become more than what you want it to be.

Fifteen to twenty percent of the participants in the divorce class don't enroll after their marriage has ended. They enroll in the divorce class when their growing relationship *after* their divorce has ended. And I also have observed that the first relationships after a marriage has ended usually don't last very long. The emotional pain is often greater when these relationships end than when the marriage or primary love relationship ended.

I believe more people will be experiencing growing relationships as we move into the 21st century, because of the many transitions taking place in society. Learning more about these types of relationships will increase the chances of them becoming more healing. Toward that end, let's take a look at two of the most common types of growing relationships: the *passionate* and the *therapeutic*.

Passionate, Emotional Relationships

Perhaps the most common of the several types of growing relationships which occur after a primary love relationship has ended is the passionate type, with its emphasis on romantic love. Here at last — or so it seems — are all of those qualities which were missing in the late marriage: passion, honesty, good communication, empathy, understanding, even good sex! No wonder the new partners want it to last forever, hang onto it tightly, and talk about their future together.

But commitments for the long term might not be healing for either party at this stage. Let's consider some of the potential pitfalls and benefits of the passionate emotional relationship:

• **Pitfall:** *Making the other person responsible for your excitement and passion.* Have you made this new attachment too important in your life? It feels so good when you are on the rough seas of your transition that you want to make it last forever. You think you can't live without this exciting new partner. What you need to remember is that you're in the process of recovery. Take responsibility for creating this relationship yourself. You have just begun to be the person you want to be; give yourself the time it takes to finish the job. It does feel good to be with that other person. But don't give away all your power by making another person responsible for your happiness.

• **Benefit:** *Your personal growth is an important reason for this relationship.* The lesson for you to learn in this relationship is to heal, to become, to be free, to be yourself. Take advantage of the lesson, and take credit for what you are learning. You have created an environment in which you can grow.

• **Pitfall:** *Putting your partner on a pedestal.* That mistake will almost surely limit the healing potential of this relationship. Try acting out this pedestal relationship by doing what the late family therapist Virginia Satir called "body-sculpture" (described in Chapter Fifteen). You and another person describe how your relationship feels by arranging your bodies in a sculpturing position. Let your partner stand on a pedestal (a chair, stool, small table) while you stand on the floor. Talk to each other. Give each other a hug. Become aware of how it feels. Your partner on the pedestal usually feels lonely, precarious, and uncomfortable.

• **Pitfall:** *Focusing too much on the future.* Because the relationship feels so good, you start thinking about the future, and what it would be like to be married to this person forever. Living in the future inhibits healing, while living in the present maximizes healing, Living in the present is an indication of a self-actualized person. You need to enjoy the sunset each day in this relationship. You need to live each day as though it were your last. You need to communicate about everything you are feeling now, and let go of dreaming about the future or how long this relationship is going to last.

• **Benefit:** *Communication is usually good in such a relationship.* You often share things about yourself and become more vulnerable than you have ever been. You treasure being open, vulnerable, and intimate. Realize that an important lesson in this relationship might be learning to be intimate and vulnerable. Remember that the communication skills and the feeling of vulnerability you are learning in this relationship will always be available to you in other relationships.

- **Pitfall:** *You believe you'll never have another relationship with such a wonderful person again.* Part of the reason you hang on to this relationship so tightly is that you see this person as your "one and only." (An expectation you learned from society?) Any other person will be dull and unexciting after this person. There is some truth in this. But the excitement you feel is not because of the other person. It is because of your own process of growth. You are living in the present, being vulnerable, feeling new feelings. Much of the excitement you feel is because you are coming out of your shell, finding yourself, "coming home" emotionally.

While you may never feel this same excitement — becoming free of your shell — again, you have the potential of feeling the joy and excitement of intimacy, being emotionally close, and feeling loving and being loved in your future relationships which may have more meaning than the good feelings you experience in this relationship when you are coming out of your shell.

- **Benefit:** *You find out how good it feels to be healthy.* As you grow and become you, you can allow yourself to be vulnerable with the resulting feelings of intimacy, to feel more secure with an identity of your own. The really important point for you to learn here is that *you can feel this way in many relationships and with many people.* So stop believing this is the only person that you can have such a relationship with. You will be able to have other healthy relationships if you choose, because you are learning to have a better relationship with yourself. But you may not feel as intense in another relationship because it won't have the neediness.

- **Benefit:** *An adult relationship can be a laboratory for growth.* Remember the themes from Chapters Three and Ten, on family of origin and childhood influences? You can rework and relearn the things you learned as a child. This growing relationship might be as good a laboratory of growth as any relationship you have had or will ever have. This new relationship is very likely much different from the relationships you built with your family of origin and with ex-love partner. This may partly explain why this relationship feels so good.

• **Pitfall:** *An imbalance of emotional investment.* It is very easy to invest 80% or more of your emotional time and energy into this relationship and neglect investing in yourself. That inhibits your healing and your growth, contributes to the relationship ending, and makes it much more painful when it does end. If you want to maximize the healing possible in this growing relationship, discipline yourself to keep investing as much into yourself as you are investing in the relationship. This will help you keep your individual identity rather than losing it in your exciting, new, passionate love relationship. If you need help in seeing how to do this, keep track of your time. How much of your free time is spent in improving yourself, such as hobbies, taking classes, time by yourself or with your friends? And how much time are you spending with the other person doing relationship activities?

Learn all you can, heal all you can, and stop holding the precious butterfly in your hands so tightly that it can't fly and be free. The energy you spend holding on tightly to the other person and to the relationship keeps you from climbing your own mountain and completing your own healing.

Friendship and Therapeutic Relationships

I mentioned previously that this growing relationship doesn't have to be with a love partner. In fact, there are tremendous advantages in having a growing relationship with a person who is not a love partner. You can have the same healing with a good friend, or a family member. You can still talk about feelings, be vulnerable, share parts of yourself that you have never shared with another. This friendship doesn't have the same thrills, excitement, and passion as the love relationship. But it is safer, seldom ends with the emotional pain present in ending romantic relationships, and can have just as deep healing. It can also be the laboratory for growth to change past patterns of relationships just as the passionate love relationship can be.

It is easy for participants in the Rebuilding class to identify with growing relationships based upon friendship. The participants are open and honest, share important aspects of themselves, feel a closeness and intimacy with others, and realize the relationships are special and often more healthy and healing than what they have known in the past. Learning to develop these kind of friendship growing relationships can be one of the most valuable learning experiences for the participants in divorce recovery classes.

Therapy can also be a growing relationship, depending upon the therapist and the style of therapy. But the same type of growth can take place and with the safety that comes from paying for the therapy and keeping it professional. A therapy relationship that helps you to become fully yourself can be a beautiful experience.

Are They Always Transitional?

People ask if every growing relationship has to end. I say no. Have you thought about how each relationship has a foundation that is unique, both to that relationship and to where you are emotionally when you start the relationship? The foundation for the growing relationship is built for growth and healing; that's its purpose. A long-term committed relationship has a foundation built for longevity. What's the difference?

When you are building a growing relationship, you are in process — unstable, continually growing and changing, healing the wounds of the past. You are different today from what you were yesterday. And you will be different tomorrow. During this period of rapid change, your foundation needs to be flexible, adaptable, changeable — allowing you to be different as you change. That isn't a suitable foundation for a long-term relationship. The contract when you started the growing relationship might not have been written or spelled out verbally but it was there. "I need this relationship so I can find out who I am" was probably in the contract. The foundation for a long-term relationship is more stable and more permanent (although not rigid). Long term unions require commitment, purpose, and stability.

If the growing relationship is to last, it needs to be jacked up and a new foundation put under it. This can be done in various ways. I have known couples who had healthy termination of their relationships so one or both of them could be the "young colt" — out running around the pasture investing in themselves rather than investing in the relationship. Then they got back together and built a relationship with a more permanent foundation.

Changing the relationship can also can be done with good communication. I believe that anything you can talk out, you don't have to act out. If you talk out with awareness and ownership that the relationship needs to be changed from a growing one to a longer, more committed one, it can be done. But without the three basic ingredients of awareness, ownership, and communication, it probably won't happen.

There is another problem. If you are truly changing, you might be a different person than you were when you started the relationship. Maybe your attraction and reason for entering into the relationship was to be with a person who was entirely different than your parents, former lovers, former friends. And when the need for a contrasting person is met, maybe you will want relationships with people more like your parents, former lovers, and former friends. So when the need for the different person passes, you may want to end the relationship. Many people in growing relationships outgrow the relationship for a variety of reasons.

Don't move too quickly to try to convert a growing relationship into one of long-term commitment. Both partners must be ready to accept themselves where they are now, and to move ahead into a more stable future.

Why Do I Have to Have So Many?

Sometimes people ask why they have to have so many growing relationships. A very good question. There are several explanations:

• The relationships may have had only a fraction of the healing possible because you loaded them down with the future, rather than focusing on the present.

• You didn't pay enough attention to your own recovery and healing process because you were so infatuated with how great the other person was.

• You terminated the relationship with a lot of pain because you weren't aware of how to do a healthy termination. (This pain increases the need for another relationship to heal the pain of ending that one.)

• You may just simply have a lot of healing needing to be done from your family of origin and childhood experiences, and it takes several relationships to accomplish that.

• You've been working through issues that have been described in the previous chapters, but you weren't aware of what these issues were. Awareness increases the healing possible in a relationship a great deal.

• Another reason you have had so many relationships is because of the passion possible in these relationships. They become so physical that the real teaching of the relationship becomes obscured. You can escape very easily into passionate sex, and not ever wake up on the awareness level.

• You may not have been able to connect effectively on an emotional level. If you are not living in the present, if you do not give your complete attention to the relationship, if you avoid intimacy rather than seek it, then you never reach closeness, connectedness, intimacy, healing in the relationship. You may have been reluctant to end it because it in essence was never consummated on an intimate level. Each relationship has contributed to your growth, and it might be helpful for you to identify and be thankful for each relationship, and each person with whom you have been in relationship. The homework at the end of the chapter suggests you write the things you learned and healed in each of your growing relationships.

Please be gentle with yourself. If you beat yourself up with your inner critic each time you enter into or end a relationship, you again have negated the healing with criticism. Give yourself a warm fuzzy for each growing relationship you have created; you'll maximize the healing that has taken place instead of negating it.

Making Your Primary Love A Growing Relationship

One of the exciting ways to have one of these healing-relationships is to make your marriage or primary love relationship into a growing relationship! It takes the same concepts to make it work: living in the present, good communication, no future expectations, and ownership (that you are responsible for carving out this new relationship).

You may find helpful material in the chapters on rebellion and healing separations to help you carve out a new relationship within your marriage. It won't be easy, but most primary love relationships can be jacked up and have a new foundation put under them. My follow-up book, *Loving Choices: A Growing Experience,* is designed to help you create a growing relationship within your committed love relationship.

Learning Good Communication Skills

The growing relationship needs good communication, and the quickest way you can improve your communication skills is to learn to use "I" messages instead of "you" messages. You messages are like poisoned darts that you throw at another person, who either becomes defensive or starts thinking what to say (throw) back at you. I messages let others know that you are accepting responsibility for (owning) your own feelings and attitudes.

I messages may be difficult for you because you haven't always thought about what is going on inside of you. I suggest an easy way for you to start using I messages. Start each sentence with the pronoun "I" when you are doing important communication with yourself and with others. Try using these four kinds of communication: "I think _____," "I feel _____," "I want _____," and "I will _____." It is helpful for us to separate our thoughts from our feelings and to use two different kinds of communication for each.

Think about what you hope to achieve with your message. If you don't *say* what you want, you probably won't *get* what you want. And you need to finish your communication with a commitment about what action *you* will take. Taking responsible action to help achieve what you want is like putting your money where your mouth is.

Men frequently have difficulty accessing and talking about feelings. Using "I feel" statements may help them overcome this handicap. On the other hand, females can often tell you what the other people around them want or need but they can't tell you what they themselves want or need.

This material on I messages builds on the work of Dr. Thomas Gordon, California psychologist who developed the highly successful "Effectiveness Training" programs for parents, teachers, and leaders. My book *Rebuilding Relationships* describes a more complicated communication model using the same foundation. If you want to learn more about how to better communicate with yourself and others, you may want to read the communication chapters in the relationships book.

Healthy Termination

Another key part of growing relationships is a process I call *healthy termination*. Because most of these relationships will end, they will be more growth-enhancing for both parties if you learn how to do a healthy termination. It's an inherent problem in these relationships: you try to make them last longer than is healthy because you've started laying the expectations of future on them.

By trying to stretch a short-term relationship into something longer than its "natural life," you make it unduly stressful. When you finish stretching it till it breaks, it snaps back at you like a rubber band — and hurts more than it has to.

If you could back it off into friendship before it gets stretched too far, you are more likely to have a healthy termination. If you live in the present, you'll notice when the "present" is less meaningful than it was. The needs that created the relationship have changed. That's the time to start terminating. Talk about your needs being different. Own what is happening with your changes, how your needs are different, and share what lessons and valuable learning you have gained from the relationship. Healthy terminations end with a fraction of the pain that could be there from trying to stretch the relationship into something it is not.

The healthy termination has its roots in openness and honesty about the needs and desires of both partners when you started the relationship. Pete was an Army Chaplain who stated it well. "I told her I was a wet little kitty, and needed someone to take care of me and lick me dry like the mother cat does. And I also told her I didn't know whether I would want a relationship with her when I finally was dry. We were able to terminate the relationship with a minimum of pain because we had been open and honest from the beginning."

So here are the characteristics of a healthy termination. I encourage you to build them into your growing relationships:

- Openness and honesty in communication.
- Living in the present. Taking one day at a time, rather than making plans for an uncertain "future" together.
- Taking responsibility — ownership — for your own feelings, and expressing them openly. Avoiding games like, "I'm fine. Nothing's wrong."
- Seeing this from the beginning as a short-term relationship. "Commitment" is not part of a growing relationship, unless it becomes a long-term union.
- Talking about your needs. Listening to your partner's needs.

Watch for clues which tell you it's time to move on. Let your partner know when they start to show up.

Plan for the highly-probable termination of the relationship. Discuss how you'll handle it when the time comes (e.g., Will alternate living arrangements be needed? Transportation? Are children involved? Will you continue as friends? How about mutual friends?

This concept of a healthy termination applies to all relationships. Each relationship has its natural cycle of growth. Some are short-term annuals, and others are long-term perennials. It's not easy to recognize just what the life-span of the relationship is. Ownership — acceptance of responsibility for yourselves, your feelings, and what's going on with each of you individually — is a tremendous help in allowing the relationship to find its own natural cycle.

Most of the pain in our lives is holding on to something too long when we need to let it go. If you believe your happiness is someone else's responsibility, you'll have difficulty letting a relationship have its natural length of life.

Do You Need a Growing Relationship?

There are a number of ways to heal without having a growing relationship. However, it does feel good to have someone's hand to hold while you are waking-up. And someone to talk to while you are learning about yourself. They contribute much to the healing experience.

If you can understand that these relationships are a place you can put into practice all the skills that you have read about and learned while reading this book, you'll see the benefits of this relationship even more. I hope that the awareness gained from reading this book will help you pursue real healing in these kinds of relationships instead of allowing them to repeat old patterns.

Awareness plus ownership will maximize the healing in these growing relationships. Most of the healing I have been talking about *cannot* happen without ownership. We can't learn the lessons the relationship is teaching us if we don't own what we are creating and what we are healing.

Children and Relatedness

Your children will probably develop growing relationships also. They may suddenly be good friends with other children whose parents are divorcing. They will find they can talk to these friends better than the "married kids" who had been their friends.

You may be surprised to find you are feeling judgemental toward the kids whose parents are divorcing and don't want your kids to associate with them. Surprise! You have found some of your own biases and prejudices toward divorce. Remember your children are going through the divorce process also, and finding friends who are in a similar situation may be helpful. And realize that anyone can go through a divorce and you don't have to persist in critical attitudes toward people who are ending relationships.

If you are involved in your own growing relationship, where does your child fit in? It depends upon the type of relationship you are creating. If you have a therapy relationship, it may be helpful to share this with your children. They will be more open to talking with others if they realize you are talking to someone. If your growing relationship is with a friend or family member, you may choose to involve your children in this relationship by sharing with them how good it feels to have a special person to talk to.

If your relationship looks like the passionate love affair kind of growing relationship, however, then you need to decide how much to include your child in this relationship. Your child has been observing the arguments between you parents and you may want to expose your child to a more peaceful and loving relationship. It is easy for the excitement of the new relationship to cloud your thinking and you may want to include the children in this relationship more than is appropriate. Having your new partner spend the night while the kids are there will usually be difficult for your children to deal with.

The chances of this relationship lasting and becoming long term are not high. Your children will have to deal with the rending of another of your relationships. Keep some perspective on how much you want to involve your children in your growing relationship.

Take responsibility for creating this growing relationship as part of your adjustment process. Awareness of this may help your children to put the relationship in better perspective. You take control of your life by making more aware, loving choices; your children can follow your example.

Homework for a Growing Relationship

Write responses to the following questions in your journal.

1. What is your response to this Chapter? Does this discussion square with your experience?

2. If you have had one or more growing relationships, describe them. How were they healing? How were they harmful? What did you learn in each one? Were they with a friend, lover, therapist, or a family member? How could you make the next one more healing and healthy?

3. If you have not had a growing relationship, do you want to? Are you afraid of becoming vulnerable? Are you unable to communicate? Are you afraid of being hurt again?

4. If you are in a primary committed love relationship and having a healing separation, do you think it is possible to experience

a growing relationship with your partner? Is this a new concept for you?

Let me give you some hope. In the many years I've been teaching the relationships class for couples, I have observed hundreds of couples create a new and loving relationship from the painful ashes of a dead relationship. You can do it! Start by both of you reading and working your way through this book. Do as much of the homework as you have time to do. Encourage and nurture each other because this process takes commitment, self-discipline, and confidence.

How Am I Doing?

Before you go on the the next chapter, take advantage of this brief self-assessment. It will help you to determine if you're ready to head on up the trail.

1. *I'm ready to forgive myself for having growing relationships in the past where I made the other person responsible for my joy and happiness.*

2. *I will make a list of what I learned in each of my past growing relationships.*

3. *I will choose, using my present awareness, what kind of growing relationship I want to have in the future.*

4. *I will take ownership for creating growing relationships as part of my healing process.*

5. *I will take ownership for feeling good in my growing relationships because I am becoming the person I choose to be.*

6. *I will put into practice all of the relationship skills I learned as a participant in the Rebuilding Class (if I took part). I will use these skills in all of my future relationships.*

7. *I am being open and honest, using good communication skills, trying out new behavior, breaking old patterns of interaction, and making my relationships as growing and healing as possible.*

SEXUALITY
"I'm Interested, But I'm Scared"

When you're first separated, it's normal to be extremely fearful of sex. During the adjustment process, you can learn to express your unique sexuality according to your own moral standards. The singles subculture emphasizes authenticity, responsibility, and individuality more than rules. You can discover what *you* believe rather than what is expected of you. The great difference in attitudes and values of male and female sexuality appears to be a myth. Your adjustment may be complicated by the major changes taking place in female and male sex roles. In any case, *safe sex* is the order of the day.

Chapter 17

Being Divorced and Middle-aged Is:
   ...Not taking out the garbage for fear you'll miss that obscene phone call.
   ...Standing out in the middle of the dark parking lot and shouting, "Hey you muggers, the muggee is here!"
   ...Telling the guy who frisked you and demanded all your money that you have no money but if he'll frisk you again, you'll write him a check.
   ...Putting a sign on your gate that reads, "All trespassers will be violated."
   ...Looking under the bed and hoping someone is there.

— Lois

Everyone looks forward to this portion of the climb with great expectations. You may have turned to read this chapter first. (If so, I urge you to read at least Chapter One first!) Maybe you have been anticipating this chapter on sexuality since the original discussion of the rebuilding blocks in Chapter One.

"I Wish I Were Single . . .?"

What was your attitude toward those swinging singles when you were married? Did you wonder if they were the sexual athletes they were rumored to be? And did you fantasize what it would be like to have a date with a different and exciting person each night of the week?

Now you are single. Look at the people around you. Many are spending evenings alone. Many are out pretending to have fun at singles parties — when in reality they are bored stiff. Many times you spend an evening with a person who makes your ex look attractive and desirable — and you never thought anyone could be worse than your ex. And everyone is going with someone and then breaking up — you can't even keep track of who is dating whom. The contrast between your fantasy of the wild single life and what it actually is adds greatly to the trauma of divorce.

"A Date? Well, I Don't Know . . ."

Take heart — the first part of this sexuality climb is the steepest and most difficult — it gets easier after you become accustomed to being single. You have not been "out on a date" for years, and the first person you ask turns you down. You attend a singles party petrified that no one will ask you to dance — and equally petrified that someone will. At the first contact with the opposite sex you feel like an awkward junior-high kid on a first date. And wow! If someone should make a pass at you — the thought is enough to make you stay home, alone, forever.

Just what is appropriate behavior for an adult who hasn't dated in years? There may have been rules and chaperons at your teenage parties. Your parents probably told you what time to be in. Now you have no one to set the limits for yourself, and your feelings are so confused and uncertain that you can't even rely on them. You envied the freedom of singleness, and now you would give anything to have the security of marriage again.

Later on in the process, when you've found your individual pathway, things will be more comfortable. After you have overcome your confusion and uncertainty, you'll find that you can express yourself through dating and relationships with the opposite sex. There may be a freedom that you didn't have when you were a teenager doing what was expected of you — or what was not expected.

"I'm Glad You Asked That Question"

In my divorce seminars, sexuality is one of the last of the sessions. This is not to save the best for last, but to give people time to become comfortable discussing such a personal and emotional issue. To help people become more comfortable, I ask them to write questions about sexuality — you know, the ones that they always wanted to ask but were afraid to. The questions are directed to either males or females, and the facilitator reads the questions aloud to ensure anonymity. These questions give us insights into the concerns of formerly married people.

Some questions recently separated people frequently ask include: 1) "What do you find attractive and desirable in the opposite sex?" 2) "What do you call going out? I hate the word *date!*"; and 3) "How do I tell the person I'm going out with that I don't want anything heavy?"

Later on in the process, people might ask these questions: 1) "What do men think about a woman who has sex early in the relationship?" 2) "How do women feel about having more than one sexual relationship at the same time?" 3) "Why don't men call again after we've gone to bed together?" and 4) "I refuse to consider having sex outside of marriage — would you want to go out with me?"

The adjustments resulting from the changing sex roles cause difficulty for both men and women: 1) "What do men think about a woman who asks you out?" 2) "Just what do women want? I hold the door open for one woman and she gets irritated. The next woman waits for me to open the door. What am I supposed to do?" 3) "I always felt comfortable making complimentary comments to a woman and asking her out. This week a 'liberated' woman told me she liked my legs, and asked me if I would like to go out with her. What do I do?" 4) "Who do you think should pay for the date?" 5) "Whose responsibility is it for birth control?" 6) "Is everybody but me comfortable about using condoms?"

Questions about kids can be difficult, too: 1) "Who pays for the babysitter?" 2) "Who takes the babysitter home?" 3) "What do you think about a member of the opposite sex spending the night when children are present?" 4) "My children don't want me to date. What do I do?" 5) "What do I say to my teenager when she tells me to get home early?" and 6) "What do I do when the kid answers the doorbell, sees me, and shuts the door in my face?"

Most formerly married people are frightened about AIDS, VD, and other sexually-transmitted diseases: 1) "I would like to have sex but I'm deathly afraid of VD. How can I be sure to avoid getting a disease?" 2) "How do I find out if the person may be infected with AIDS before we have sex?" and 3) "What is herpes? Is it really dangerous?"

Formerly married people have many understandable concerns about sexuality. These questions reflect only a few of their anxieties. Dorothy reflected the emotional impact of sexuality, reporting, "I became extremely depressed last week when I realized I was 40 years old, divorced, and might never get laid again!"

Take It One Stage At A Time

I've had a conflict about having sexual relations while I am single. One part of me says that sex is important to my personal growth, and the other part says that I feel guilty having sex with a woman I'm not married to. What do I do?

— Tom

On this part of the climb up the mountain you'll want to find your own pathway. Each of us has an individual morality that will largely determine our direction. Because this area requires an effort not only to climb, but also to find your way, you may feel more hesitant and less confident. Take your time and make sure the path you choose really suits you. Of course, you can change paths if one is not appropriate. But some people have paid a tremendous price — emotionally and physically — because they experimented with behavior that was not really compatible with their own values.

There are three stages in this rebuilding block. Each of the stages of sexuality affects us personally a great deal as we go through the adjustment process.

You had an available sexual relationship for all those years that you were married. Suddenly, your love relationship is not available. You are faced with all of the emotional and social adjustments of ending a love relationship, including what to do with your sexual desires.

"Not Tonight, Thanks"

The first step of the process, while you are in deep grief, is a *lack of interest* in sex, or maybe a complete inability to perform sexually. Women tend to be completely uninterested in sex, men often are impotent. Just when you are feeling a great deal of emotional pain, the fact that you are uninterested or unable to perform sexually adds to the pain. Many people come to me saying, "I was already hurting so much, and now I find that I can't perform sexually. It feels like hitting rock bottom." When they learn that it is perfectly normal and natural to be uninterested in sex while in deep grief, they feel greatly relieved.

Honk If You're . . .

"I became so horny after my separation that I called my friend asking for suggestions of what I could do. Having sex with someone I was not married to was out of the question for me.

— Raquel

Somewhere along the divorce process, perhaps near the end of the Anger rebuilding block, you get through this stage of not being able to perform sexually. At that point, you will probably go to the other extreme and reach the *horny* stage. Your sexual desires are greater than you have ever known in your whole life. It is almost frightening because you feel unable to control the sexual desires. Bonnie described this stage as "delicious torture." Because the needs and desires of this stage are so overwhelming, it is important to understand the feelings and attitudes as much as possible.

Among the many feelings present in the horny stage is a need to prove that you are okay, personally and sexually. It is as though you are trying to solve not only your sexual problems but all of the other rebuilding blocks as well, using sex as the method. Your behavior at the horny stage may be somewhat compulsive because of this. You are trying to overcome loneliness, to feel lovable again, to improve your self-concept, to work through some anger, to develop friendships — and all of these things are concentrated in the sexual drive. It is as though your body is trying to heal itself through sexual expression alone.

One-night stands are a popular way that people try to solve this horny stage. We see this portrayed in books and movies about divorce. The need to go out and "prove that you are okay" may be so great that you will do something sexually that you had not ever done before.

Another important understanding about the horny stage is that there is a great need for touching during this stage. As you go through the divorce process, you will probably experience a heightened need to be physically touched. Touch has remarkable, healing qualities. Depending upon the warmth and closeness of your relationship, you likely received much physical touching in your marriage. Suddenly that touching is not there anymore. Many people will try to meet their need for physical touching with sex, not realizing that there is a very real difference between physical touching and sexual touching. Although the two are entirely different, you can resolve much of your need for sexual contact by getting the physical touching that you need.

You can resolve the needs of the horny stage by methods other than direct sexual contact. If you understand that a part of the compulsive drive behind the horny stage is to prove that you are okay, and to feel good about yourself again, then you can work directly on that. Building your identity and self-confidence, and understanding that you are lovable can overcome the loneliness and take away some of the pressures of the horny stage. And if you can reach your quota of hugs, this will also take away some of the pressures. Together, these steps may go a long way toward resolving your needs at this difficult time.

The stereotype about the divorced person being sexually an "easy mark" results from the horny stage. During this period, the divorced person is an easy mark. The sexual drive is tremendous. Many people going through the divorce process have sexual relationships somewhat promiscuously. Not a recommended practice in the age of AIDS.

Getting Back to Normal

*Sex in our marriage was not good. We separated and experienced
sexual relationships with other people. Then when we came together
again, we were surprised that sex with each other was good. It seemed
to free us to be apart and to be with others.*

— Mike and Jane

Eventually you will overcome the horny stage and get into the
third stage of post-divorce sexuality in which your *normal sex drive*
resumes. (There is, of course, a great deal of variation in sex drive
from one person to another.) Because the horny stage is so compulsive and so controlling, people often find it a relief to be back to their
normal sexual desires.

Not everybody going through the divorce process goes through
these three stages of sexuality. Some people do not go into the
celibate stage of being uninterested in sex, and some do not experience the horny stage. However, the stages are very common
occurrences which need to be recognized.

During the early stages of sexuality you are doing what you
should do; then you go through a stage of doing what you *want* to do.
Most people going through the divorce process experience the evolution of becoming free sexually in the sense that they are suddenly
aware of who they are and what their sexual nature is. This is another
beautiful part of the divorce process.

Many people were sexually monogamous in marriage because
that is what they believed they *should* be. Then when they go through
the horny stage, they may have many sexual relationships.

Finally, they decide to be monogamous again because this is
what they want to be. Consider the impact of this process upon future
love relationships. The need for sexual experience outside of a committed relationship is greatly diminished when one arrives at this
third stage. As long as you are in the *should* stage sexually, there is
always the temptation to do what you *should not* do. But when you
reach this third stage, doing what you want to do and expressing
who you really are, the temptation for sex outside a love relationship
is greatly diminished.

There's More to Life

I've agreed with everything you have said until now, but when you state that experiencing sexual relationships while single can be a personal growth experience, I have to strongly disagree. Sex is sacred, and should occur only between two people in a sacred marriage.

— Father John

We have blown sex out of proportion in our society, perhaps because we hid it and denied it for so long. With so much emphasis on sex in the last few decades, it appears to have lost some of its reality. Advertising is full of sex in order to sell products. We revere youth and the supposed beauty, aliveness, and sexuality of youth. With such a daily overdose in the media, it is tough to keep a proper perspective on sexuality when it comes to love relationships and marriage.

Usually missing from popular presentations is the spiritual dimension of human sexuality. Sex is one way of transcending our normal means of expressing ourselves, and it allows us to show our love and concern for another person in a very special and positive way. Sex can be a method of transporting oneself to levels beyond everyday, to become something greater than what one normally is. But this spiritual dimension that is present in sexuality is also present in overcoming anger, in our ability to communicate, in learning to like another person, and in learning to accept and deal with all of the human emotions. Sexuality, when placed in perspective, may be seen as only one of the many beautiful things that occur in our expression of concern for other people.

Our society has traditionally placed extreme emphasis on having a sexual relationship only with the person to whom we are married. The messages are mixed and quite confusing. Many divorced people are amazed to learn that they can have very enjoyable and beautiful sex without being in love with the person. Others feel a great amount of guilt if they have sexual relationships outside of marriage. A number adopt a morality that is concerned only with not catching a disease and not becoming pregnant.

Healthy divorce adjustment requires that we grow beyond an undue emphasis on sex and arrive at the point where we can understand the beauty of our sexuality as a special way of sharing and communicating with another person. A personal morality which includes sexuality as an expression of your individuality and your uniqueness, and which is concerned with the needs and well-being of your sexual partner(s), is socially responsible, self-actualized, ...and human.

To be specific, each person has to develop a personal and individual sexual morality appropriate for her or his own values, personality, background, attitudes, and experiences. Many people will choose to have no sexual relationships outside of marriage, and this may be appropriate for them. Others may find sexual experiences an appropriate way of resolving the horny stage and a way of healing themselves after ending the love relationship.

I have found that most divorced people are more comfortable having only one sexual relationship at a time, and this can be a very positive decision for a person to make. The evidence seems pretty clear that most divorced people must have an emotional relationship to support a sexual relationship. When people have communication, trust, understanding, and respect for each other, they are comfortable having a sexual relationship. If you are able to reach this level of self-actualization in your sexual relationships, I believe you will find less need to have relationships outside of marriage if you remarry in the future.

Can We Talk About It? Open Communication About Sex
Let's now look at some of the other adjustment problems that you may experience as you end a love relationship and enter the formerly married subculture. I frequently hear complaints, especially from women, that all the opposite sex is interested in is going to bed with them. When I go to social gatherings, that is the topic of most discussions. Yet very few formerly married people are genuinely able to enjoy cheap and casual sex that has a lot of elements of using. There are, unfortunately, many people in our society who have not developed ways of interacting with the opposite sex beyond the sexual area. It can be and often is the easiest avenue open for contact and, after all, is one where the potential payoff is great. Nevertheless,

there are many aspects of interaction other than sexual, and your life will be so much richer if you fully develop your range of choices. For example, in the previous chapter we looked at developing friendships with the opposite sex that are non-romantic and non-sexual.

It is interesting that, on the questionnaires in my classes asking people what they would like to talk about, the number two choice (after relationships) differs between men and women. The second choice for women is sexuality in almost all classes, and the second choice for men is love in almost all classes. Not only does this break up the stereotype, but in class it is very common for women to be much more comfortable talking about sexuality than men are. After one sexuality class, Burt confided to me that he went home and was unable to go to sleep because he was so shocked by how freely the women in the class talked about sexuality.

I believe that openness is a very healthy response style. (You'll recall our discussion in Chapter Thirteen, dealing with dropping our masks and being more open in our communication.) Sexuality used to be such a sacred cow that it was impossible for people to talk and communicate about it. We were thus prevented from understanding and dealing with our sexuality. Now because of the openness, we are able to understand and develop our sexual feelings just as we understand and develop all of the other human emotions we feel.

The openness in sexual matters allows us another avenue that is very freeing. When you are dating in the formerly married society, you can discuss sexual concerns openly and early in the relationship, minimizing all of the little games that go on concerning, "Are we going to bed or not?" Many of the dating relationships that you have will never include sexual intimacy; it will simply not be appropriate. By discussing this and getting it out in the open, it frees you to allow the relationship to develop more naturally and normally, free of the games that go along with not knowing where you stand sexually with the other person.

If you are early in the rebuilding process, and the idea of having sexual relationships is extremely frightening, you can share this with the other person. You can say, "I really need to get out and be with a friend, but anything beyond friendship is more than I can stand emotionally at this point." You will be surprised at the favorable response from others after you have shared yourself openly like this. Most will understand and accept you because they have been through the divorce process and have experienced some of the same feelings.

Without Using Each Other

The many desperate, lonely people introduce another problem to the formerly married subculture. They make the whole problem of sexuality even more difficult because these people are basically looking for somebody to use. If you are a kind and caring person, seeing all of the needy people around you may tempt you to help them meet their needs, some of which may be sexual.

The great deal of loneliness and neediness out in the formerly married subculture causes special adjustment problems for those of us who are caught in the *compassion trap* — the need to nurture and give to others in response to their apparent needs. If you tend to be that way, you will have to be somewhat selfish and learn that there is no way you can meet the needs of all those who are desperate and lonely. You must meet your own needs and take care of yourself first, and do so without using other people or allowing others to use you. Do everything you can to feel good about yourself and to grow within yourself so you can become as complete and whole as possible, and can overcome your own loneliness and neediness. That will provide you a solid foundation for future relationships, and for helping others who are in genuine need.

Roles and Rules: Who Does What to Whom?

Another big problem for many people entering the formerly married subculture is the question of rules. You may feel as though you are a bewildered teenager, not exactly understanding and knowing how to behave. There has been a great deal of change in our society regarding sexual behavior and attitudes. Most of this change is a freeing from set rules of conduct prescribed by the courting game into a freedom to be ourselves. Freedom to be yourself is very difficult if you do not know who "yourself" is. Thus the problem is not really so much that the rules have changed, as it is that certain behavior was expected before. Now you need to find your way, and follow your own unique style as you go. To become open and honest with who you are, and to express that unique individuality as much as possible, will be much more difficult than just following the established rules of dating that were prevalent before.

Another problem results from the fact that sex roles are changing, and women are initiators in everything much more than before. Women quite frequently now are expected to initiate sexual behavior, and this is all very upsetting for many people of both sexes. Women in class during the sexuality discussion ask, "How do men feel about women being the initiators?" The typical male response is that they find it very freeing to have the woman be the initiator. They have had to deal with all the fears of rejection that have been inherent in asking and initiating with women. They say that it feels good to have women now deal with the risk of being turned down, and that they are free from the burden of being the initiator all the time.

While men in the seminars talk about "how good it feels" to have women take the lead, women report that in the real world outside of the seminars, many men are threatened by assertive women. Although men say they like to be asked out, often they are uncomfortable when the actual situation arises. It appears that *intellectually* men like women to initiate, but *emotionally* men have more difficulty handling sexually assertive women.

The problem is not limited to males. Females report confusion also. The woman may say she would like to ask the man out, but when the time comes the old morality takes over and the woman never gets around to asking. For many women there is a double adjustment process happening — adjustment to becoming single, and adjustment in finding identity as a woman. It is not easy to question the old roles and try out new behavior when you are rebuilding after the loss of a relationship. On the other hand, it is an appropriate time to do it. Everything else in your life is changing. Why not try out some changes in sex roles at the same time?

Many of the new roles affect the interaction between sexes

profoundly. Many women report they like the freedom of paying their own way on a date, since this frees them from the expectation of sex in return for dinner. Some women enjoy responding to sexism by telling the male he has "a nice ass." Some even go so far as to let men know how it feels to be used sexually, by taking them to bed, then getting up, putting on their clothes, and leaving.

It appears that the end result of the changing sex roles will be more equality between the sexes and more freedom for individuals to be themselves. But we see the pendulum of social mores swing back and forth. In the 60s and 70s and early 80s, the movement was strongly toward sexual freedom and gender equality. As we begin the 90s, more traditional values are re-emerging. It's not a smooth road, and the period of change causes much uncertainty and confusion. Now more than ever, perhaps, it is necessary to know yourself, to adopt values which are both self-fulfilling and respectful of others, and to act in accordance with those values.

Let's Be Careful Out There

A couple of words about safe sex: *practice it!*

Safe sex is really important today. A decade or so ago, the fear of Herpes started to affect the sexual behavior of our society. AIDS (acquired immunodeficiency syndrome), virtually unknown then, now has made a major impact upon sexual behavior around the world. The number of people in all walks of life who are dying from AIDS appears likely to increase. Science and medicine will continue to seek ways to deal with the disease, but in the meantime you and I will have to take responsibility for preventing AIDS — along with Herpes, Hepatitus B, and other sexually transmitted diseases — by adopting safe sex practices. Many are choosing to be much more selective and/or to curtail their sexual activity.

One woman told me her dilemma: She felt that to be responsible she needed to share with a sexual partner before sex that she had genital Herpes. She read the manuals on how to share this information, but found them lacking in one major respect. They failed to tell her that some males you share this information with will become impotent. At least that's what she experienced.

Impact Publishers Statement on Safe Sex

Impact Publishers, Inc. recognizes safe and healthy approaches to sexual expression as one of the principal health and social issues of our time. We offer the following statement for your serious consideration:

• Sexual expression is a basic, normal, positive, intensely personal and highly satisfying human activity. Although sexual practices are often publicly regulated by social mores, religious values, and law, individuals and couples decide privately whether or not to follow such regulations.

• Responsible sexual practice requires good information, including knowledge of the fundamentals of human sexuality, responsible family planning, contraceptive choices, and protection against sexually transmitted diseases.

• Sexually transmitted diseases, such as Acquired Immune Deficiency Syndrome (AIDS), various forms of Herpes, Hepatitis B, and the several Veneral Diseases, are serious and widespread public health problems, both in the United States and throughout the populated world.

• "Safe sex" — minimizing the risks of sexually transmitted diseases — includes at minimum the following:
  - an absolutely certain, long-term, exclusively monogamous relationship, *or ALL of the following*:
  - regular periodic physical examinations;
  - conscientious unfailing use of condoms (preferably with spermicides) during intercourse;
  - awareness and avoidance of common risk factors in STD's (e.g., intravenous drug use, high-risk populations);
  - honest and open discussion of sexual habits and preferences with potential partners;
  - infrequent changing of partners.

• Each individual — married or single — has the right to freedom of choice in sexual expression, so long as the practice involves consenting adults and consciously avoids physical or psychological harm to any person.

• No one is obligated to have a sexual relationship with another person — including a marriage partner — unless he or she wishes to do so.

• The following AIDS facts are reproduced from the brochure, *Understanding AIDS: A Message from the Surgeon General,* released in 1988 by C. Everett Koop, M.D., then Surgeon General of the United States:

- *Who you are has nothing to do with whether you are in danger of being infected with the AIDS virus. What matters is what you do.*

- *There are two main ways you can get AIDS. First, you can become infected by having sex — oral, anal, or vaginal — with someone who is infected with the AIDS virus. Second, you can be infected by sharing drug needles and syringes with an infected person.*

- *Your chances of coming into contact with the virus increase with the number of sex partners you have.*

- *You won't get AIDS through everyday contact...a mosquito bite...saliva, sweat, tears, urine, or a bowel movement...a kiss...clothes, a telephone, or from a toilet seat.*

- *A person can be infected with the AIDS virus without showing any symptoms at all.*

- *The AIDS virus may live in the human body for years before actual symptoms appear.*

- *Condoms are the best preventative measure against AIDS besides not having sex and practicing safe behavior.*

- *RISKY BEHAVIOR*
    Sharing drug needles and syringes.
    Anal sex, with or without a condom.
    Vaginal or oral sex with someone who shoots drugs or engages in anal sex.
    Sex with someone you don't know well (a pickup or prostitute) or with someone you know has several sex partners.
    Unprotected sex (without a condom) with an infected person.

- *SAFE BEHAVIOR*
    Not having sex.
    Sex with one mutually faithful, uninfected partner.
    Not shooting drugs.

- *If you know someone well enough to have sex, then you should be able to talk about AIDS. If someone is unwilling to talk, you shouldn't have sex.*

We need to communicate with potential sexual partners the need for safe sex practices even if it is difficult to do so. We need to take control of our lives around the area of sexuality and make careful loving choices. Never was the old adage, "better to be safe than sorry," more appropriate.

My publisher has prepared the statement on the preceding pages regarding sensible safe sex. I encourage you to read it and to think about how it may apply to your life.

Sex and the Formerly-Married

Is the area of sexuality really so very different now, when you are re-entering the ranks of single persons, than it was when you were single before marriage? It is more open, and allows for more individual and unique expression of ourselves, rather than simply following the rules of the courting system. What you must learn in order to function in the formerly-married subculture is to find yourself, express yourself, communicate, and relate with others without losing your identity. In short, simply learn to be yourself in your interactions with others, including your sexual contacts. Sexuality — as it always has been — is an important part of learning to be and to express yourself.

Children and Sex

Children of divorce also have the rebuilding block of sexuality to deal with. When their parents' relationship ends, where do children find role models for relationships, sexuality, becoming an adult man or woman and a mature person?

It is often confusing for children to see their parents get involved in another love relationship. Somehow children sense that it may include sex. (I think kids know more about which parents are going to bed and which are not than the parents believe!) And if the parents are in the horny stage and sending out all of the sexual vibrations which accompany that stage, what do the children do with that? How do they handle this new behavior in their parents?

Communication may sound like an old answer, but it is critically important at this point. When parents talk with their children *frankly* and openly about sexuality, it is very helpful for the kids and for the parents. Although there is much anxiety and insecurity in the children's lives, that very turmoil can be the beginning of learning. Children may well gain a far deeper understanding of sexuality — including their own — as their parents go through this stage of rebuilding.

Children can find role models in relatives, grandparents, and their parents' male and female friends. As one teenager stated to me, "It seems I've got more models around now than I ever had before!"

"How Are You Doing?"

We have covered a lot of ground in this chapter, and there is much we have not explored. Sex is often a stumbling block for the divorced person, so be sure you have dealt thoroughly with these issues before you go on. Here are some trail markers for assessing your progress.

1. *I am comfortable going out with potential love partners.*
2. *I know and can explain my present moral attitudes and values.*
3. *I feel capable of having a deep and meaningful sexual relationship if it were appropriate.*
4. *I would feel comfortable being intimate with another love partner.*
5. *My sexual behavior is consistent with my morality.*
6. *I am satisfied with my present dating situation.*
7. *I am behaving morally the way I would like to have my children behave .*
8. *I believe that my personal sexuality expresses my individual and unique morality.*
9. *I feel satisfied with the way I am meeting my sexual needs.*
10. *I take responsibility for my interaction with others.*
11. *I have learned that male and female sexual attitudes and values may be more alike than different.*
12. *I feel comfortable being with a member of the opposite sex.*
13. *I am secure enough to behave the way I want even if it does not conform to the expectations of others.*
14. *I am not letting the compulsive needs of the horny stage control my behavior.*

15. *I am solving the neediness of the horny stage in a manner that is acceptable to me.*

16. *I understand and accept that many people will have no desire and may be unable to perform sexually while in deep grief.*

17. *I am getting my "quota" of hugs every week.*

SINGLENESS
"You Mean It's Okay?"

In the singleness stage, you emphasize investment in your own personal growth rather than in other relationships. A period of singleness enables you to build confidence in yourself so you can experience and enjoy being single as an acceptable alternative lifestyle, not as a time to be lonely. It is easy, however, to become stuck in this rebuilding block as a means of avoiding another intimate love relationship.

Chapter 18

I've become aware that living as a single person is an affirmation of strength and self — not an embarrassing admission of failure. I'm more relaxed in the company of others — I'm no longer wasting emotional energy being a social chameleon. Post-marital guilt, self-doubts, and questions like "Will I ever love again?" are greatly diminished. I am happy as a single person — something I had not thought possible before.   *— Larry*

Have you ever been on a hike when a member of the hiking party decided to walk on alone instead of staying with the group? Sometimes people want and need to be by themselves, with their own thoughts, and to enjoy the view alone.

You'll notice a number of people walking by themselves during this part of the climb. They've gained enough confidence in their climbing ability that they choose to walk at their own pace, rather than following the crowd. They choose time to be alone as a way of investing in themselves. I call it the *singleness stage*.

Were You Ever Really Single Before?

Many people never learned to be single persons before they married. They went from parental homes to marriage homes, never even considered that one could be happy living as a single person, and never questioned the myth that one married and lived happily ever after.

Mona lived with her parents until she married Joe. She went from pleasing one man, her father, to pleasing another man, her husband. When Joe first talked about leaving, she clung to him because the thought of living alone was terrifying. She had never learned to please herself. She had always been a dependent person, and now the thought of being independent, although challenging, was frightening to her. She was embarrassed because it really sounded silly to her that a woman of 25 did not know her own mind, or know what to do with her life.

Only gradually did she adjust to being alone. At first she searched for other relationships, something/someone to lean on. As she became more and more confident, she began doing more things for herself and enjoying it. She wallpapered a whole bedroom; sawed the boards and pounded the nails for a new patio fence; went to a movie by herself one afternoon while the kids were with Joe, and even enjoyed stumbling alone in the dark trying to find a seat. She invited the whole neighborhood in for a party. These activities left her feeling exhilarated, knowing that she did not need anyone. She became a good example of what it means to be an independent person.

Jim represents the male side of this same coin. He had been well cared for by his mother. The clothes were always washed and ironed, meals were on time, and even his room was kept clean. He could devote his time to school, school activities, and his job. When he entered college, he lived in a dorm. Again his meals were provided and he had a minimum of housekeeping chores. When he married Janet, she took over all the things his mother had always done. He felt independent and didn't realize how dependent he actually was. He found out when he left Janet. He was helpless in the kitchen, even in preparing the simplest meal. He had very little understanding of how to wash his clothes, and ended up with pink underwear when he put them in the wash with his red socks! You can pay for car maintenance, but it is difficult — and very expensive — to hire a full-time cook and housekeeper.

Gradually Jim's self-prepared meals improved. Finally he got brave enough to invite a female friend to his home to eat, and she was delighted with the meal he prepared. His clothes began to look more cared for. He was very pleased and proud when he learned to iron his own shirts! Learning to care for himself was like growing up — and each accomplishment gave him a feeling of success and achievement.

"Me and My Shadow"

But the singleness I am talking about is much more than learning to do the tasks that someone else has done for you. It is a whole way of life. Dating and love relationships are a good example. A typical comment from a recently-separated person might be, "I'll never make it as a single person; I need another love relationship." During the singleness stage, the same person might say, "Why get remarried? I can come and go as I please. I can eat whenever I feel like it. I don't have to adjust my daily living habits to another person. Being single sure feels good!"

Before the singleness stage, one may be looking for the "lost half." But during this stage one reaches the point of comfort in going out alone. No longer is a "date" necessary to avoid embarrassment or a feeling of failure. The quality of relationships improves: now you're choosing the person you go out with, rather than taking whoever seems available. And the whole evening out may be spent *sharing* rather than *needing*. Other persons may be encountered and enjoyed for who they are, rather than as potential lifetime companions.

Single and Loving It

One of the homework assignments in the divorce seminars has to do with developing new interests in the singleness stage. Many have spent their free, recreational time in the past doing what the spouse wanted or what they had learned to do with their parents.

The assignment now is simply to take the time to develop a new interest, or to pursue something you may have wanted to do for a long time. It might be to learn to play the guitar, to paint, to drive a car, or to play a new sport. Participants who take this homework seriously find many new activities that *they* really enjoy; they no longer settle for what someone else enjoyed.

Singleness is a time for being a responsible adult. Because the roles we act out in our relationships are so closely related to our internal attitudes and feelings, we change inside as we change our external roles. It is easier to do this in the singleness stage than when we are in permanent love relationships. A neutral environment facilitates both internal and external changes. The singleness stage is a key period to make the internal changes in attitudes and feelings necessary for personal growth.

"I'm Glad To Be Single Again . . . Or Am I?"

Not everything is rosy in the singleness stage, of course. Research shows that single people may still not fare as well economically. Single persons are passed over for promotions, looked upon as fair game romantically and sexually. Despite recent laws prohibiting sexual harassment, single women in particular may be pressured in the workplace, expected to trade sexual "favors" for promotions and other opportunities. The tax laws favor married couples, who may file income tax jointly. Big changes have been made in obtaining credit for single people; nevertheless, there remain many forms of economic discrimination against singles.

There are other situations that make single people feel uncomfortable. Alexa complained about her child's Sunday School class. When the teacher asked the children to draw pictures of their families, Alexa's son drew a picture of himself, his sister, and his mother — which was his family. The teacher made him draw a picture of a man in the family because, "We all know that a family consists of both a father and a mother!" Alexa expressed her negative feelings by talking directly with the minister of the church.

Ursula went to church on Mother's Day and the sermon was about marital love. Although she was a mother, she felt completely left out of the sermon. It was a depressing day in church for her. She wrote a letter to the minister explaining her feelings.

Schools are often an irritating problem when you are a single parent. The PTA chairperson calls and asks that Johnny's parents run the dart show. The single-parent father explains that he is single but would be willing to come alone. The chairperson informs him that it takes two to run the show and she will ask someone else to handle it. PTA meetings themselves are often couple-oriented; you can feel really single and alone when you attend without a partner.

You come alone to a parent-teacher conference, and the teacher informs you that "all of the *problem children* in the room have just one parent," and that's why she wanted to see you. Your child may not be getting "the parenting she needs," and perhaps that's why she is doing so poorly in her school work. What's more, your daughter is "so boy crazy for a sixth grader!" It is implied that if Mom had a "permanent" relationship with one man, Janie would have a better attitude toward males. You feel angry, vulnerable, and defenseless. What can you say?

You can develop some assertive responses for the most common put-downs and discriminatory acts. You can help to educate others, while maintaining your own integrity, by responding firmly. You'll feel better inside, too, rather than going away fuming!

Here's an example: in response to the teacher who insists Janie would be better off in a two-parent household, you might try something like this, "You're right — being a single parent isn't easy. In fact, in 1992 Vice President Dan Quayle called single mothers 'genuine heroes.' But Janie and I are doing fine these days, and I don't agree that her school performance is suffering because of my divorce. I'll be glad to work with you on special homework or tutoring or other efforts to improve her schoolwork. What suggestions do you have for her study habits? Will you give her extra assignments?"

That way, you're not accepting her put-down, or letting her blame your personal life for Janie's school problems. The responsibility for school work is focused back where it belongs — on teacher-student-parent cooperation, not on your love life.

Successfully Single

It often takes a great deal of inner security to handle the single-ness stage successfully. Much of the discussion in this chapter concerns the internal feelings present in the singleness stage. If you have worked your way through the prior rebuilding blocks, it is likely that you will be able to experience the peacefulness and calmness that occurs in the singleness stage. You may become slight-ly upset about the attitudes of others, but you'll be strong enough to handle them. Learn from the external prejudices and use them to become more secure in your own internal feelings.

Singleness can be one of the most productive stages you go through in the climb, in the sense that the old wounds can really be healed. Dealing with the external discrimination may help you to become stronger inside.

One caution: Singleness is an easy stage in which to become stuck. If you have not worked through all of the leftovers concerning marriage and intimacy, you may use the singleness stage as a place to hide. It may sound like the singleness stage when you hear someone say, "I'll never marry again." But in many ways that is the opposite of genuine singleness. Fear of intimacy, avoidance of feel-ings, and opposition to marriage as though it were the worst institution in our society — all indicate that the person is *stuck*. The goal is to be free to *choose* singleness or remarriage, not to stay single forever.

Singleness has become an acceptable alternative in our society. When I was a child, a single person was looked upon in our com-munity as somewhat weird, one who just did not quite make it to the altar. It was patriotic to be married because, after all, the family was the cornerstone of society. Attitudes are changing; at a talk I gave on love relationships, one woman wanted to know why we had to keep talking about *relationships.* Was not it just as valid to talk about remaining single? Did we have to keep looking toward being in a relationship as the ideal? The fact that there are approximately a million divorces in the United States each year makes singleness more acceptable for many. The large number of formerly married people in our society has brought about many changes in attitudes toward singleness. Perhaps we are becoming more accepting of individual differences? Let's hope so!

Children and Singleness

Singleness is an important rebuilding block for children, too. They need to learn to be single, individual, independent-from-parents people before they marry for the first time. If children can see and understand the importance of singleness, it will give them a much better chance to develop successful love relationships in their futures.

Parenting is different during the singleness stage. In earlier stages parents frequently bend themselves out of shape trying to make sure they are lovable, datable, and okay in many other ways. The kids often suffer; their needs are put on the "back-burner." In the singleness stage, parents usually are more responsive to the needs of the kids. Susannah had been volunteering in the seminars because she "needed" to feel worthwhile by helping others. When she began to reach the singleness stage, she resigned as a volunteer because she wanted to spend more time with her children. Parents in the singleness stage have begun to rise above their own emotional needs.

How Are You Doing?

At this point, the climb up the mountain has the big advantage of a view above the timberline. You can see forever. And the singleness stage is definitely above the timberline. You can see the real world much better. You can know yourself much better. You understand people, and your interactions with people, much better. Your viewpoint of life is much broader. Down in the plains before the crisis occurred, your vision was limited. Now you see and understand concepts never before understood. At the singleness stage, we're almost to the top. Let's hurry and see the view from the peak!

Here are some items to check yourself with before the final climb.

1. *I am comfortable being single.*
2. *I can be happy as a single person.*
3. *I am comfortable going to social events as a single person.*

4. *I see being single as an acceptable alternative lifestyle.*
5. *I am becoming a whole person rather than a half-person looking for my other lost half.*
6. *I am spending time investing in my own personal growth rather than looking for another love relationship.*
7. *I can look at my friends as people I want to be with rather than as potential love partners.*
8. *If I have children and family, I can spend time enjoying being with them rather than begrudging the time they take from my personal life.*
9. *I have found internal peace and contentment as a single person.*

PURPOSE
"I Have Goals for the Future Now"

Recently separated people tend to be living in the past, and tend to be very dependent upon others. After they have worked through the divorce process, they begin to live more in the present and to be less dependent upon others. Now you can plan for your future as an independent person, with or without a new love relationship.

Chapter 19

When I started this divorce seminar I dreamed I was driving a car that went off a mountain road and I was balancing on the edge of a cliff, too scared to move. When I completed this divorce seminar, I dreamed I was in a big, dark pit with my car but there was a cement ramp at the end of the pit where I could drive my car out. — Bob

Take a look back down the trail. Hasn't this been a rewarding climb? Our highest priority, when we were back in the divorce pits at the bottom of the mountain, was to survive. We weren't thinking about setting any goals for the future. We were getting along from hour to hour, day to day.

Things have changed a lot as we've "gained altitude"! It was hard work climbing the divorce process trail, but now that you're almost at the top, you have some perspective. You can look back at your past to see how you got to where you are today. You can look at your present situation and recognize how much you have accomplished. You can look at your future, and know that you can determine for yourself who you will become.

Looking at Your Past, Present, and Future Life

The trauma of divorce motivates us to take a good hard look at our lives. We tend to go back into the past and dwell a great deal upon the things that we would have done differently if we could live our lives over again. We tend to be so engrossed in the present scene that we are unable to think about the future.

I suggest that it is time for you to get out of some of the past thinking and the present pain and to start thinking about goals and decisions for the future.

I know that people in a great deal of emotional pain cannot make plans and set goals for the future, and if you are still in a great deal of emotional pain, then you may find it difficult to read this chapter which has to do with setting goals. If you've read this book too fast and haven't allowed all of the emotional learning to take place, then you may need to set aside this chapter for now, take some time to go back over the previous material, and do the emotional learning that you need to do.

My research shows that people who have recently separated have very low scores in the *Tennessee Self Concept Scale*. Other research that I've conducted using the *Personality Orientation Inventory* indicated that recently separated people, and especially dumpees, have a great deal of "living in the past" in their thinking and attitudes. People in the divorce pits have very little hope and goals for the future. They feel they have entered Dante's *Inferno*, where the words above the gates read, "All Hope abandon, ye who enter here."

But chances are, if you have worked your way carefully through each of the preceding chapters, that you are ready to get on with your life. In this chapter, you'll be building on your successful climb up the mountain and doing some goal setting for your future.

Let's get started!

Your Lifeline: An Exercise in Setting Goals

I have an experiential exercise for you that will help you to look at your past, your present and your future life: I want you to draw your own "Lifeline." This lifeline is a graphic "time line," drawn across a sheet paper from left to right, showing the ups and downs of your life. (Illustrated on the following page is an example of one person's lifeline, to give you an idea of how the finished work might look.)

Keep in mind that this project is only for yourself; it is *not* an art project to be graded! Erase and/or start over as you need to, so that the final product is realistic and valuable *for you*. Here's a step-by-step guide to the process:

• The first step is to find as big a piece of clean paper as you can find. The bigger it is, the more freedom it gives you to draw your lifeline. A few feet of butcher paper is ideal.

• Next, think about your present age and then think about how long you expect to live. Most people, when they think about it, will have a feeling about how old they are going to be when they die. They may feel they are going to live to be very old, or they may feel they are going to die young. Get in touch with this feeling and see what kind of a life expectancy you have for yourself. Then think about your present age, what percent of your life you've already lived, and what percent of your life you've got left to live. For example, if you feel that you may live to be 70 years old and you are presently 35 years old, then you have lived half your expected life.

• Take your clean sheet of paper and draw a vertical line that will signify to the left of the line how much life you've already lived and to the right of the line how much you've got left to live. If you've lived half of your life, the line would be in the middle. If you've lived a third of your life, the line would be a third of the way across the paper. Think about how many years you've probably got left to live compared to how many years you've already lived. I wonder what you are going to do with the remaining years of your life?

• Think about whether your life has been basically happy or basically unhappy so far. Draw another line horizontally on the paper reflecting your basic level of happiness. If you have been basically unhappy all your life, draw the line lower down on the page. Now you are ready to start drawing your lifeline.

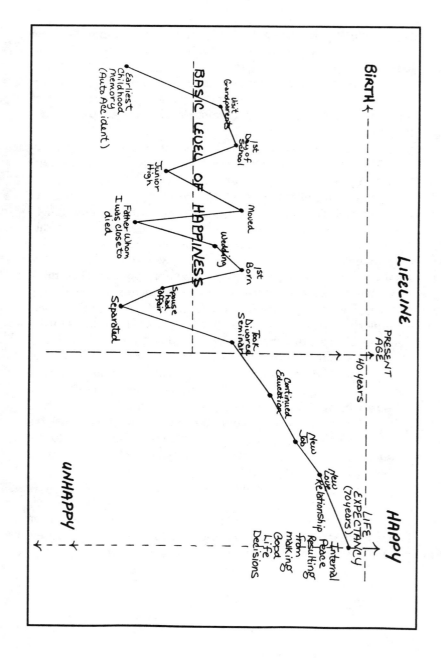

Your Lifeline: The Past:

- I want you to start your lifeline by trying to remember the earliest childhood memory that you have. Think about this early childhood memory for a little bit. It may tell you a great deal about yourself and about the rest of your life. Then start your lifeline reflecting on the happiness and unhappiness of this earliest childhood memory. The more unhappy this earliest memory was, the lower you start on the page.

- Next, think through the important things you can remember in your early childhood. Identify them in your mind and mark them on your lifeline. If there was an extremely happy event that you remember, mark that on your lifeline, putting it higher on the paper. If there were extremely unhappy things such as loss of somebody in your family through death, mark that as something more unhappy. Keep working through your life as you enter grade school, junior high, high school, and keep marking the important milestones that stand out in your memory. Think of doing this lifeline as though you were telling a story to a friend and you were to tell them about the important things that have happened to you in your life. Include your marriage, and any children that you may have.

Your Lifeline: The Present

- Now think about your divorce, and your present emotional situation. Many people who have recently separated will draw their lifelines with the divorce crisis as the lowest point in their lives. This kind of leaves you at a bad place in your lifeline, but remember that you still have all of the future left to work on it, and to improve yourself to become the kind of person you would like to be. Draw your lifeline to show your level of happiness at your divorce and since.

Your Lifeline: The Near Future

• Now you have passed the present, and it's time to start thinking about the future. Make some short-term goals of what you are going to be doing next month, the next three months, the next six months. Predict what you are going to be doing, and how you are going to be feeling, in your life. Is it going to be a happier or less happy time than the present? Do you still have some pain to work through, such as the trauma of the final hearing of the divorce decree, a property settlement, a poor financial condition with many financial obligations and very low income? Draw the next few months on your lilfeline as realistically as possible.

Your Lifeline: The Long-Term Future

• Start making longer term goals. Ask yourself, "What am I going to be doing a year from now, five years from now? What am I going to be like in my old age? Is my face going to reflect the happiness that I've known in my life, or is my face going to reflect sadness, bitterness, anger, or negative feelings of some sort? How will retirement affect me? Will I be ready for retirement? Will I be able to handle the adjustment of not working any more? Have I taken care of my financial needs in old age? How do I feel about major illnesses occurring in my future life? Do I feel as though I have developed a healthy life style that will prevent me from having major illnesses? Is my life full of negative feelings that are going to be turned into physical illness as I become older?"

You have planted a life into a seed-bed and you're going to grow and mature and harvest the crop. What kind of crop are you going to harvest with your life? Are you going to look back and say, "I've lived the type of life that I liked to live and I am ready to die." Or are you going to look back and say, "Life has somehow or other passed me by. I'm not ready to die yet."

What about the person you will be living with? Is it important for you to have another love relationship? To share your life with somebody else as you become old? Or would you like to live as a single person and enjoy all of the freedom of being single?

What is important to you in your life? Is it important to make money, to become famous, to have good health, to be successful? And what is success to you? What does it mean? What would you do with your life to make it successful? Will you be comfortable with your answers to these questions: "What contributions will I be remembered for?" "Will I leave the world a better place?"

Are you becoming the type of person that you'd like to be? When are you going to start changing and becoming that person? Today, next week, next month? Or are you never going to get around to being the person you want to be? Today would be a good time to start.

Today is the first day of the rest of your life.

Kids Need Goals Too!

Children feel very confused when their parents are divorcing. While the parents are going through their own pain in the divorce process, the needs of the children are often overlooked. They have no idea where they are going, what's going to happen to them, how they'll feel tomorrow. They often feel lost, without any goals or direction.

Children have their own stumbling blocks to change into rebuilding blocks (see Appendix A). If they are given a chance to work through the process themselves, they can begin to develop goals for themselves and for their new family structure. If not, they probably feel they are going nowhere.

A structured personal or group growth program, such as the Children of Divorce workshop described in the Appendix, can be very valuable for children at this time. Such experiences develop children's skills for dealing with their parents' pain, and for meeting their own needs.

Divorce is an uncertain and unstable time for kids. It's particularly important that we help them to maintain hope for the future, and that we give them opportunities to develop their own goals.

How Are You Doing?

Now that you've thought about your life and your future, and completed your lifeline chart, take a few moments to assess your progress before you go on to the mountain top. I know it's tempting to sprint to the top when you're this close, but after all your work to get this far, it's worth maintaining a steady pace. Answer these few questions, then go on to the top-of-the-mountain chapter:

1. *I have worked my way through each of the rebuilding blocks on the climb up the mountain.*
2. *I have thought about my life and drawn a lifeline chart.*
3. *I have set some achievable goals for my future, and have a tentative plan for reaching them.*
4. *I have gone back over the blocks which were problems for me, and feel I've dealt with the issues.*
5. *I'm ready to accept the joys and responsibilities that Freedom can bring!*

FREEDOM
From Chrysalis to Butterfly

By working through the rebuilding blocks, you can build more meaningful relationships in your future. You will have the freedom to choose to be free and happy either as a single person or in another love relationship. Freedom is being able to be fully yourself.

Chapter 20

I felt many times in my marriage that I was trapped in a prison of love. It was hard to be myself when there were so many demands and expectations placed upon me. When I first separated I felt even worse. But now I have found that I can fly. I can be me. I feel as if I left the chrysalis and have become a butterfly. I feel so free. — Alice

Wow! Would you look at that view from here on top of the mountain!

After this page, I want you to stop reading for a moment and take time to go on a fantasy trip. Imagine being on top of a mountain with a view of other peaks and valleys below. Smell the pine trees; let the clear, bright high-altitude sun warm your skin. Notice the clouds lower than you are, and feel the cool breeze blowing off the snow glaciers. Notice how far away the horizon is out over the plains, and how far you can see.

Think back about the climb. What was the most enjoyable and interesting portion for you? What was the most difficult part? The most painful? Can you identify the many changes that have taken place within you? Have you really reached the top emotionally or are you only at the top in your mind? Think about how it feels at the top, having worked so hard in your climb of personal growth.

Take as much time as you want with this fantasy before you go on reading. When you have thought about your fantasy carefully, turn the page and continue reading.

How Far You Have Come!

On the singleness portion of the trail, I hope you found not only that it feels good to be single, but that it may have been the most productive lifestyle for you during the climb. Now it's time to think about relationships again. How did the process of working your way through these rebuilding blocks affect the way you deal with others? The way you react to loneliness, grief, rejection, guilt, anger, and love significantly determines how you handle your daily life and your interactions with those around you.

If you really work at the rebuilding process, overcoming each stumbling block — including the ones you've had a lot of trouble with — you'll be able to enter into another love relationship and make it more productive than the last one. You'll be prepared to meet your own needs, and the needs of your loved one(s), much better than in the past. Rebuilding not only helps you to survive the crisis, but it also enhances your future love relationships. That feels good!

A Word to the Widowed

Perhaps you were widowed and were satisfied with the happiness you felt in your last relationship. Research indicates that people who were widowed have remarriages which are more likely to last. Being widowed is a painful and very difficult adjustment process, and most of the rebuilding blocks are helpful to those who are going through that crisis. Many widowed persons, however, do not have to deal with one of the toughest parts of the adjustment — a previous, unhappy love relationship.

The Air Is Pretty Thin Up Here

For many people, the climb is so difficult that they feel like quitting before reaching the top. I have heard countless people say, "I want to stop climbing and take a rest! I'm tired of growing." And many do stop along the way because they are tired, frightened, or feel unable to handle the changes. My response is the same as that I would offer to someone who gets tired on a hike: sit and rest, get your energy back, then keep on climbing. The view at the top is worth it.

I find support, hope, and a belief that you can make it are helpful. But it's up to you in the end. Probably the best evidence of the difficulty of the climb comes from the small percentage of people at the top. Do you have the self-discipline, desire, courage, and stamina to make it?

Now comes the "truth in packaging" disclaimer: I cannot promise that you will be happier, or wealthier, or more fulfilled if you complete the climb. I can assure you that there are fewer turkeys and more eagles at this altitude, but I cannot promise that you will find an eagle for yourself (except when you look in the mirror!). The plain hard fact is that you will not necessarily find another "just right" person with whom to create a lasting relationship. What you will find is that you like yourself better, you can enjoy being alone and single, and the people whom you meet up here will be pretty special — after all, they made this tough climb, too!

It is true that there are fewer persons here from which to choose. An awful lot of folks just did not make it this far — indeed, many are still at the base camp, playing social games, hiding behind emotional walls, and finding excuses not to undertake the climb. The lack of numbers here may make the process of finding new friends and potential lovers more difficult. But I have found that relationships with others at the top have such a higher quality that quantity is not so important. When you're really at the top, giving off those good vibrations, there are many people attracted to you. I don't think the top of the mountain is as lonely as parts of the trail were on the way up. And if you are still feeling lonely, maybe you haven't reached the top emotionally.

Take a Deep Breath...

You may get discouraged at times when you realize that the old patterns have crept back and you really haven't changed as much as you thought. Do you normally put on your right or left shoe first? Try to reverse your routine this next week and put on the other shoe first. I'll bet you forget and go back to the old way. It is difficult to make changes in your daily living habits, and even harder to make changes in your personality. Keep up your determination and you will make it. Don't get discouraged — it may come slowly!

You may greatly fear the unknown future. You're not alone! It may be learning to be single; it may be not knowing what to expect or what is expected of you. How do you feel the first time you drive or ride in a new city that is unfamiliar to you? Confused, lost, uncertain? How about the way you feel the first time you go to a singles party? There is a certain amount of comfort in the known. Your old relationship may look good even if it was like living in hell. I hope that if you go back to the old relationship, it will be for more positive reasons than fear of the unknown future!

Beyond Singleness

I've talked a great deal during the climb up the mountain about the importance of learning to be single. Let me get in a last word about the importance of relationships. We can become whole by emotionally working hard at becoming whole. But I believe there is a part of each of us that needs another person to help us become completely fulfilled. A love relationship is more than icing on the cake, but that analogy seems to fit: the cake is whole without icing, but ever so much sweeter with it! I think each of us needs another person to help us become completely fulfilled, and to make life sweeter!

Becoming Free

When you were in the pits of the crisis, you gave no thought to plans and goals for the future. Part of your grief was concerned with loss of future, since you had to give up the plans and goals you had in that love relationship. But when you came out of the pits, you began looking to the future and making plans again.

Ernie, a member of one of my seminars who worked in a hospital, told the group one evening, "It's like the process in the hospital psych wards. There's a crafts room where the patients spend time. When patients first are admitted, they have no energy to work on crafts. But when they begin to be really interested in crafts, this is a good indication that they're ready to be discharged. I felt ready to be discharged from the divorce pits when I started making plans for the future!"

My research has found that recently separated people, and especially dumpees, are very much "living in the past," thinking mostly about how it "used to be." Further along in the process, people stop living in the past and start living in the present, enjoying the sunsets. I hope by now you have stopped living in the past, and are living in the present and making plans for your own future.

Recently separated people, and again especially dumpees, are very dependent upon others, according to my research. As people grow further in the process, they gain more independence, and find a good balance between independence and dependence. Have you found a good balance between dependence and independence?

The Children of Freedom

Children need to work their way through the rebuilding blocks, and to learn the freedom to be themselves, free from all the unhealthy needs that control so many people. They need to be free to choose marriage. Quite frequently children of divorce say that they will not get married because they saw how devastating divorce was to their parents. Children need freedom of choice in what they will do with their lives, rather than to follow or contradict their parents' pattern.

All children are not the same, nor do they have the same needs. Although I have been generalizing a great deal about children, in reference to each of the rebuilding blocks, remember that each child is a unique human being, and that it is as important for them as it is for adults that they be respected and treated as such! Their differing needs depend upon age, sex, cultural background, number of children in the family, health, availability of extended family and/or friends and neighbors, physical environment, conditions at school, and the nature of their parents' breakup, as well as the individual personal characteristics of each child.

Kids are stronger than you think, and can grow through the rebuilding process right along with you. I encourage you to help them do so! You'll find the material in Appendix A helpful if you take this charge seriously.

How Are You Doing?

I thought you might like a self-evaluation report card to help you see how you are doing in your personal growth. You may wish to check yourself now and occasionally in the future, say once a month, or at least in two months, six months, a year. The list includes some important aspects of personal growth that you need to be aware of in order to keep growing. Most of these are areas I've talked about as we climbed the mountain, and you may want to go back and review them in the book.

"How Am I Doing?"

1. *I am able to put into words what I am feeling.*
2. *I am able to communicate to another person what I am feeling.*
3. *I have at least one life-line friend of each sex that I can ask for help when I feel I am drowning in the river of life.*
4. *I can express my anger in a positive manner that is not destructive to me or to those around me.*
5. *I am keeping a journal of my feelings and attitudes as I adjust to my crisis.*
6. *I have made at least one new friend, or renewed an old friendship in the past month.*
7. *I have invested quality time with at least one friend this past week.*
8. *I have identified which of the rebuilding blocks I need to work on, and have made a plan to start my further work.*
9. *I have invested time into a growing experience such as reading a good book, taking an educational class, attending an interesting lecture, or watching an educational program on TV this past week.*
10. *I have seriously considered if I would benefit from a therapy relationship in order to enhance my personal growth or to speed up my adjustment process.*
11. *I have received my quota of hugs from my friends this week.*
12. *I have spent time by myself either in prayer, meditation, or solitary thought this past week.*

13. *I have nurtured myself with a kind deed this past week.*
14. *I listen to the aches, tensions, and feelings in my body to learn more about myself.*
15. *I exercise regularly.*
16. *I have made at least one change in my daily living habits that I feel good about this past week.*
17. *I nourish my body with an adequate diet.*
18. *I have given emotionally of myself to at least one friend this past week.*
19. *I have invested in my spiritual growth this past week.*
20. *I like being the person I am.*
21. *I am making plans for my future.*
22. *I have let the "natural child" within me have fun this past week.*
23. *I am not carrying around pent up feelings of anger, grief, loneliness, rejection, or guilt but have learned to express them in order to rid myself of them.*
24. *I am much more in control of my life than I was when my past love relationship ended.*
25. *I am experiencing the feeling of freedom to be myself.*
26. *I am actively using the concepts learned from this book to help speed up my adjustment process.*

Well, how *are* you doing? Are you satisfied with your self-evaluative "report card?" Get it out again from time to time. It will help you keep track of your progress, and remind you of some of the important concepts we've talked about in this climb.

Are You Ready to Fly?

What is this freedom we all seem to be striving for? Freedom is something you find inside you. And you find it by becoming free from unmet needs which control you, such as the need to avoid being alone, the need to feel guilty, the need to find a critical parent to please, or the need to get free from your own "parent within you."

The butterfly at the top of the mountain stands for the freedom you find to fly and land where you choose. You can be free from the bonds that have kept you from being the person you would like to be. The person you were meant to be. The person you are capable of being. Our worst enemies are those within us, and it is those demons from which we need to free ourselves.

Of course, our best friends are inside us as well. Climbing the mountain not only gives us the freedom of choice to seek happiness — either alone or in another love relationship — it also gives us the freedom to be ourselves. And that makes the climb of personal growth worthwhile.

It is tough for me to end this book, because I know it represents just a beginning for you. I have watched thousands of people go through the rebuilding process. They have taught me a great deal. You could help me learn more by dropping me a note, in care of my publisher, to let me know how *REBUILDING* has helped you, and how I could make it even better.

If you think it would help to hear me talk about the process, you might want to listen to the audio cassette I've recorded. It's not a reading of the book, but a summary of my thoughts in a conversational style. The tape runs about 90 minutes, and is available from Impact Publishers (see page 326).

I hope you will not put this book away on a shelf, but that you will use it, as often as you need to, as a tool to help you rebuild. Share it with a friend, or perhaps give your friend his or her own copy.

Most of all, I wish you success in your continuing personal growth.

APPENDIX A

KIDS ARE TOUGHER THAN YOU THINK
The Rebuilding Blocks Process for Children

Bruce Fisher, Ed.D. and Robert Stewart, M.A.

"I thought everything in my life that could go wrong had. But now my kids are acting out. I really don't know what to do."
— Corinne

"Sure, single working mothers have problems — real ones. But what about fathers who have custody of their children after a divorce? If you're a man trying to work and raise a child alone, you get no support from anyone. Women are uncomfortable around you — they either think you're on the make, or they want to mother you and your child to death. You can't talk to other men: they think you're a little weird if you're worrying about toilet training, while they're planning a golf game or a camping trip.
As a single custodial father I didn't know:
    a) what to do when my son woke up screaming with a nightmare,
    b) how to go about finding a good baby-sitter,
    c) how to plan my son's birthday when he turned three,
    d) how to plan the weekly meals and bake cookies and cakes,
    e) how to answer questions like, 'Why did she go? Where is she?
    Will I see her again? Does she love me? Will you leave me?
    Why do I have to go to the baby-sitter's?'
Harboring all of these insecurities, we both cried a lot."
— Bill

"Remember the good old days, Dad — the days before you left home?"
— Sheila

Children go through an adjustment process similar to the adult's process, but the feelings and attitudes in each rebuilding block may be somewhat different for children. It helps if we realize that our children are also in process, with a mountain of their own to climb.

As family therapists, we believe we are obligated not only to help children adjust to their parents' divorce, but also to help them adjust to the transformation that took place while the parents were reading the *Rebuilding* book or attending the Fisher ten-week Rebuilding seminar.

There is a great deal of research about the effect on children of their parents' divorce. Some say the children are scarred for life, others say the children can actually benefit from their parents' divorce. The Fisher books and workshop are designed to facilitate the latter.

The people who have done a good job of adjusting are typically better parents. Their children reinforce what much of the research says: children whose parents are adjusting well tend to adjust better also.

Thoughts on Children and Divorce

Many parents try to make up for the guilt they feel about hurting the children when they get divorced by playing "super-parent." This is usually not helpful to the children.

Kids tend to become stuck in the same building blocks as their parents. *The nicest thing you as a parent can do for your child is to get your own act together — to work through your own adjustment process —* so you can be the warm supportive parent you are capable of being.

Many times the children remain strong and supportive to the parents until the parents get their act together. Finally, when the children perceive their parents are strong enough, they take their turn at working through the adjustment process.

There are many reasons we were motivated to add this Appendix on children to the book. First, in almost every class at least one person is working through his or her parents' divorce of twenty to forty years earlier. We hope your children will not take that long to adjust to the ending of your relationship.

The second reason is important to us as marriage and family therapists. Participating in the ten-week class often results in tremendous personal growth. This can result in changes affecting the children. They not only have to adjust to their parents' divorce, but also to the changes one or both parents may have made. We need to do all we can to help our children adjust to what can be major changes in our lives.

We hope the material in this Appendix, together with the material on children in the chapters, will help both you and your children to make this crisis into a creative experience. We also hope this Appendix will provide an outline and some motivation to provide a workshop for children wherever the ten-week adult class is taught.

A Good Divorce Is Better than a Bad Marriage.

When I [Bruce] was a juvenile probation officer in the early seventies, I at first thought one of the major reasons teenagers were in trouble was because their parents had divorced. This was reinforced by the fact that 48% of the children we worked with came from a home other than a two-parent family. After I went through my own divorce, I was able to understand that I had been guilty of prejudice against divorced families. It wasn't the divorce that was the major cause of kids having difficulties, it was the dysfunctional family which often ended up divorced.

Research is showing today that maybe a third of children whose parents divorced are doing above average in school and adjustment, another third are doing about average, and one-third are doing below average. In contrast, children who are living in a two-parent dysfunctional family are almost all doing below average.

I also have a bias about the adversarial process in our divorce courts. I saw the benefits of the adversarial process when I worked in the juvenile justice system, because the process helped find the truth and bring about justice. But after working for more than two decades with people going through the divorce court, I have decided that the adversarial process contributes to the anger and vindictiveness of the divorce process, and ultimately makes the adjustment much harder for the children of divorce — not to mention its effects upon their parents.

The judge in one case allowed the father to force five custody hearings for the three children over a two-year period. I viewed this as the court abusing the children. Again it may not be the divorce, but the court's handling of the divorce, that contributes to the children's adjustment difficulty. Children suffer minimal emotional and psychological damage when their parents have an amiable divorce. The children's pain is magnified several times when their parents divorce is acrimonious.

Fortunately, parents, and subsequently their children, have a much better opportunity of adjusting to the trauma of divorce today than they did in the forties. I went to the library and copied articles on divorce from a *Saturday Evening Post* of 1948. An example of one headline was, "Children are semi-orphaned by their parents' divorce." It is my hope that we are approaching the time when the possibility of children having four parents instead of two will be looked at favorably.

I don't want to minimize the difficult adjustment for children when their parents go through a divorce. The consequences of divorce can affect children for many years. Where do the divorced parents sit at the daughter's wedding? How do the children have a close relationship with grandparents when the parents are continuing the divorce battles? How much more likely is it that the children will divorce after they marry if their parents divorced when they were young?

I believe that: a good divorce is better for children than living with their parents in a bad marriage; if parents are able to adjust to their divorce, the chances of the kids adjusting are greatly increased; many adults are able to be better parents after the divorce and the children often benefit from this improved parenting; divorce is often the most traumatic event in a child's life, and we need to do what we can to minimize the emotional and psychological hurt and pain.

The Effects of Parental Adjustment on Children.

We've been perplexed and amazed at this phenomenon for years: When we adults are in the divorce pits, why do all of our mechanical appliances break down? Does our washing machine and our car know we are going through divorce? I don't laugh anymore at my friend who gives the copy machine a small blessing before she uses it so it won't misfeed.

When we are in the stage of mechanical breakdowns all around us, our children are often emotionally supporting us more than we would like to admit. They often behave better so they don't upset us. They often are doing things for us they wouldn't have thought about doing when we were married. They don't let us know how much pain and anger they are feeling. They in essence put their adjustment process on hold because they don't want to upset us any more than they have to.

When we parents begin to sit back and relax because we think we are adjusted, feeling stronger, and over the divorce, look out! That's often when our children sense at some level *they* can start working through the rebuilding blocks; they don't have to walk around on tip-toes anymore.

Corinne told the class, "I thought everything in my life that could go wrong has. But now my kids are acting out. I really don't know what to do." I pointed out to her that her kids may have been giving her a compliment! What the children are really saying might be, "You've adjusted and are strong enough that I can now work through my process. I need to cry, to be angry, and act out my hurt. I think you're finally ready to handle me while I work through my pain." I enjoy watching the parents' faces light up when I explain this because many times that is exactly what has happened to them and their children.

Kids *are* tougher than you think.

There Are Stumbling Blocks for Children
As your children make the climb up the divorce recovery mountain there are seven stumbling blocks they may encounter.

The first stumbling block your children may be experiencing is, *"I don't know what divorce is."* Your children may not know what the word "divorce" means or how it will work in your lives together. It's not uncommon for children to hold myths about divorce, or to drift toward believing their worst fears when left to discover things on their own.

The second stumbling block is, *"I don't like all the changes happening around me."* Divorce has brought a complete overhaul of life as your children knew it. There are many logistical changes your children may have needed to adjust to, (residence, neighborhood, school, friends, personal space,...) perhaps in a short period of time.

The third stumbling block is, *"I have all these different feelings stuck inside me."* Your children are most likely experiencing a wide range of emotional responses related to the divorce. They may be feeling sad, angry, worried, confused, relieved, and many other emotions without any knowledge of what to do with their feelings.

The fourth stumbling block is, *"I wonder if I am responsible for my parents' divorce."* Children feel responsible in a variety of ways. Some believe they actually did something bad to cause their parents to get divorced. Other children feel responsible to help their parents feel better about what has happened. Finally, some children believe there is something wrong with them that they do not get to see the non-custodial parent more often.

The fifth stumbling block is, *"I don't know if we are a family any more."* Your children may be wondering how to relate to you and your former partner now that the two of you are no longer in relationship. Some children wonder if it is okay to love both parents, or if they need to pick a side. Children also wonder what it means to be a family now that everyone no longer lives together.

The sixth stumbling block is, *"I wish my parents would get back together."* It is a fantasy your children may keep alive because they are unhappy with what divorce has meant for their lives. Many children kindle hope as a way of moderating the stress of watching their parents separate. Other children who are having difficulty with the other stumbling blocks may want to change what they are experiencing by wishing for something different.

The next stumbling block is, *"I think it will be all good, or all bad, if my mom or dad finds a new partner."* This block concerns your children's view of the future. Some children think if you find a new partner everything will be okay; somehow the family is incomplete until they have a new mommy or daddy. Other children resist their parent's interest in someone new because it is a concrete sign that their parents will not get back together. Children who view your finding a new partner through either the "all good" or "all bad" lens may be stuck at this block.

The last stumbling block is *"I feel like the only child in the world whose parents are divorcing."* During the divorce process, children often believe they are alone, and have no friends. They are lonely, usually have low feelings of self-worth (as they wonder what they did wrong to cause the divorce), and keep looking for new friends.

What Are the Rebuilding Blocks for Children?

Remember the analogy of tripping over a log? While the stumbling blocks trip children up, rebuilding blocks are the process of getting them back on their feet. The experience of divorce is accepted, and the foundation for recovery built, with the rebuilding blocks. The crisis becomes an experience that may actually encourage your children's growth and maturity. As children change each of the stumbling blocks into rebuilding blocks, they become stronger.

The first rebuilding block is, *"I know what divorce is and what it means for me."* At this block your children gain a clear understanding and definition of divorce. They also learn what it will and won't mean for their individual lives.

The second rebuilding block is, *"I'm finding out how to handle the changes I am experiencing.* Here, your children discover some healthy ways to cope with the various events taking place around them. They may not like the changes, but they are finding non-destructive ways to work with them.

The third rebuilding block is, *"I'm letting my feelings out without hurting myself or others."* At this block your children become more aware of their feelings, and discover appropriate ways of expressing them. To reach this block, children usually need to feel safe sharing their feelings with at least one parent.

The fourth rebuilding block is, *"I know divorce is a grown-up problem."* Your children are letting go of their need to take responsibility for what has happened between you and your former partner. Your children develop good boundaries, learning the difference between what they can and cannot control.

The fifth rebuilding block is, *"I can still love my mom and my dad."* Your children realize they do not have to choose sides between their parents. They have a new definition of family that includes both mom and dad, separately.

The sixth rebuilding block is, *"I'm accepting that my parents will not get back together."* Your children grow toward accepting that you and your former partner will not be back together. They learn to feel safe even as they acknowledge that their wish won't come true.

The seventh rebuilding block is, *"I can see things I will like, and things I won't like, if my mom or dad finds a new partner."* Your children are moving away from viewing your dating as either all good or bad. They find a balanced perspective on both the positive aspects and the challenges that will arise if you find a new partner.

The next rebuilding block is *"I'm learning to be a friend to myself through my parents' divorce."* A child who is able to say this has neared the end of the climb. The feeling of self-worth in this statement makes the climb worthwhile. At this stage, children have grown from loneliness into a feeling of emotional closeness with themselves and others.

The last rebuilding block doesn't have a corresponding stumbling block: *"I have the freedom to be myself."* When you and your child(ren) reach the top of the mountain, the view of yourself, others and life itself is spectacular. The personal freedom and intimacy both children and parents feel is great. Together you and your children have transformed the crisis into a creative experience.

Each of the rebuilding blocks represents an adjustment for children as they experience the stages of divorce recovery. It is likely that your children will gain in wisdom, strength, and maturity as they climb to the top of the mountain.

Rebuilding Together

One symbolic activity you could do with your children is to take them for a hike. This is especially good if you live close to mountains or foothills, so you can pick a trail and climb to the top. Shared outdoor activities can really bring children and parents together. You and your children already know that adjusting to divorce is a lot like climbing a mountain. All of you could gain powerful insights by physically hiking even part way up. In urban areas, you could plan a challenging course in a safe neighborhood, and include some stair climbing along the way. If you decide to do this activity, it will help if each of you pays attention to the feelings you notice on your journey. Which aspects of your hike were exciting? Which were frustrating? What challenges did you encounter? How did you feel at the end of your hike? How about when you reached your goal? What was it like for you and your children to accomplish this goal together? What are you learning about adjusting to the ending of your love relationship? What are you learning about your children? What are your children learning about you?

Divorce Recovery Mountain for Children

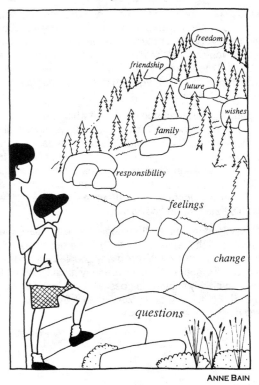

ANNE BAIN

APPENDIX B

THE HEALING SEPARATION
An Alternative to Divorce

"I have a vision of a relationship more beautiful and loving than both of us can imagine or know. It is truly a relationship that is a laboratory for growth, where we are able to grow and completely be ourselves, while still in relationship with each other. I am not a whole enough person to be able to have such a healthy relationship with you without building a better relationship with myself first. I think I will need to separate and live apart from you for a while. I love you."
— Nina

For many years, a popular "women's" magazine ran a monthly columm called "Can This Marriage Be Saved?" which gave advice to couples who were really in trouble. There's a resurgence of interest in saving marriages these days, and I'd like to share with you one very powerful tool which has helped a number of relationships. While it's too early to call this a thoroughly tested and proven process, it has such promise that I urge you to give it thoughtful consideration if you've not yet actually divorced.

A Healing Separation is a structured time apart which can help a couple heal a relationship that isn't working. It can also help revitalize and renew a relationship that is working. The Healing Separation is designed to transform the basis of a love relationship — moving it from neediness to health. A successful Healing Separation requires that both partners be committed to personal growth, and to creating healthier relationships with themselves and each other. Such a framework will allow them to carve out a new and more fulfilling relationship than they've known in the past.

When a relationship is in trouble, the couple has essentially three choices: 1) continue as is, 2) end the relationship, or 3) carve out a new relationship. If the relationship is already crumbling, not many couples want to continue it as is. That leaves choices 2 and 3. Chances are they hadn't thought much about the third choice — it probably seemed impossible. What's more, they don't know know how to go about it. So their choice, almost by default, is to end the relationship. And up goes the divorce rate.

There is another alternative: partners can work out a new relationship with themselves and with each other. The Healing Separation offers a process within which to do just that.

What is a Healing Separation?

The Healing Separation, like the old-style "trial separation," involves living apart for a while, with the decision as to whether or not to end the relationship put off until some future time. Unlike unplanned and unstructured separations, however, the Healing Separation is a working separation, in which you and your partner dedicate yourselves to investing in your own personal growth. If you can create a better relationship with yourself, that can allow different and healthier relationships with others. Sometimes your work during a Healing Separation may be on "the old relationship," and sometimes it may be on "the old you." The Healing Separation is a creative way to strengthen both partners and build a new relationship without dissolving the partnership.

A relationship between two people is analogous to a bridge. Each partner forms one end and provides half the support for the bridge. The connection between the two — the bridge — is the relationship itself. A Healing Separation gives the partners time to concentrate on themselves, on their own supportive end structures, rather than on the relationship. It's a scary process because neither person is tending the relationship bridge for a while — it could collapse. Nevertheless, it may be worth the risk. When the two ends eventually are rebuilt, the possibility exists for a new healthy relationship bridge to be built, supported by bridge ends which are now stronger.

What Are the Purposes of a Healing Separation?

The goals of a Healing Separation are more profound than simply whether you continue your love relationship. I have found a high correlation between the amount of personal growth each person does and the success of the Healing Separation. If both parties are committed and motivated to work on their self-relationship, the chance of their new relationship lasting is good.

The following list of purposes for a Healing Separation may help you determine if your own separation is successful:

• *To take the pressure off a troubled relationship.* A love relationship is a changing pattern of interaction between two people who themselves are changing as they develop emotionally, socially, physically, and spiritually. This evolution of the relationship may result in strains and pressures upon the relationship and a crisis may develop. During this crisis, it is difficult for the partners to make rational and objective decisions concerning their future. A time apart pending a final decision may be an advantageous alternative for the couple to consider.

• *To enhance your personal growth* so that you can work through the stumbling blocks mentioned in this book. Changing stumbling blocks into rebuilding blocks can be the end result of a successful Healing Separation.

• *To transform your relationship* into something more beautiful and loving then you ever thought possible. You could find yourself in a relationship that not only allows you to be yourself, but enhances your individual identity, and offers more love and joy than you ever imagined. You could deepen your definition of what love is, and create a relationship that has no boundaries or limits, one which has evolved and transformed to a level of love usually associated with spiritual love — a good imitation of God's love.

• *To end your love relationship on a positive note* and have the ending a creative and constructive experience. To reach this goal might mean the ending has a minimum of stress, anxiety, court battles, with everyone feeling good about the way it worked out. Remaining friends and being able to co-parent peacefully could be important by-products of this healthy ending.

Who Should Have a Healing Separation?

Here are some key characteristics of partners who might want to consider a Healing Separation:

• *You are experiencing sad and unhappy feelings,* or feeling suffocated, or experiencing tremendous pressures, or feeling depressed, possibly even suicidal. You need to separate in order to survive and continue living.

• *Your partner has refused take any responsibility for the relationship difficulties* and has refused to become involved in counseling or other growth activities. The separation is one way to "hit your partner over the head with a two-by-four" in order to get his or her attention.

• *You are going through the rebellion process* identified in Chapter Twelve. You feel the need for emotional space and decide to separate to relieve the internal pressures.

• *You are in the process of healing your childhood abuse and neglect* and need to be alone in order to complete the process.

• *You have begun an important personal transformation,* perhaps psychological or spiritual in nature, and you want to invest as much time and effort as possible into your own process. You find the time and effort spent in the relationship competes with and limits the amount of time you can spend with yourself.

• *You have not been able to gain enough emotional space* in the love relationship and need more space to survive, to grow, to evolve, or to transform.

• *You're caught in conflict:* wanting to continue the love relationship, but unable to break the old patterns. Living together encourages continuing the old patterns of interaction. You want to "divorce the old relationship" so you can carve out a new one that is more healthy and less needy. A time apart may allow you to create new ways of interacting by developing a new and different relationship with yourself.

• *You need an understanding of how it feels to be single.* You may have gone directly from your parental home to a marriage home without experiencing the single life. You missed experiencing one of the developmental stages of growth and development — that of being an independent adult. Many people wrongly believe the single life to be one of freedom with no responsibilities — an escape from the stress of living with a love partner. Having some time apart from the love partner may provide a more realistic view of the difficulties of living as a single person.

• *You may need to express your independence from your family patterns* for the first time. You may have built a love relationship bridge much like your parents' bridge. Now you're attempting to get free from your parents' influence, and you need to have distance from your love partner because your patterns with your partner are too similar to those you experienced with one or both parents.

• *You and your partner are projecting your unhappiness onto each other,* making the other "responsible" for your unhappiness. You have not learned to take individual ownership of your own feelings. Time apart — with a plan for personal growth — could help both of you learn to accept adult responsibility for your lives.

Dumpers and Dumpees Again: The 80-20 Rule

A separation is seldom started as a mutual decision. In the Fisher divorce classes, some 84% of couples ended their relationships when the dumper decided to leave. I estimate a similar division in the decision to have a Healing Separation; that is, one partner is the initiator and the other is reluctant perhaps 80% of the time. Sounds like quite an obstacle to the success of the Healing Separation, doesn't it? How can a couple overcome the differences in attitude, goals, and motivation of the initiator and the reluctant one?

First of all, couples must re-think the question of "Who's to blame?" When a relationship is not working as well as it should, *both parties are equally responsible for the malfunctions.* It has taken me a long time to understand and really believe that statement. But the longer I work with couples, the more I find that when you peel off the layers of pain and get to the core issues, *the responsibility for the problems is equal.* Thus the problems are mutual even though one person was the initiator in the separation. When you begin to understand and accept the notion of mutual responsibility for the problems, you have begun to build a foundation for a successful Healing Separation — and a successful new relationship.

My research on the divorce process indicates the dumpee experiences much more anger and painful feelings than the dumper. Probably the reluctant one in a Healing Separation will experience more emotional pain. Whatever strong feelings are experienced by either party will need to worked through before the separation truly becomes healing.

The parties in a Healing Separation have more alone time, to work on themselves, on their careers, on projects and hobbies. This can be a positive aspect and helpful to both parties. The reluctant one may learn to appreciate having extra time to work on personal growth and eventually appreciate the initiator's decision to have a Healing Separation.

When the reluctant one finally understands that the initiator had so much internal pain and emotional pressure that separation was a matter of survival, it helps the reluctant one to understand and accept the initiator's decision.

In the "Rebuilding Relationships" classes, it is usually the female partner who is more motivated to take the class. After about five weeks of the class, however, men admit, "I didn't think I needed this class. I was just taking it for her because I thought she needed it, but the learning of this past five weeks has helped me discover I needed the class more than she did." Education and awareness helps the reluctant one to appreciate the benefits of a Healing Separation.

My experience has been that it is more likely for the initiator to be female. Among the reasons for this: 1) Research indicates married females are more unhappy than married males. 2) Females are more likely to be open to new ways of improving relationships. 3) The person who is experiencing personal change and transformation — perhaps one who is healing past abuse, usually female — will seek time and space to do that work. 4) The person who is going through a spiritual transformation is usually female. 5) The female partner, most often the submissive one in our male-dominated society, is more likely than the dominant one to seek equality. 6) When a relationship is not working, the male often will leave the relationship, not knowing or believing there is a possibility of changing it. If the female partner initiates the separation, the traditional "macho male" will often seek the ending of the relationship rather than agree to a Healing Separation. It takes a male who is sensitive, patient, caring, flexible, and open to change to participate in a Healing Separation.

Guidelines for a Successful Healing Separation
Following the guidelines below will improve the chances of success of your Healing Separation. They're not all absolute rules, but if you ignore more than one or two, your prospects will be hurt:

1) Probably the most important requirement for both of you is *a strong*

commitment to make the Healing Separation work. Feelings of love and commitment are tremendously helpful to motivate you both.

2) *Make a list of what your ideal love relationship would be like.* Think of what aspects would be important to you. Allow yourself to develop a fantasy role model of what your relationship might be like after the Healing Separation. *Share and discuss your lists with each other.*

3) *Commit yourselves to communicating with each other in an open and honest manner.* Learn to use "I" messages rather than "you" messages. Communicate by stating, "I think ____," "I feel ____," "I want____," "I need ____," and "I will ____." Learn to be as honest as you can be with yourself and with your partner. Learn to say what is true for you. Complete honesty may include owning that portion of the relationship problems for which you have been responsible. Are you part of the problem, or part of the solution?

4) *Do not file for divorce or start any court proceedings during the Healing Separation.* You must agree to not take any legal action without first conferring with the other person. The adversarial legal system is antithetical to the goals of a Healing Separation. Even the threat or the thought of the other person filing is enough to release the brakes of the train headed for dissolution, so you need to make it clear in the "separation agreement" that neither of you will consider undertaking any court action. The exception to this is when one or both of you needs to let the old relationship die by having a final decree stating you are divorced. You need to work toward obtaining the final decree together and avoid the adversarial court process. Anything you can do to help end the old relationship is helpful in the Healing Separation. This may be the step that really gets your partner's attention and let's the other person know you are serious in your need for emotional space.

5) *Quality time together might nourish this new relationship.* (See the following section.) It is helpful to think of the new relationship as a tender young plant just emerging from the seedbed. It needs frequent tender, loving care in order to grow and not be squashed by the storms of the Healing Separation.

6) *Continuing a sexual relationship may help* nurture the relationship, but it could also hurt. Review the material in Chapter Seventeen for cautions.

7) Sometimes you will need to *talk out issues with another person* other than with your partner. You will need a good support system, or a therapy relationship, or both, to resolve these issues without them being added to the storms that will most likely occur during a Healing Separation.

8) It is a great time to *keep a personal journal.* You will need a place to express and dissipate the strong feelings which are bound to emerge during

this difficult time, and a place to sort out the many thoughts and feelings you are experiencing.

9) *Read, take classes, attend lectures and seminars.* Awareness can really help to put the brakes on your runaway relationship train. Reading and learning all you can will help make the process healing rather than destructive.

10) You will need to *do some self-care* so you don't become emotionally and physically drained. The whole process can be very draining emotionally, and sometimes you feel like giving up because you don't have enough energy to continue. What can you do to restore yourself and keep from becoming emotionally drained?

11) *Use the "Healing Separation Agreement"* in Appendix C — with modifications to suit your relationship needs — as a firm commitment to each other. A formal agreement such as this will give your Healing Separation the best chance of success.

12) *Seriously consider a (joint) ongoing therapy relationship* with an accredited Marriage and Family Therapist.

Other Considerations
   Quality Time Together. You may find it beneficial to set times to be together on a regular basis during the separation, as often as feels right and okay. It should be agreeable to both of you to spend "quality time" together. This quality time might include one or more of the following activities: a) important sharing and active listening, using good communication skills, b) verbal intimacy and/or sexual intimacy, if appropriate, c) time to nurture each other, d) trying out new patterns of interaction leading to carving out a new relationship, e) doing fun activities together, f) sharing your personal growth with the other person. When your old dysfunctional patterns of interaction start happening, you need to be apart rather than continuing the old unproductive patterns of behavior together. Remember to stay honest with each other!

   Length of separation. You may be asking, "How long are we going to be separated?" Part of the goal for this process is to encourage and support you to be as fearful and insecure as possible! It would be easy for you to make a commitment for three months, and then use that deadline as a way of not dealing emotionally with the problems. "I can put up with anything for three months," might be your attitude. My suggestion is for both of you to agree on a time limit for your Healing Separation, but realize it can and should be re-negotiated. This insecurity of not knowing how long you will be separated may help to keep you on your toes, and you may be able to use the insecurity of no time limit as motivation to keep growing.

Insecurity about the future of your relationship can be frightening. You don't know how much to work on yourself, and how much to work on the relationship. (If you've been trying to change your partner, that may be one of the reasons you're having a Healing Separation!) Sometimes it feels as if you are walking on ice. One false step and down you go, into the icy water of loneliness, rejection, guilt, anger, and the other feelings of the divorce pits.

The Healing Separation will probably consume a year or so of your life.

Timing of When To Move Back Together. I've found the question of when to end the separation by moving back together to be crucial. Usually the couple is uncomfortable living apart, and the pain motivates them to move back together too quickly. One party is usually pushing to live together more quickly than the other. Males usually want to move back together quicker than the females. The reluctant partner usually wants to move back together before the initiator does. Time itself is a factor: early in the process, one or both are eager to move back together; the longer the separation lasts, the more hesitant both partners are to move back together.

It is very destructive to move back together too quickly and have the patterns of the old relationship come back. This increases the possibility of separating again, and each separation increases the chances of the relationship ending.

Take your time about moving back together. Beware of the "honeymoon phase." You may start to feel emotionally close, intimate; sexual satisfaction may improve (maybe because you have let go of sexual expectations); you want to live together again — but maybe for the wrong reasons. I suggest you wait until you both agree that you sincerely choose to be in relationship with each other, and to share the rest of your lives with each other. Paradoxically, when you both believe you can live *alone* the rest of your lives and be happy, it may be a good indicator you are ready to move back and live *together* again.

Outside love relationships. As a general rule, having an extra love relationship during a Healing Separation will diminish your chances of improving your relationship with yourself. Time and energy invested in the outside relationship diminishes the time and energy available to invest in your own growth as a person.

Partners who initiate the separation seeking personal growth, healing, or transformation, are so involved in their personal growth process that an extra relationship is often not of interest. They have a strong commitment to the Healing Separation, and are willing to risk everything in their relationship with their reluctant partners just so they can work toward becoming whole persons.

Reluctant partners have many opportunities for outside relationships, but they usually find out they are more "married" than they thought. Often they discover that a potential new partner has a multitude of new problems. Dating may leave them much more committed to the Healing Separation.

The person, male or female, who initiates a separation while in the rebellion process is much more likely to have an outside relationship which looks like an affair and may include sexual intimacy. He or she usually thinks of it as part of the process — the primary purpose is to have someone to talk intimately with — and does not think of it as an affair. This extra relationship may become a long-term union, but the chances of it becoming a healthy relationship are small.

Outside relationships usually have an adverse effect upon a Healing Separation because the people involved make the extra relationship more important than it is. A partner who is in rebellion finds it exciting and believes it has much promise for the future. (This excitement rarely lasts beyond the early or "honeymoon" stage.) The other partner will feel hurt, rejected, and angry about the extra relationship, and may decide to end the Healing Separation and let go of the relationship altogether.

Lack of support. Another area of difficulty in a Healing Separation is your support system. Both partners need an emotional support system to help deal with the pressures of the difficult situation. The problem is that very few people have seen a Healing Separation work, and the view of many friends and relatives will be that the relationship is going to end. They don't believe there is such a concept as a Healing Separation. Thus when you need emotional support the most, your friends are urging you to end the relationship, saying things like, "You're still in denial. Can't you see that the relationship is over?" "Are you co-dependent? You don't seem to be able to disentangle." "You are just opening yourself to be taken into court with some shark attorney. You better get your partner before s/he gets you." "Why are you staying in limbo? You need to get on with your life." "Why don't you get rid of that bum?"

The idea of a Healing Separation is contrary to the values and beliefs of many people. A commitment "till death do us part" is a strong belief in our society, and a Healing Separation is somehow undesirable, not spiritually okay, a form of radical behavior. That's one of the reasons people are unable to support and accept the couple attempting this alternative to divorce.

You need your support friends, but it often makes you more insecure when your friends tell you the relationship is going to end. Continue to reach out and build your support system, but understand they may not always be there to help you make the Healing Separation succeed. Maybe having them read this Appendix will help them be more supportive of you.

Paradoxes of a Healing Separation.
There are many paradoxes (and contradictions?) I have observed in Healing Separations. Here are some of the more important ones:

1) The person who initiates often does it out of a need for emotional space. But the reluctant one often uses and benefits from the emotional space as much as or more than the initiator.

2) Initiators appear to be selfishly seeking ways of meeting their own needs, but often are providing an opportunity for their reluctant partners to meet their needs.

3) The initiator appears to be leaving the relationship, but may actually be more committed to the relationship than is the reluctant one.

4) As soon as initiators feel they have the emotional space they need, they reach out and ask for more closeness with the reluctant one.

5) The initiator wants the separation, but is not looking for another relationship. The reluctant one wants the relationship to continue, but is more likely to enter into another love relationship.

6) When the partners separate, they are often more "married" than they were when they were living together.

7) Most love partners project some of their hang-ups onto the other person. The Healing Separation makes these projections more obvious and identifiable. It's harder to blame another person for what happens when he or she doesn't live there any more!

8) One of the reasons initiators give for wanting a separation is so they can enhance their personal growth. But reluctant partners may experience as much or more personal growth during a separation.

9) The initiator may actually elect to have the marriage legally ended by a final court dissolution so the partners can begin again to build and create a new and different relationship.

10) The Healing Separation makes it look to others as if the relationship is not working, when in reality it may be the healthiest it has ever been.

11) In the process of seeking a clearer personal identity, the initiator may find a stronger sense of "relationship identity" — personal identity as part of a relationship.

12) Initiators often give reluctant partners what they need rather than what they want.

Is This a Healing Separation or Denial?

It is a time for action, not promises. If both parties are not actively engaged in working on themselves and rebuilding their ends of the relationship bridge, it is probably not a Healing Separation but a step toward the ending of the relationship.

Here are some important questions. Are you both working at this Healing Separation or is only one of you investing in your own personal growth? Are both parties involved in counseling? Are both parties reading self-help books? Are both parties spending time alone or are they continually with people in situations that are not growth-producing? Are both parties avoiding excessive drug and alcohol use? Are both parties investing in themselves or are they investing in another relationship outside of this one? Are the two people having any quality time together which includes good communication? Are both parties attempting to become more aware of their individual contribution to the difficulties in the relationship? Are both parties looking at how they can grow, instead of expecting the other person to make all the changes? Do both believe the partner is the problem and there is nothing one can do to change or grow until the other changes?

How does your Healing Separation rate on these questions? Are both of you working at the relationship? If only one is, then most likely you are in denial and your relationship is going to end.

Afterword

The structure of the Healing Separation is designed specifically for couples in a primary love relationship; the lessons are most relevant to their needs. Nevertheless, the lessons presented in this Appendix will work for many kinds of relationships, including friendships, family relationships, co-workers in a business setting, therapy. A "time out" is often helpful to allow the people involved to gain breathing space and perspective — a chance to take a fresh look at what's actually happening in the relationship, and to build a foundation for a stronger partnership in the future.

Appendix Check List

Both partners in a Healing Separation will benefit from reading this Appendix and completing the following check list.

1. *I recognize the reasons I entered into my past love relationship which contributed to my need for a Healing Separation.*

2. *I have identified and own some of my contributions to our need for a Healing Separation.*

3. *I am committed to working on my own personal growth and development during this Healing Separation.*

4A. *I am aware of my own personal process that has resulted in my need for more emotional space at this time of my life. OR*

4B. *I am aware of my own contributions to my partner's need for more emotional space.*

5. *I am working on my own personal growth so I will have a healthier relationship with myself.*

6. *I am committed to make this Healing Separation a creative experience.*

7. *I am committed to learning as much as possible from my relationship partner during this Healing Separation.*

8. *I am avoiding the behaviors which may lead this Healing Separation toward the rocks of divorce.*

9. *I am working on relieving the internal pressures which contributed to my need for more emotional space.*

10. *I have completed my part of the Healing Separation agreement form.*

11. *When the time is appropriate, I will communicate with my partner about ending the Healing Separation, either through ending the relationship or moving back and living together again.*

12. *I am avoiding blaming and projecting upon my partner.*

13. *I am avoiding the "helpless victim" role; I don't believe there is "nothing I can do" about my situation.*

14. *I will either read the follow-up book,* Rebuilding Relationships, *or enroll in the ten-week "Rebuilding Relationships" class, or both.*

APPENDIX C

A HEALING SEPARATION AGREEMENT FORM

(A healing separation is a very challenging experience, which may result in increased stress and anxiety for both partners. Some structure and awareness can help improve the chances of success of the healing separation. Unplanned and unstructured separations will most likely contribute to the ending of the relationship. This healing separation agreement attempts to provide structure and guidelines to help make the separation a more constructive and creative experience, and to greatly enhance the growth of the relationship rather than contributing to its demise.)

A. Commitment to Do a Healing Separation.

With the awareness that our love relationship is at a point of crisis, we choose to try a working and creative healing separation in order to obtain a better individual perspective of the future of our relationship. In choosing this healing separation, it is acknowledged there are aspects in our relationship which are destructive to us as a couple and as individuals. Likewise we acknowledge there are positive and constructive elements in our relationship which could be called assets and upon which we may be able to build a new and different relationship. With this in mind, we are committed to do the personal, social, psychological, and spiritual work necessary to make this separation a healing one.

At some future time, when we have experienced the personal growth and self-actualization possible in a healing separation, we will make a more enlightened decision about the future of our love relationship.

B. Goals of Our Healing Separation.

Each partner agrees to the following goals for this separation:

1. To provide time and emotional space outside of the love relationship so I can enhance my personal, social, spiritual, and emotional growth.

2. To better identify my needs, wants, and expectations of the love relationship.

3. To help me explore what my basic relationship needs are and to help me determine if these needs can be met in this love relationship.

4. To experience the social, sexual, economic, and parental stresses which can occur when I have separated from my partner.

5. To allow me to determine if I can work through my process better apart than I can in the relationship.

6. To experience enough emotional distance so I can separate out my issues which have become convoluted and mixed up together with my partner's issues in our relationship.

7. To provide an environment to help our relationship heal, transform, evolve into a more loving and healthy relationship.

C. Specific Decisions Regarding This Healing Separation.
1. Length of separation.
We agree our separation will begin on (month and day) _____
19____, and end on _____, 19____.

(Most couples have a sense of how long a separation they will need or want. It may vary from a few weeks to six months or longer. The length of time agreed upon may be re-negotiated at any time by the initiation of either partner. The length of time would be a good topic for a communication exercise.)

2. Time to Be Spent Together.
We agree to spend time together when it is agreeable to both parties. This time might be spent having fun, talking, parenting together, or sharing my personal growth process. We agree to meet for _____ hours _____ times the first week, and to negotiate the time together for each succeeding week. We agree to discuss and reach an agreement if this time together is to include a continuing sexual involvement with each other.

(A healing separation ideally should include some quality time together on a regular basis. Some people will enjoy their new-found freedom and desire very little quality time. On the other hand when the person needing more emotional space separates, they may want more time together. This may be confusing to the person who wasn't desiring the healing separation. Partners who feel suffocated emotionally desperately want out. But when they get out of what feels like a tight place, the need for emotional space is decreased tremendously.

It is important that the time together be quality time and be spent creating a new relationship. When the old pattern starts occurring in whatever form that may take, one solution is to end the quality time together and be apart. There are arguments for and against a continued sexual involvement with each other. Ideally sexual contact will enhance intimacy and make the separation less stressful and hurtful. Sex can, however, result in problems of the sort discussed in Chapter ___, creating confusion for the potential dumpee if the dumper is just trying to "let him/her down easy.")

3. Personal growth experiences
Partner A (_____) agrees to participate in _____ individual counseling, _____ the Rebuilding class, _____ the Rebuilding

Relationships class, _____ marriage counseling, _____ other growth experiences such as reading self-help books, keeping an individual journal, dream interpretation, exercise programs, diet programs, growth groups.

Partner B (_____) agrees to participate in _____ individual counseling, _____ the Rebuilding class, _____ the Rebuilding Relationships class, _____ marriage counseling, _____ other growth experiences such as reading self-help books, keeping an individual journal, dream interpretation, exercise programs, diet programs, growth groups.

(Ideally a healing separation would include as many personal growth experiences as feasible, practical, and helpful.)

4. Relationships and Involvements outside of the relationship.

Partner A agrees _____ to develop a support system of important friends, _____ to become more involved socially with others, _____ to not date potential love partners, _____ to remain emotionally monogamous , _____ to remain sexually monogamous, _____ to become involved in clubs, church singles groups, etc.

Partner B agrees _____ to develop a support system of important friends, _____ to become more involved socially with others, _____ to not date potential love partners, _____ to remain emotionally monogamous , _____ to remain sexually monogamous, _____ to become involved in clubs, church singles groups, etc.

(Ideally a joint decision and compromise should be made concerning social involvement, romantic, and sexual relationships outside of this relationship.)

5. Living arrangements.

Partner A agrees to _____ remain in the family home, _____ move and find an alternative living arrangement, _____ alternate living with partner so the children can remain in family home.

Partner B agrees to _____ remain in the family home, _____ move and find an alternative living arrangement, _____ alternate living with partner so the children can remain in family home.

(My experience has been that the in-house separation, with both parties continuing to live in the family home, results in a less creative experience. It seems to dilute the separation experience and keeps both parties from experiencing as much personal growth as is possible with separate living arrangements. It may not give enough emotional space to the person who needs more space.)

7. Financial decisions.

Partner A agrees to ____ maintain joint checking account jointly, ____ maintain joint checking account separately, ____ open new checking account, ____ pay auto expenses, ____ pay household living expenses, ____ pay child support of $____ monthly, ____ pay home mortgage and utilities, ____ pay medical and dental bills.

Partner B agrees to ____ maintain joint checking account jointly, ____ maintain joint checking account separately, ____ open new checking account, ____ pay auto expenses, ____ pay household living expenses, ____ pay child support of $____ monthly, ____ pay home mortgage and utilities, ____ pay medical and dental bills.

(Some couples will decide to continue joint checking accounts, savings accounts, and payment of bills. Other couples will completely separate financial aspects of the relationship.

My experience with divorcing couples indicates that many times one person will completely close out checking accounts and savings accounts without the other person's knowledge or consent. I suggest if there is any chance for potential disagreement, that each person take out half of the assets and open separate accounts.)

8. Motor vehicles.

Partner A agrees to operate _____ vehicle, and Partner B agrees to operate _____ vehicle.

(It is suggested ownership and titles not be changed until a decision has been made about the future of the love relationship.)

D. Children involved in this relationship.

1. We agree to ____ joint custody, ___ solo or physical custody be given to _____.

2. We agree to the following visitation schedule.

3. The medical and dental expenses and health insurance will be the responsibility of partner ____.

4. We agree to the following suggestions, designed to help the healing separation be a positive experience for our children:

a. Both parents remain committed to maintain a good quality relationship with each child involved. Each child should continue to feel loved by both parents.

b. Parents be as open and honest with the children about the healing separation as is appropriate.

c. The parents will help the children see and understand the physical separation is an adult problem and that the children are not responsible for the problems in the parent's love relationship.

d. The parents will not express anger or negative feelings towards the other parent through the children. It is very destructive to children to become caught in the emotional crossfire of the parents.

e. The parents will avoid forcing the children to take sides in the parental arguments concerning differing attitudes and viewpoints.

f. The parents will not put the children in a position of spying and reporting on the behavior of the other parent.

g. Both parents will remain committed to work with each other on parenting the children and to effectively co-parent with as much coopera- tion as possible.

(It is important when a couple does a Healing Separation to minimize the emotional trauma for the children involved.)

E. Signing the agreement

We have read and discussed the above Healing Separation Agreement and agree to the above terms of the agreement. Each of us furthermore agrees to inform the other partner of any desire to modify or change any terms in the agreement, or to terminate the agreement.

_____

Partner A   Date

_____

Partner B   Date

Suggestions

I have found that couples reading this book helps them to build and create more healthy relationships. Of even more help is enrolling in the ten-week Rebuilding Class. It is helpful to think about taking the Rebuilding class with the goal of the class participation to be "divorcing the old relationship" rather than divorcing your former love partner.

A Healing Separation is very difficult to pull off. I suggest a) you work with a marriage and family therapist, b) read my book, *Loving Choices, A Growing Experience,* which is a follow-up book to this one, c) enroll in the "Hart-Fisher Loving Choices Seminar" ten-week class if it is offered in your community, and d) create a support system to help you grow through this difficult time. If you haven't been able to make your relationship work before the Healing Separation, you may have difficulty making it work without outside help, guidance, information, and support during the Healing Separation.

APPENDIX D

PROGRAMS OF
THE FAMILY RELATIONS LEARNING CENTER

Rebuilding: When Your Relationship Ends
- Ten-week class for individuals
  (Based on this book.)
- Weekend training workshops for facilitators
  (Preparation to lead the ten-week class. Held four
  times a year in Boulder.)
- *Rebuilding Blocks 60-minute Video*
  (Dr. Fisher discusses the climb up the "mountain"
  of Rebuilding blocks.)
- *When Your Relationship Ends six-hour audiotapes*
  (A 45-minute tape for each of eight sessions from the
  ten-week class.)
- *Fisher Divorce Adjustment Scale*
  (An inventory to measure individual adjustment after divorce,
  used as a pre-test, post-test for participants in the ten-week class.)

Loving Choices: A Growing Experience
- Ten-week class for singles
  (Based on the book by Dr. Fisher: *Loving Choices:
  A Growing Experience.)*
- Ten-week class for couples
  (As above for couples who wish to work together on an
  existing relationship.)
- Weekend training workshops for facilitators
  (Preparation to lead the ten-week class. Held four times
  a year in Boulder.)

For further information on these and other programs, please contact:
Family Relations Learning Center
450 Ord Drive
Boulder, Colorado 80303
Telephone: 303-499-1171

BIBLIOGRAPHY

Further Reading On Chapter Topics

The Divorce Process

Bloomfield, H., Colgrove, M. & McWilliams, P. (1976, 1991) *How to Survive the Loss of a Love.* Los Angeles, CA: Prelude Press.

Limon, W. (1991) *Beginning Again: Beyond The End Of Love.* New York: Harper/Collins Publishers.

Progoff, I. (1975) *At a Journal Workshop. The Basic Text and Guide for Using the Intensive Journal Process.* New York: Dialogue House Library.

Robertson, C. (1980) *Woman's Guide To Divorce & Decision Making. Supportive Workbook for Women Facing the Process of Divorce.* New York: Simon & Schuster.

Smoke, J. (1985) *Growing Through Divorce: With Working Guide.* Eugene, Oregon. Harvest House.

Stearns, A. (1988) *Coming Back.* New York: Ballantine Books.

Trafford, A. (1982) *Crazy Time: Surviving Divorce.* New York: Bantam Books.

Wilson, C.A. & Schilling, E. (1990) *Survival Manual for Women in Divorce: 150 Questions & Answers.* Boulder, CO: Quantum Press.

Wilson, C.A. & Schilling, E. (1992) *Survival Manual for Men in Divorce: Straightforward Answers About Your Rights.* Boulder, CO: Quantum Press.

Fear

Jampolsky, G. (1970) *Love is Letting Go of Fear.* Toronto: Bantam Books.

Jeffers, S. (1987) *Feel The Fear and Do It Anyway.* New York: Fawcett Columbine.

Adaptation

Abrams, J. (1990) *Reclaiming the Inner Child.* Los Angeles, CA: Jeremy P. Tarcher, Inc.

Berman, C. (1991) *Adult Children of Divorce Speak Out.* New York: Simon & Schuster.

Bradshaw, J. (1990) *Homecoming: Reclaiming and Championing Your Inner Child.* New York: Bantam Books.

Brissett, M. & Burns, R. (1991) *The Adult Child of Divorce.* Nashville: Oliver Nelson.

Kellogg, T. (1990) *Broken Toys, Broken Dreams: Understanding & Healing Boundaries, Codependence, Compulsion & Family Relationships.* Amherst, MA: Brat Publishing.

Paul, M. & Chopich, E. (1990) *Healing Your Aloneness: Finding Love and Wholeness Through Your Inner Child.* San Francisco, CA: Harper & Row.

Whitfield, C. (1989) *Healing The Child Within.* Deerfield Beach, FL: Health Communications.

Guilt/Rejection

Borysenko, J. (1990) *Guilt is the Teacher, Love is the Lesson.* New York: Warner Books.

Grief

Fintushel, N. & Hillard, N. (1991) *A Grief Out Of Season.* New York: Little Brown.

Tatelbaum, J. (1980) *The Courage to Grieve: Creative Living, Recovery, & Growth Through Grief.* New York: Harper & Row.

Westberg, G. (1962) *Good Grief.* Philadelphia, PA: Fortress Press.

Anger

Alberti, R. & Emmons, M. (1990) *Your Perfect Right: A Guide to Assertive Living* (sixth edition). San Luis Obispo, CA: Impact Publishers.

Lerner, H. (1985) *The Dance of Anger: A Woman's Guide to the Changing Patterns of Intimate Relationships.* New York: Harper & Row.

Tavris, C. (1982) *Anger: The Misunderstood Emotion.* New York: Simon & Schuster.

Warren, N. (1990) *Make Anger Your Ally.* Brentwood, TN. Wolgemuth & Hyatt.

Weisinger, H. (1985) *Anger Workout Book.* New York: Quill.

Self-Worth

Bloomfield, H. (1985) *Making Peace With Yourself: Turning Your Weaknesses Into Strengths.* (1985) New York: Ballantine.

Books.Briggs, D. (1977) *Celebrate Your Self: Enhancing Your Own Self-Esteem.* New York: Doubleday.

Branden, N. (1983) *Honoring The Self.* Toronto: Bantam Books.

Palmer, P. and Froehner, M. (1989) *Teen Esteem: A Self- Direction Manual for Young Adults.* San Luis Obispo, CA: Impact Publishers.

Powell, J. (1976) *Fully Human, Fully Alive.* Allen, TX: Tabor Publications.

Powell, J. (1969) *Why Am I Afraid to Tell You Who I Am?* Allen, TX: Tabor Publishing.

Satir, V.A. (1988) *The New Peoplemaking*. Palo Alto, CA: Science & Behavior Books.
Wegsscheider-Cruse, S. (1987) *Learning To Love Yourself: Finding Your Self-Worth*. Deerfield Beach, FL: Health Communications.

Letting Go
Kingma, D.A. (1987) *Coming Apart: Why Relationships End and How to Live Through the Ending of Yours*. New York: Fawcett Crest.
Wanderer, Z. (1952) *Letting Go: 12 Week Personal Action Program to Overcome a Broken Heart*. New York: Bantam.

Transition
Bridges, W. (1980) *Transitions: Making Sense of Life's Changes*. Reading, MA: Addison-Wesley Publishing Co.
Spencer, S. & Adams, J. (1990) *Life Changes: Growing Through Personal Transitions*. San Luis Obispo, CA: Impact Publishers.

Love
Buchler, R. (1987) *Love: No Strings Attached*. Nashville, TN: Thomas Nelson Publishers.
Keyes, K. (1990) *The Power of Unconditional Love*. Coos Bay, OR: Love Line Books.
Lee, J.A. (1974) The styles of loving. *Psychology Today*, 5:45-51 (October).
Powell, J. (1978) *Unconditional Love*. Allen, TX Tabor Publishing.

Trust
Larsen, T. (1979) *Trust Yourself: You Have The Power*. San Luis Obispo, CA: Impact Publishers (out of print).

Relatedness
Bloomfield, H. (1983) *Making Peace With Your Parents: The Key to Enriching Your Life and All Your Relationships*. New York: Ballantine Books.
Campbell, S. (1980) *The Couple's Journey: Intimacy as a Path to Wholeness*. San Luis Obispo, CA: Impact Publishers.
Campbell, S. (1984) *Beyond the Power Struggle*. San Luis Obispo, CA: Impact Publishers.
Emmons, M. & Alberti, R. (1991) *Accepting Each Other: Individuality and Intimacy in Your Loving Relationship*. San Luis Obispo, CA: Impact Publishers.
Fisher, B. & Hart, N. (1995) *Loving Choices: A Growing Experience*. Boulder, CO: Family Relations Learning Center.
Keyes, K. (1983) *Your Heart's Desire: How to Create a Loving Relationship*. Coos Bay, OR: Love Line Books.

O'Mara, P. (1991) *The Way Back Home: Essays on Life and Family.* Santa Fe, N.M: Mothering Publications.

Sanford. J. (1980) *The Invisible Partners: How the Male and Female in Each of Us Affects Our Relationships.* New York: Paulist Press.

Smith, R. & Tessina, T. (1987) *How To Be A Couple & Still Be Free.* North Hollywood, CA: Newcastle Publishing Co.

WelWood, J. (1990) *Journey Of The Heart.* New York: Harper/ Collins Publishers.

Woititz, J. (1985) *Struggle for Intimacy.* Deerfield Beach, FL: Health Communications, Inc.

Sexuality

Calderone, M. & Johnson, E. (1989) *The Family Book About Sexuality.* New York: Harper & Row.

Woititz, J. (1989) *Healing Your Sexual Self.* Deerfield Beach, FL: Health Communications.

Singleness

Larson, S. & Larson, H. (1990) *Suddenly Single: A Lifeline For Anyone Who Has Lost a Love.* San Francisco, CA: Halo Books.

Children of Divorce

Briggs, D. (1970) *Your Child's Self-Esteem.* New York: Doubleday.

Brown, L. & Brown, M. (1986) *Dinosaurs Divorce: A Guide for Changing Families.* Boston MA: Little Brown & Company.

Fleming, B. (1992) *Scott The Dot: A Self-Esteem Tale for Children.* San Luis Obispo, CA: Impact Publishers.

Francke, L. (1983) *Growing Up Divorced.* New York: Fawcett Crest.

Freed, A. (1973) *T.A. for Tots: Transactional Analysis for Everybody Series.* Rolling Hills Estates, CA: Jalmar Press.

Lansky, V. (1989) *Vicki Lansky's Divorce Book for Parents: Helping Your Children Cope With Divorce And Its Aftermath.* New York: Signet Books.

Newman, G. (1981) *101 Ways To Be A Long Distance Super-Dad: Don't Divorce Your Kids.* Saratoga, CA: R & E Publishers.

Palmer, P. (1977) *Liking Myself.* San Luis Obispo, CA: Impact Publishers.

Palmer, P. (1977) *The Mouse, The Monster and Me.* San Luis Obispo, CA: Impact Publishers.

Ricci, I. (1980) *Mom's House, Dad's House: Making Shared Custody Work.* New York: Macmillan Publishing Co. .

Rofes, E. (Editor) (1981) *The Kids' Book Of Divorce: By, For & About Kids.* New York: Vintage Books.

Virture, D. (1988) *My Kids Don't Live With Me Anymore: Coping With The Custody Crisis.* Minneapolis, MN: CompCare Publishers.

Readings on Related Topics

Inspirational
Gibran, K. (1923) *The Prophet*. New York: Alfred A. Knopf, Publisher.
Miller, R. Editors of New Age Journal (1992) *As Above So Below: Paths to Spiritual Renewal in Daily Life*. Los Angeles: Jeremy P. Tarcher.
Peck, S. (1978) *The Road Less Traveled: New Psychology of Love, Traditional Values and Spiritual Growth*. New York: Simon & Schuster.

Stepfamilies
Burt, M., Editor (1991) *Stepfamilies Stepping Ahead: Eight-Step Program for Successful Family Living*. Lincoln, NE: Stepfamily Assoc. of America.
Einstein, E. (1982) *The Stepfamily: Living, Loving & Learning*. Boston: Shambhala.
Visher, E. & Visher, J (1979) *Step-Families: Myths and Realities*. New York: Citadel Press.

Women and Men
Austin, N. & Phelps, S. (1987) *The Assertive Woman: A New Look* (second edition). San Luis Obispo, CA: Impact Publishers.
Bly, R. (1990) *Iron John: A Book About Men*. New York: Vintage Books.
Keen, S. (1991) *Fire In The Belly: On Being A Man*. New York: Bantam Books.
Wetcher, K., McCaughtry, F., Barker, F. (1991) *Save The Males: Why Men Are Mistreated, Misdiagnosed and Misunderstood*. Washington, D.C: The PIA Press..

INDEX

Rebellion, 169, 174-175
external, 170-171
internal, 171
partner involvement, 172
relationship healing, 175-176
"Rebound" relationships, 21
"Rebuilding Blocks," 6-8
Rebuilding Relationships, 164,
234
"Rebuilding Relationships"
(class), 68, 127, 164, 300
Rejection, 13, 48
anger, 132
children, 103
dumpees, 92-93
Relatedness, 21, 222-223
affairs, 225
children, 238-239
friendship/therapeutic relationships, 230-231
good communication, 234-235
growing relationships, 224-
226, 231-234
healthy termination, 233-234,
235-236
homework, 237-238
passionate, emotional
relationships, 227-230
Relationships. See Love
relationships
Relationship styles, 211-215
Religion, 26, 59
Rogers, Carl, 204
Runaway syndrome, 144-145

Safe sex, 253-256
Satir, Virginia M., 1-2, 168, 204
Saturday Evening Post, 295
Scapegoat, 129-130
Self-esteem. See Self-worth
Self-love, 199-201, 203-205
Self-talk, 58
Self-worth, 16, 41, 150-151
childhood influences, 167-168
children, 160
importance, 152-153
steps to greater, 153-159

Separation (healing), 296-307
See also Healing Separation
Agreement
Sexuality, 22, 240
being single, 241-242, 256
children, 256-257
compassion trap, 251
dating, 242
morality, 244, 248-249
open communication, 249-251
roles, 252-253
rules, 251-252
safe sex, 253-256
stages of, 244-247
Shell/Rebel/Love Theory, 172,
174
Shell stage, 169, 172, 174-175
"Significant parent," 164-166
Singleness, 23, 260-263
children, 267
dating, 263
developing interests, 263-264
problems, 264
sexuality, 241-242, 256
Sleeplessness, 111
Smothering Relationship, 212
Suicidal feelings, 112, 115
Support groups, 28
church, 30-31
friendships, 84-85

Teachers Guide, 30-31
Tennessee Self-Concept Scale,
152-153, 272
Transition, 16-17, 162-164, 172-
175
childhood influences, 167-168
children, 178
easing, 178-179
family of origin, 164-167
leaving leftovers behind, 177-
178
power struggles, 176-177
rebellion, 169-172, 175-176
Trust, 20, 208-211
children, 220-221
rebuilding, 219-220

MORE BOOKS BY BRUCE FISHER

REBUILDING WORKBOOK
Bruce Fisher, Ed.D., and Jere Bierhaus
Softcover: $10.00   116pp.
For use with *Rebuilding: When Your Relationship Ends* in the "Fisher Rebuilding Ten Week Educational Seminar," it will enhance your progress and assist in your adjustment process. Helpful even if not participating in the Seminar.

REBUILDING FACILITATOR'S MANUAL
Bruce Fisher, Ed.D., and Jere Bierhaus
Softcover: $50.00   197pp.
Designed to be used with *Rebuilding: When Your Relationship Ends* and the *Rebuilding Workbook* in the "Fisher Rebuilding Ten Week Educational Seminar." Answers questions relating to facilitating a Seminar and includes the Fisher Divorce Adjustment Scale scoring and research data.

LOVING CHOICES
A Growing Experience
Bruce Fisher, Ed.D., and Nina Hart
Softcover: $12.00   240pp.
Helps individuals and couples to develop healthy, healing relationships. Especially useful for those who have gone through divorce. Emphasizes good communication. Views relationship as a laboratory for growth.

LOVING CHOICES WORKBOOK
Bruce Fisher, Ed.D., and Nina Hart
Softcover: $12.00   120pp.
Workbook with exercises designed for both singles and couples of all kinds. Can be used individually, in connection with therapy or in informal groups to enhance relationships in all areas of life.

Please see the following page for more books.